CALL OF THE WHITE

WHITE

TAKING THE WORLD TO THE SOUTH POLE

EIGHT WOMEN
ONE UNIQUE EXPEDITION

FELICITY ASTON

summersdale

CALL OF THE WHITE

Summersdale Publishers Ltd
46 West Street
Chichester
West Sussex
PO19 1RP
UK

www.summersdale.com

Printed and bound in Great Britain

ISBN: 978-1-84953-134-4

CONTENTS

PROLOGUE

SWEPT UNDERWATER

My eyes snapped open as the tent above me was raked by yet another violent gust. The fabric of our flimsy shelter writhed in the wind like the loosened sails of a yacht in a hurricane. The whole tent seemed to contract with each blast of the storm, like a lung trying to breathe. The wind tore at the tent in a fury from all directions, as if there were physical beings outside, tugging at our refuge, incensed by its presence and intent on its removal. Lying in my sleeping bag on the tent floor, I was jolted violently by the vibration of the squalls. The movement would have kept me awake even if the noise hadn't already made sleep impossible. The roar of the wind, the clatter of ice blown against the tent and the snapping of fabric filled my brain until I could think of nothing else. It was all-consuming.

Abruptly, there was a change. One side of the tent sounded particularly noisy. Something had come loose. As I strained against the restrictive hood of my sleeping bag to peer around me, I could see the far corner of the tent bulging inwards. One of the guy ropes that anchored the outside of the tent to the ground had come free or snapped. It wasn't serious but it made me anxious about the other identical anchors holding the tent down. In Antarctica, a tent is more than just a shelter, it is a lifeline. Without the protection of a tent, a person can't survive in the open. We couldn't risk our tent blowing away or getting damaged. I wriggled out of my sleeping bag, anxious to get outside and re-anchor the free material. I punched my arms into the sleeves of my down jacket, ignoring the involuntary shiver as the super-cooled lining touched my skin, and kicked my feet into my down booties. Next to me were the worm-like forms of my three tent-mates, cocooned deep in their sleeping bags. I could sense that they were all awake – nobody could sleep through such a storm – but none of them moved as I squeezed out of the tent door.

Outside, I had to push myself away from the tent and I tottered on the spot for a moment as I steadied myself in the gale. The force of the wind felt oppressive, as if the air itself was thicker out here. I glanced around at the brightly lit Antarctic night. As I squinted into the glare of the sun reflected by the flawless white of the snow, it could have been two in the afternoon rather than two in the morning. This far south there is no darkness during the summer. Instead, the sun makes endless circles in the sky, never lowering itself towards the horizon. Despite the sunshine, it was still breathtakingly cold. I readjusted my face-covering to protect the exposed skin that was already burning with the sting of the subzero temperatures.

Our tents were pitched on the fringes of a small base camp. A few hundred metres to the right was a cluster of rigid tents and containers used for the logistical operation that stretched across Antarctica and to South America. We had arrived at the camp from Chile the day before, spilling out of a large cargo plane after a six-hour flight in its windowless belly. The plan was to stay in the base camp and acclimatise for a few days, before being flown by a small ski-plane to the point on the Antarctic coast where we would start our expedition to the South Pole. I ran my eyes over the long lines of small geodesic tents used as sleeping accommodation by the staff running the camp. They seemed to be part submerged in a broiling haze of snow-filled air. As I watched, my eyes grew wider; the snow was being drawn upwards, forming a towering cloud of whirling eddies that looked like a blanched sandstorm. The cloud drew more snow and ice into itself as it churned and swept across the camp, advancing towards me like a tsunami. I watched it till the last second, before turning and crouching low to the ground as my back was pelted with fist-sized lumps of ice carried by the wind. As the violence died down I stood to see yet another icy squall in the distance, rising up a dozen metres into the air, screening the sunlight and creating its own shadow. The noise of the oncoming mass of snow and ice was as loud as a low-flying military jet, but it had a menace to it, as if the storm were alive. My body reacted to the noise instinctively, tensing every muscle; each sense so alert that it was almost painful. Within minutes, the squall had reached me and yet again I crouched low into the snow, lost in a violence of wind and a swirling mass of ice-hard spray that for a few seconds made it hard to breathe. It felt like being swept underwater.

Beside me, our two lightweight tents billowed and bucked in the Antarctic gale. I found the loose guy rope and anchored it deep in the snow, stamping my boot around the attachment to make the powder snow as hard and firm as ice. The restored tension in the tent seemed to enrage the storm even further; the next squall sent the tent into a spasm that looked even more dramatic from the outside than it had sounded from within. Between gusts I shovelled spadefuls of snow onto the sides of the tent, which were already piled high with snow blocks to weigh them down. Still, the tent threatened to pull free. The vibration of the tent shrugged off the larger blocks of compacted snow faster than I could replace them and as I frantically shovelled snow onto one weak spot, another appeared elsewhere. I called for help through the tent fabric to my teammates inside. The first well-covered figure appeared out of the tent door just as another blast struck. Without time to explain, I grabbed her shoulder to spin her against the wind and bring us both down into a crouch on the snow as we were pelted with rocks of ice by the fury sweeping over us.

As soon as the gust passed I ducked my head into the tent to warn the others to watch for the approaching squalls on their way out but, halfway through my sentence, the tent closed in around us. The poles caved inwards, drooping silently while the material billowed as delicately as a falling parachute. Scrambling out of the tent we grabbed at the tent poles, trying to find where they had broken, but we were too late. Another gust hit us and, as the tent struggled, the jagged edges of the broken poles tore through the outer fabric with a sickening wrench, shredding our precious shelter.

We worked quickly to isolate the broken poles, holding them firm through the gusts to prevent any further damage but, even as we struggled, I could see the extent of the ruin and my mind worked rapidly through the consequences. We didn't have a spare tent so we would need to repair the damage. We had limited repair materials with us that I doubted would be sufficient to piece together all the torn fabric and broken poles. Even if we could scavenge enough glue and spares from the workshops around base camp, the repairs would need to be reliable enough for us to entrust our lives to the restored tent. There was no question of starting the expedition with equipment that might fail and therefore put our lives at risk.

I felt my insides tighten, pulling the blood away from my face as I realised, fully, what I had instinctively known from the moment the tent had collapsed. Without a suitable tent, there was no expedition.

Our expedition was over before it had even begun.

CHAPTER ONE

BEGINNINGS

I stood in the centre of London on a traffic island in the middle of a pedestrian crossing. A stampede of distracted commuters jostled either side of me. Dressed in my smartest business suit, I looked like anyone else rushing from tube station to office in the morning drizzle. Nobody could tell that the day before I had been huddled in a slightly damp sleeping bag in a cold corner of a soot-filled military tent in a freezing part of central Norway. I could barely believe it myself. For the previous fortnight my world had been drifting snow, pink-lit peaks and glimpses of musk ox as I taught others how to travel through that bitter cold. Now, after a 24-hour dash by train and plane, I found myself in a landscape of belching buses, aggressive taxis and an unyielding workforce marching towards their day.

Taking my time, I walked along Gloucester Road to the headquarters of the Winston Churchill Memorial Trust. In a grand-fronted building with fat white pillars and a glossy black door, I sat in front of a panel of four very stern-looking men and told them my idea: I wanted to take a team of eight women from across the Commonwealth to the South Pole. The team would not be experienced adventurers or seasoned polar explorers but 'ordinary' women who wanted to show the world what they were capable of. The trust awards a number of grants every year to people who want to travel overseas for career-enhancing study or to complete projects that will bring benefit to themselves, their community and, ultimately, the UK. My application was unusual in that I wasn't asking for funds towards the main project, the expedition to Antarctica. Instead, I asked them to finance my journey to eight carefully selected Commonwealth countries to interview candidates and find an expedition team. I needed a team before I could go in search of sponsorship for the main expedition and I was hoping the trust would help me fund this initial step.

The interview didn't go well. I'm usually confident at interviews but this time I felt nervous; perhaps an indication of how badly I wanted this panel of strangers to support my wild idea. One member of the panel announced that he was an expert in Commonwealth matters and then fell silent. His lack of opinion on my idea didn't seem favourable, neither did the fact that the chairman of the panel (who asked all the questions) seemed keen to move on swiftly, repeatedly cutting short my answers before I'd had time to make my case. The sticking point seemed to be a concern that the support of the trust would be overshadowed by all the other organisations and sponsors that I would need to involve in order to fund the actual expedition. 'Regardless of the future support or outcome of the expedition, if the trust supports my recruitment journey then it will always be the very start of our story,' I tried to reassure them. 'It will be the very important initial seed that makes everything else possible.'

Twenty minutes later I sat in a nearby coffee shop, trying to overcome my disappointment. I had attended so many interviews for grants and funding over the years that I had developed an instinctive sense of the outcome. I called my mother but didn't get the sympathy I was looking for. 'You always do this,' she sighed down the phone. 'You think you've done badly and then a few weeks later it all works out fine.' I rang off feeling frustrated. Just because things had gone my way in the past didn't mean that they always would.

That night I flew back to Norway to become an instructor again for a few more weeks and my days were absorbed by pulling sledges, tent routines and ice-breaking drills. Unfortunately, open wilderness can be a surprisingly claustrophobic place. The constant driving snow forced me to retreat into my goggles and the hood of my jacket, which formed a tiny protective cocoon from the brute forces beyond. Days were spent skiing along silently in my own personal bubble of thought, mulling over my plans. I kept telling myself that rejection from the trust was likely to be the first of many obstacles that I would have to overcome. If the expedition was truly an idea worth pursuing, it had to be strong enough to withstand setbacks like this. Still, it was hard to see how I would be able to move forward without funding, and there were precious few sources of finance.

The expedition was an idea that had gestated in my brain during dozens of similarly long ski journeys. While making slow progress through white landscapes, numerous ideas float into my head; many roll around for days, perhaps even weeks or months, but generally they fade and disappear. The good ideas are the ones that refuse to leave, the ones that keep coming back. The Commonwealth Women's Antarctic Expedition wasn't an idea that had arrived fully formed. It had grown slowly, taking on different formats as I thought through all aspects of the plan. The motivation had accumulated just as slowly during my travels over the previous five years. The more I saw of the world, the more I realised that the majority of women on the planet, even now in the twenty-first century, are unable to make their own choices in life. Whether the cause is economical, political, cultural or religious, many women are still considered to be inferior by the society in which they live. The realisation made me sad and frustrated. Gradually, I began to feel an unshakeable sense of responsibility. I was one of the lucky ones that had the freedom to live my life as I wanted. Shouldn't I be doing something to help those women around the world that weren't so lucky? Forming an all-female team to ski to the South Pole might seem like a bizarre way to address inequality, but skiing to the South Pole is widely seen as more than just a physical journey; it has become a well-understood metaphor for overcoming obstacles and reaching a common goal. It struck me that an all-female team completing a journey so readily associated with heroic male explorers sporting icy beards would send a very strong and positive message about what women are achieving today, despite obstacles that are far more challenging than the subzero temperatures of Antarctica.

My first problem in planning the expedition was deciding which countries to include. There had to be some common theme that drew the countries involved together. I considered all the groupings I could think of: the United Nations seemed too vague; NATO was far too military and political; the European Union didn't strike me as a terribly innovative basis for an expedition; but what about the Commonwealth? I read through the list of just over fifty states that form the Commonwealth. It was an intriguing roll call of nations: developed countries were listed alongside those that were emerging onto the international stage; countries with troubled or tragic histories were mixed with those facing difficult futures; countries that were instantly familiar were as common as those that I wasn't able to point out on a world map without some hesitation. It was an eclectic and exciting list. It fitted. Even better, the Commonwealth would celebrate its 60th anniversary year in 2009, making a Commonwealth expedition very timely.

There was just one reason to pause: I had to be sure of what the Commonwealth, as an organisation, stood for. Its original purpose 60 years ago had been to retain a degree of connection between the newly independent countries of the devolving British Empire. To some, its survival into the twenty-first century is a slightly embarrassing and anachronistic reminder of a colonial past, but I needed to make up my own mind. Skimming over the endless debate about what political influence the Commonwealth should have, what became clear from my research is that the Commonwealth remains a channel through which nations from a diverse economic, cultural and geographical spectrum communicate with each other – and that struck me as something that deserved credit. As I delved further into the work of the Commonwealth, I was impressed by the number of projects designed to share skills and knowledge between countries. These range from media training to encourage free speech, to experts sharing ideas on health care and social services. I saw the very modern concept of global social responsibility reflected in the work of the Commonwealth. Rather than a staid old dinosaur, I found a vibrant global community and felt proud that the UK had been so instrumental in its foundation.

I needed to be sensitive about which countries I approached, avoiding those that had recently experienced intense political or social turmoil. The obvious choices would have been the rich, developed Commonwealth countries, such as Canada, South Africa and Australia, but this seemed too easy and would represent only one side of the Commonwealth. Many Commonwealth nations are in Africa or the Caribbean, so this is where I focused first.

Jamaica appeared to be one of the only Caribbean nations large enough to provide the support a team member would need. It has a fiercely patriotic diaspora that would be likely to add their backing to anyone flying the Jamaican flag at the South Pole and although adventure sports are not an established pastime in Jamaica, there is a Jamaican ski federation, a dog sled team that competes internationally and the legendary Olympic bobsleigh team – all of which gave me hope that the expedition might win support. Turning to Africa, I looked for a Commonwealth country relatively free of political and economic chaos. Ghana in West Africa stood out, with its comparatively free press, stable economy and robustly democratic political system. In addition, it had been the first African country to join the Commonwealth, a distinction that seemed to make it fitting that a Ghanaian would represent Africa on the expedition team.

Likewise, India's place in history as the country whose independence had prompted the formation of the Commonwealth in the first place made it a clear candidate for being included in an expedition to mark the event. India is an enthusiastic mountaineering nation and has a long association with Antarctica, having operated research stations on the continent since 1983. An association with Antarctica similarly prompted me to involve New Zealand. New Zealanders consider Antarctica to be their own backyard, and many were astounded by the fact that whoever joined this expedition would be the first New Zealand woman to ski to the South Pole. Most assumed that the record had been claimed years ago.

Looking at Asia, Brunei Darussalam stands out within the Commonwealth as one of only three absolute monarchies (the others being Swaziland and Tonga). It would also be the only Muslim country to be represented on the expedition. Its near neighbour, Singapore, is a small but wealthy city-state that is carefully multicultural, representing the incredible diversity of the Commonwealth.

Finally, my attention switched to Europe. There are two Commonwealth countries within Europe apart from the UK: Malta and Cyprus. For its size, culture and complex political history, I chose Cyprus. I now had the complete composition of my team. The countries involved would be Brunei Darussalam, Cyprus, Ghana, India, Jamaica, New Zealand, Singapore and the UK.

I wasn't surprised to arrive home from Norway to find a very thin letter on my doormat stamped with the logo of the Winston Churchill Memorial Trust. My heart sank. It was a thin business envelope with no more than one sheet of paper inside. Experience has taught me that thin letters indicate a negative reply: positive replies come with information leaflets and papers to sign. Putting the envelope to one side I fought my disappointment. I had suspected that this would be the outcome but even so, it was a blow to have confirmation. I'd have to find another way to make my project happen but, right then, I was physically and emotionally drained from a month instructing others and didn't feel able to shrug off a setback just yet. All afternoon I pottered around my flat unpacking, doing washing, gazing out of the window and reinserting myself into my life after weeks of being away. That evening, glass of wine in hand, I finally sat in my front room and steeled myself for the rejection inside the envelope. I'd had all afternoon to get used to the idea. I unfolded the letter and read the first line.

'I am very pleased to inform you that you have been selected for the award of a 2008 Winston Churchill Travelling Fellowship; I offer my warm congratulations.'

I had to read the letter again to make sure I'd understood. I read it a third time before it sank in. I dropped the letter and skipped stupidly around the room, laughing at the unnecessary agony I'd been putting myself through for hours – so much for experience! As quick as the laughter (and the skipping), came another thought and a slowly rising panic from the pit of my stomach. Now I had to turn this big idea into a reality. The trust's panel of four had believed in me and with that belief came the pressure to deliver. The volume of work to be done filled my head and I started scribbling down a colossal to-do list that just kept getting longer. As the size of the project became clear, I felt my confidence begin to waver. I wanted to get to work straight away, worried that otherwise I'd never have the courage to begin. But there was a delay: I was due to spend the next ten weeks on back-to-back expeditions in remote locations without the means to access the Internet or the free time to spend planning the project. I put my to-do list away, knowing that it would be mid May before I would have a chance to look at it again.

It wasn't unusual for me to disappear to far-flung, and usually frozen, destinations for weeks at a time. If I were able to travel back through time and appear to an 18-year-old me for long enough to describe to her what her life would be like in a dozen or so years, I often wonder what she would make of it. I worked hard at school, and I was good at it, but I never really had any strong preference for one subject over another. When it came to A levels, I hated deciding what subjects to study; it felt like I was narrowing down my options. Choosing a subject to read at university was even worse. I remember sitting in the small careers room at school flicking through a book of degree subjects arranged in alphabetical order. I started at the back and worked my way forward. I'd nearly finished the book before I got to astrophysics – the physics of the stars, understanding the rules of the universe, learning what is beyond our own existence. It was the only subject that I could imagine would hold my attention for the next three years. I went to University College London in the centre of the capital. It was a fantastic place to be a student but, as the years rolled by, the pressure grew to decide on a career, a direction.

Finding myself back in a careers office, I explored the possibilities. I loved the astronomy I was learning but, as I neared graduation, it was becoming clear that I was reaching my intellectual limit in aspects of the subject. As my lectures delved deeper into cosmology and quantum mechanics, my brain felt warped. It was time to bow out. I needed a new focus.

For several years I had been vaguely aware of the British Antarctic Survey but I had assumed that to be sent to Antarctica you would need to be a serious scientist – to have a PhD at the very least – so I was surprised, and excited, as I read through their adverts asking for graduates to fill assistant roles. With conviction, I knew that I had found the new direction I had been looking for.

After graduation I spent two and a half years, without a break, at Rothera Research Station on the Antarctic Peninsula with the British Antarctic Survey. Rothera is the largest British base on the continent but it is still relatively small. The station itself covers an area barely a kilometre square, containing a few dozen buildings of all shapes and sizes, and houses a transient population of 85 in the summer season that shrinks to a permanent crew of just 20 during the seven-month winters. I was in charge of ozone and climate monitoring on the base but it was the place that fascinated me more than the science. At times it was hard to be cut off from the rest of the world with a random group of people, some of whom I periodically neither liked nor understood, but I never once lost my complete awe of the landscape that surrounded us. It was such a privilege not to simply visit Antarctica but to actually live there and have the chance to get to know the continent and all its sublime faces, both wonderful and terrifying at the same time.

I learned a completely new set of skills in Antarctica, from the abstract to the practical. I learned how to deal with the cold; how to be respectful but not scared of it. I learned how to refuel planes, how to talk clearly on the radio, how to get a reluctant skidoo started without flooding the engine and, most importantly, I learned about people. I saw leaders and teams; I witnessed groups form and fall apart. I saw personalities that thrived in the centre of things and those that pulled themselves away. I didn't realise it at the time, but the experience was to give me the best foundation possible for putting together and leading teams of my own.

I returned from Antarctica firmly bitten by the polar bug. I lacked any clear ambition and yet I felt sure that, this time, I wasn't going to find the answer in a careers office. I hopped from one project to the next, grabbing any opportunities that were offered. I took a job at the Royal Geographical Society, organising expeditions for large groups of 16- to 19-year-olds, and convinced two of my colleagues to take part in a race with me across the Canadian Arctic. We became the first ever all-female team to complete the 500-kilometre event, finishing in a respectable sixth position out of 16 teams. A year later I put together my own expedition, forming the first team of British women to cross the Greenland ice sheet. We made the 560-kilometre crossing in just 16 days, instead of the usual 30 or so, and when we reached the far coast, we made the unusual move of turning around and skiing back again; taking just 15 days to complete the return crossing.

Since then, I've combined organising my own expeditions with working as a cold-weather instructor, including training other novices to compete in the annual race across the Arctic. It's a hand-to-mouth existence that is surprisingly stressful at times. Despite shying away from a traditional office job, I still find myself glued to a laptop for days at a time completing mundane administration work and, although I spend time in some amazing places, between expeditions I can easily go an entire week without seeing another soul. And then there are the finances: sometimes I would do anything just to have the peace of mind of knowing there was a pay day at the end of each month and to know how much is going to arrive. Many times I've scanned the newspapers, ready to give it all up for a regular job, but somehow I just can't seem to visualise myself doing anything else.

I returned from the Arctic in mid May knowing that I had a daunting task ahead of me. I was due to depart on my journey to select an expedition team in mid August, which left me just three months to create a website, generate enough publicity to attract hundreds of applications, devise some kind of selection procedure, find free venues in seven countries for the candidate interviews and arrange high-level support from each of the countries as well as from the Commonwealth. It was a list, and a task, capable of deflating the most potent enthusiasm. I began by setting up a website. I wrote a rather hopeful email to a web design company and was delighted, if not a little surprised, to receive a phone call from them the very next day. Simon Meek was one of two designers that ran the company and my email had struck a chord with him. 'I'd love to go to Antarctica but I know I never will,' he explained. His reaction to the project would become a familiar one: Antarctica is an emotive place; so much so that people who have never been there and who never intend to visit, still hold it very close to their souls. Its very existence seems to make people feel better, to give some kind of comfort. It's as if we think the world can't be all that bad if somewhere like Antarctica exists. Antarctica itself became the project's very first patron, allowing the expedition to benefit from its reflected glow. Simon offered to create a website completely free of charge.

Preparing the content for the web pages was the first time that the plans for the expedition, in its entirety, moved from within my head onto paper. I started thinking about the application form that would appear on the website. What questions did I want to ask? I was clear in my mind about the sort of person I wanted on my team. I was determined to make the expedition open to as many women as possible. It would have been easier to seek applications from experienced travellers, adventurers, athletes and skiers, people that already had some of the skills and experience needed for polar travel but I felt taking that approach would have been missing a huge opportunity. I wanted to create a team of ordinary women so that anyone who read about the expedition would be able to identify with at least one of those involved and to know that, if they wanted to, they could just as easily do something as ambitious and outrageous as skiing to the South Pole.

I saw the expedition as an opportunity to test this belief but I also had to be realistic. There were practical considerations as well. Firstly, everyone needed to speak English because it was hard enough to communicate with a team above the roar of an Antarctic blizzard and the muffle of three layers of face-covering without adding a foreign language to the mix. This wasn't as prohibitive a restriction as it sounded. Most Commonwealth countries still use English as an official language, so for many applicants it would be their first language, or at least a language that they used on a regular basis. Secondly, everyone needed good access to the Internet because, in the months leading up to the expedition, constant communication was going to be vital and this couldn't be done realistically, and cost-effectively, without the Internet. I needed women with motivations strong enough to see them through all the inevitable setbacks and I felt confident that I would know as soon as I read the sentiments of someone I wanted on my team. Eventually, I settled on a format for the application form. It would demand just five answers:

Explain why you want to be involved in the expedition.
Outline your outdoor sport or adventurous activity experience, if any.
What additional skills will you bring to the team?
How would you describe yourself?
Is there anything that you would like to add to your application?

Consciously, there was no requirement for information on a person's age or appearance on the form and I had kept the questions deliberately open to give applicants the freedom and opportunity to write whatever they felt they wanted to say. Simon sent me a test application through the website as a trial run. Bizarrely, this would turn out not to be the only application I would receive from a man.

On 30 June 2008, the website was ready to be launched. All that was left to do was the very first blog entry, which would set the tone of the whole endeavour by introducing me, the expedition and the ideals behind the project. I knew what I wanted to convey, all I needed were the words. I sat for hours in front of a blinking cursor, occasionally typing frantically for a few minutes, before deleting the lot. Finally, I had something I was happy with, but I was still unsure.

There is only one person I go to for reassurance about problems like this: Paul Deegan. Paul is a three-time Everest mountaineer, expedition leader and award-winning travel writer. The first time I ever called him, I was a 26-year-old wannabe author who had just quit her job in order to prepare for a race across the Arctic. Despite my lack of credentials, Paul spent an hour on the phone with me talking over my plans, offering advice and building my confidence. Not once did he express any doubt that I would achieve exactly what I had set out to do. He asked tough questions, challenged my thinking and cut through my self-indulgent waffling without mercy but, in the five years I've been talking to him since that first call, he has always taken me and my ideas seriously and has never once skimped on his time.

Paul's response to my drafted blog was swift. 'This kind of soul-bearing is what I'd expect to read in a book about the expedition, not on the expedition blog,' he typed back. 'This is not what potential applicants need to hear.' He was absolutely right of course – Paul invariably is – but it was advice that I took on board in a much wider context. In heading up a project like this, I had to understand what people expected of me. No matter how I felt about myself, I had to present the attributes that would be anticipated in a leader of such a large project. That is not to say that I set out to misrepresent myself, but in order to have confidence in the project, people needed to have confidence in me. I deleted what I had written and started again:

What difference can eight people skiing across an icy, uninhabited continent make to the world?

I believe that the answer is: *plenty*.

Only eight women from a Commonwealth of nations that represents more than two billion people will physically make the journey to the South Pole, but many thousands more will join the team in spirit, lending support, willing them forward and following their progress across Antarctica.

If the people with whom we share our experiences are inspired to follow their own dreams or make just one change for the better in their lives, then the Commonwealth Women's Antarctic Expedition becomes much more than just an adventure, it becomes a force for change – and that is the exciting part.

Our expedition won't solve world famine or global poverty, it won't reverse global warming or prevent climate change, but it might alter the way people think, shift attitudes or plant the seed of an idea – and who knows what that seed will grow into?

When I interview candidates for the Commonwealth Women's Antarctic Expedition, I won't be looking for the most athletic, the most accomplished or the most widely travelled – I will be looking for women who inspire me, women who are reaching beyond the expectations of others and following their own path.

Are you who I am looking for?

Perhaps you have never thought of travelling to Antarctica before. Or maybe it has always been an ambition that you never got around to doing anything about. Either way, something about this opportunity has caught your imagination and now all you have to do is fill in the online application form.

I look forward to hearing from you and perhaps, on New Year's Day 2010, we will be standing together at the centre of Antarctica, at the South Pole.

Felicity
x

I saved the post, pressed a button and there it was: the entire site was on the web and available for anyone to see. It was a strange moment. I felt weirdly vulnerable, as if I'd just allowed the world to look at my secrets. A part of me wanted to pull it all back and keep it all to myself, safe from criticism and scorn; but the larger part of me was thrilled that the whole world could now read about my plans. In fact, they didn't feel like my plans anymore. They were now a beast of their own, a separate independent entity. It was out there. Several times I searched for the site from other people's computers, both horrified and thrilled when the familiar pages popped up in front of me.

It was exciting to think that anyone, at any time, could browse the website; but I needed to let people know that it was there. I wrote a press release and sent it to the big media channels and newspapers in each of the eight targeted countries. Trawling the Internet for newsroom email addresses, I sent hundreds of messages and would expectantly open my inbox every morning to see if there had been any applications, only to find it empty. The only reply I received was from a national radio station in Cyprus who wanted to interview me over the phone on a morning talk show. A few days later I waited on hold for my turn to go on air with the radio live into my ear. 'She's as cold as ice!' belted out the chorus of the song they were playing. It was a long interview with plenty of opportunity to explain all about the expedition, the type of teammate I was looking for and how listeners could apply. The interview worked; the next morning I opened up my inbox to find four new messages, all from women wanting to join the expedition. I squealed like a child: I had my first applications! I opened the message at the top of the list:

Name: Nicky
Nationality: Cypriot/New Zealander
Occupation: Writer

Explain why you want to be involved in the expedition:
It's 11.30 on a Sunday morning. I've picked up the local paper and I'm having a slow start to the day. I come across an article about an all-women trek across Antarctica and I feel my chest expand. Yes. This is it. I know with absolute certainty that this is what I want. I jump on the computer and flick through the

website, knowing I would eventually come to this question. So many reasons crowd through my mind. From my earliest memories of walking the arid hills of Cyprus with my grandfather, to the sea voyage as a five-year-old journeying to New Zealand, to a passionate life in the theatre mixed with travel, adventure, beauty, art and people. Musings on the ideas of immigration and displacement, and the personal versus the social. A sense of love and duty that brought me back to Cyprus and the realisation that life's journey is not a linear path, but one that loops back on itself, yet keeps moving forward nonetheless. I want to be involved as every fibre of my being feels it. This is who I am.

How would you describe yourself?
Happy. Confident. Get on with all types of people of all cultures. Good sense of humour and compassionate. Good in a team, unafraid to lead but willing to follow. Resourceful and able to handle stressful, tricky and even dangerous situations.

Is there anything that you would like to add to your application?
Meet me.

Nicky sounded great. For a moment I wondered if it was possible that I'd found my first teammate in the very first application. Perhaps recruitment was going to be a doddle after all. Over the days that followed, the applications continued to trickle in and I read them all carefully. What became clear is that the applicants all thought they were writing to some big, well-funded operation. They had no idea that it was just one woman with a grand idea behind it all. Looking around at my office – an ageing laptop balanced on a salvaged desk much too big for the clutter-filled room – I couldn't shake off the guilty feeling that I was just a big fraud. I lived and worked in a two-bedroom flat on the north coast of Kent that I shared with my boyfriend, Peter, taking over one of the bedrooms as my workspace. With big plans to renovate, we were still a long way from making it completely habitable. My office had faded woodchip on the walls, cobwebs in the corners and a carpet with swirls of autumn leaves that made it look permanently dirty. The carpet regularly had to be pulled back to allow access to pipes and wiring as the other rooms were slowly transformed. Never a tidy person, I found the disruption caused terminal chaos to an already faulty organisational system. I seemed to spend my life searching for things and then losing them again.

Sitting in my haphazard workspace, reading any new applications became addictive. It was fascinating to be allowed a glimpse into the lives and hearts of women I had never met. I was taken aback by the sincerity and openness of their answers. It was also clear that the expedition had touched on a frustration shared by many women about continued inequality. A lawyer in India wrote, 'Working in women's rights, I have seen how women do not have the space to dream of being explorers or travellers or are denied the luxury of just travelling their own chosen paths. It would be very fulfilling to be a part of an expedition that can – in its own way – make a difference to how women see themselves.'

Another application from India said simply, 'This mission will act as a reminder to all parents to be equally proud of their daughters.'

The applicants and their stories made me feel miserably unworthy. Who was I to be choosing from among such an admirable group of people? I wanted to reach out to them all. It seemed criminal that all this potential and strength of feeling was not being harnessed in some way. Often, as well as being profound, the writing in the applications bordered on poetic and I was regularly moved to tears. Up until now, the expedition had been motivated by my own personal philosophy, but now I had a new inspiration: I had to make this expedition happen for these women. Only a handful of the applicants could be on the team but the fact that the expedition was happening at all was obviously extremely important to everyone that applied. The applicants became a potent source of motivation and I kept particularly striking extracts from the application forms to provide additional inspiration whenever I might need it in the coming months.

Throughout school I was a keen football and volleyball player; however, I didn't get financial support from my school, which meant I couldn't take my ambition further. This was just one of the injustices that has given me the determination to fight for equal opportunities and the development of education. I lead a running club. A mixed group of 14–18-year-olds attend, most of whom don't go to school because of their financial situation. I want to teach the importance of health and physical education and that, no matter who you are, you can achieve your dreams. My club is also a way to ignite girls' passion for creating a better life for themselves before having a family.
Ama, Ghana

I had breast cancer three years ago and underwent surgery, chemo and radiotherapy, which were all successful. I am free of cancer now, and healthier and fitter than I have ever been. When I saw an article in the *Cyprus Weekly* about the expedition, I was immediately drawn to the idea and felt it would be the most amazing accomplishment after everything I have been through.
Rosie, Cyprus

I am a Khasi tribal female (belonging to a matrilineal society) from the beautiful and enchanting hill city of Shillong, in the

state of Meghalaya, in north-east India, on the border with Bangladesh. Even though I come from the most remote corner of north-east India, which is affected by insurgency-related problems and mainly regarded by the rest of India as backward, I would love to prove to the world that the majority of people living in our state are friendly, peaceful, fun-loving, God-fearing and decent human beings.
Sirrah, India

However, while some forms filled me with renewed belief in the beauty of the human spirit, others made me wary of the bizarreness of strangers, or left me completely baffled:

With my experience I will prove to be an aggressive member resulting in the team's success in achieving the ultimate goal. Good at building team spirit even in adverse situations (if otherwise mean to the team, Ha ha ha....!)

Love Life. Love dogs and cats and animals. Love musical instruments, my family and friends. Biggest fear at the moment: attack from a shark.

As the applications continued to arrive, I wrote to the high commission of each country that would be represented on the team and asked for a meeting, in the hope that I would be able to request information on the major national media outlets and other contacts that might be useful. The responses varied widely from country to country. The High Commission of India left me in the hands of a minister of undefined responsibility (his business card said simply 'Minister' in capital letters under the impressive gold embossed seal of the high commission). He listened politely, drinking sugary tea, as I told him about the expedition before dismissing me with a weary shake of the head, terribly sorry (so he said) that he couldn't help. At the Singapore High Commission I was met by the first secretary, who seemed convinced that the expedition was a ploy to criticise the Singaporean government. After weeks had passed without a reply from the High Commission of the Republic of Cyprus I rang to check that my letter had been received. The switchboard put me through to the high commissioner's office and a man answered. I was a little taken aback when it turned out to be the high commissioner himself. He hadn't read my letter, but put me through to his press officer, who sent me a contact list of every media outlet in Cyprus, as well as the contact details of several Cypriot government ministers who might have an interest in my project.

That same week I received a slightly bemusing letter from the New Zealand high commissioner that was less than enthusiastic, seemingly due to weariness. 'New Zealand receives many requests for support,' it read. 'While New Zealand identifies with the aim of raising awareness of the value of the modern Commonwealth, I regret to inform you that the New Zealand government is not able to lend your expedition its support at this stage.'

Having experienced such a mixed response, I wasn't sure what to expect when I received an invite to meet High Commissioner Burchell Whiteman at the Jamaican High Commission in London. While working at the Royal Geographical Society on the same street, I had walked past the high commission twice a day on my way to and from work and had often noticed the Jamaican flag flying high above a red-brick staircase. I always get a ridiculous thrill of excitement walking past embassies and high commissions – as if they offer a more literal doorway to their country. The high commissioner was a slight man with a clipped, greying beard and heavy eyes that made him look as if he were on the brink of sleep. He sat me down with tea and biscuits and looked through the expedition information I had given him as I talked about my plans. Occasionally, he exclaimed in amazement or shook his head in disbelief, always with a smile, pointing out that the highest point in Jamaica was more than 2,000 feet below the altitude of the South Pole and that Jamaicans were more accustomed to temperatures of 30 degrees above zero than 30 below. When I had finished, he picked up his cup and saucer and took a thoughtful sip. I resisted the urge to fill the silence.

'Jamaicans are adventurous people,' he said finally. 'I remember a man who came to visit me who had been involved in a project to take medical supplies to a remote part of the Himalaya. It had taken them weeks to drive there and they had barely been able to get the permissions they needed. When they got to the tiny clinic they were surprised to find a Jamaican nurse working there. So you see, Jamaicans are everywhere. I think you will find someone.' The high commissioner gave me a list of potential contacts in Jamaica and introduced me to his press attaché, who promised to put news of the expedition on the Jamaica Information Service, a news website that feeds the Jamaican press. As I stepped out of the high commission and into the rain I felt pleased. The meeting had gone well and I think I knew, even then, that Burchell Whiteman would prove to be one of our most faithful supporters.

Up until this point, the Commonwealth Women's Antarctic Expedition hadn't actually had any approval from the Commonwealth itself. The Commonwealth is a many-tentacled beast that can sometimes seem as hard to grapple as melting ice. The nucleus is the Commonwealth Secretariat in London, which is the diplomatic and political heart of the organisation, as well as its most tangible point of contact. Then there is a spongy plethora of associations, programmes and initiatives that surrounds it, including Commonwealth associations of professions as diverse as tax administration, human ecology, dentistry, forestry and archiving. I wrote to Commonwealth Secretary-General Kamalesh Sharma, and his reply was encouraging. 'I commend you warmly for this exceptional initiative and the effort being made to enhance intercultural understanding and to raise awareness of the work and value of the modern Commonwealth,' he wrote.

As July turned into August, my only real problem was that I just didn't have enough applications. There had been a steady trickle, but very few struck me as realistic possibilities. When I allowed myself to dwell on the issue I felt a brewing dread. I'd been so confident that I would find women with the mental strength and determination needed, but what if I was wrong? I renewed my publicity efforts and was rewarded with two more significant media interviews. The first was with an early-morning radio show in Singapore. The show would catch listeners on their way to work so I was keen to make a good impression, but the time difference meant that I had to be on air at 3 a.m. my time. I set my alarm for 2.50 a.m., hoping I'd left enough time to shake off the gravelly, just-woken edge to my voice. When the alarm rang, I made a cup of tea, hoping to trick my brain into thinking it was morning. I gazed out at my dark, quiet street, sipping my tea and waiting for the call. The phone sounded ridiculously loud when it rang, and the breezy presenter on the line seemed equally out of place. As she prepared me for the interview, I could tell from her voice that, although the appeal of the story was clear, she could not conceive of anyone who might actually want to ski to the South Pole. It was obvious that I was the 'oddball' story of the day.

On air I was asked to explain what it was like to ski for days on end in a place where there is nothing to look at. I started to talk about the need to spend a lot of time inside your own head on long expeditions, the difficulty of finding something to think about, and that sometimes I would spend a whole day simply thinking about what to think about. Suddenly, I realised I was rambling so I abruptly stopped talking. The presenter scrambled to fill the unexpected silence, 'Well... aside from the schizophrenia, what kind of person are you looking for?'

I tried to give a neat and interesting answer, but instead it all came out as incomprehensible gabble. 'After all, I've never led a team like this before so this is new for me, too!' I prattled. My brain couldn't believe what was coming out of my own mouth. I sounded insane. As the presenter dutifully wrapped up the interview, I sat with my head in my hands. On the basis of the interview, the only people who would let me lead them anywhere were the equally barmy. I felt like I'd just been on national radio to announce that I was heading to the moon in a watering can powered by a firework, and would anyone like to join me?

The second interview was with *The Telegraph*, a Calcutta-based newspaper. I took the train into London to meet the journalist in a busy cafe on the South Bank. He clipped a small microphone onto my shirt and asked why I had decided to organise the expedition. I felt under pressure to produce some wise and profound words, but the truth was that the strain of organising the expedition was so immense that I could barely put sentences together, never mind interesting sentences. I felt that he went away disappointed and slightly bemused. I could see in his face that he clearly couldn't believe that an expedition with such ambitious aims was just the daydream of this one woman sitting in front of him – surely there was a support team and a publicist and a web manager and high-level liaison with the Commonwealth Secretariat and the British Council and the governments abroad? Well, no. There was just me and my computer and 24 hours in the day.

I left the cafe and walked back across Hungerford Bridge to make my way home. I stopped halfway and looked out across London, feeling totally overwhelmed. In just six days I was due to start a journey to seven different countries, one after the other, spending just a week in each. I'd made all the arrangements for the journey but it had been like organising seven mini-trips, not just one. As I stood there watching the wobbly reflections of tower blocks in the Thames, my mind wandered through all the issues I had to tackle in the next week. Cyprus was my first destination, but I still had nowhere to stay and nowhere to hold the interviews. From Cyprus I would travel to Ghana, but I only had three applications from there. India and Singapore were next and, although most of the arrangements had been made, I had also agreed to give several talks about Antarctica during my flying visits. I would travel to Brunei the following week, where I had no accommodation and little else had been organised. I had no venue in New Zealand to hold the interviews and in Jamaica I had hardly any applications and nowhere to stay. On top of that, I had no money. I'd been refused two credit cards and had no idea how I was going to manage financially when I got back from the trip. Organising the expedition and my recruitment journey had left me with no time to earn a living.

It was a lot to digest.

The next morning I moped around my flat lacking the will to do anything. I was still miserably drinking coffee when I was called to the door to sign for a parcel. Inside was a copy of Robert Swan's book *Icewalk*, an account of an expedition he led to the North Pole in 1989 with an international eight-man team. There was no card but I knew exactly who it was from: my motivation guru, Paul Deegan. Even for Paul, this was timing of the finest order. With the wrapping still on my lap, I read the entire book in one sitting.

Robert Swan's expedition had not been an easy experience for him. Right from the outset, money had been short and finding additional finance had been his primary preoccupation. The members of his team were mostly experienced explorers but the dynamics were tense even before they'd reached the ice, with one member in particular frequently undermining his leadership. The vivid demonstration of the pitfalls and challenges of leading such a complex team was, I was sure, the reason Paul had sent me the book. It was a cautionary tale that I was later to recall ruefully. But for the moment, it was the boost I needed. If Robert Swan could make such an expedition possible in 1989, then surely I could do the same 20 years later. As I switched on my laptop and looked again at my to-do list, I remembered a passage in the book that I'd underlined in pencil, 'it seemed to me important to rekindle interest [...] in our planet and to show by example that high adventure was still at hand, that quite ordinary people without advanced skills can realise the most astonishing and ambitious of goals if they set their minds to it.'

CHAPTER TWO

WHAT IS SKIING?

Cyprus

Arriving in Cyprus, I was blasted by the heat as I left the airport. On the bus into the capital, parched Mediterranean scenes flicked past the window as I tried desperately to stay awake. The juddering of the bus, the enveloping heat of the sun and the chatter of my fellow passengers conspired to lull me to sleep. Safely delivered to the right hotel, I decided to go for a run in the cooling breeze of the early evening. The sun was dissolving into a white sky and crickets filled the air with their vibrations. I was staying in a small, family-run hotel tucked away deep in the suburbs of Nicosia and, although I'd been checked in by the father, the son now sat behind the front desk. I asked him which way I should go for my run. 'Well, don't go too far that way,' he said, pointing right, 'otherwise you'll need your passport.' I must have looked blank because he added an explanation, 'Turkey is just over there, so don't go jumping over any barbed wire.'

Running to the end of the road, I saw what he meant. A tall white wall topped with rolls of razor wire and fringed with a neat curb-stoned lawn stretched across my path. To the left was a squat watchtower and beyond were a number of official-looking buildings bristling with antennae and satellite dishes. I turned right and ran along the wall for a while. Eventually, it was replaced by a wire fence allowing a glimpse of the buffer zone; a broad swathe of scrubland scattered with rubble, rusting debris and abandoned houses. This was the physical evidence of Cyprus' complex political history. In 1974 the Turkish Army occupied the northern third of the island in an intervention that lasted barely a month but left some 200,000 people displaced. While politicians argued over the validity of Turkey's actions in the months and years that followed, the front line, cutting right through the centre of the capital, became entrenched. Nicosia remains the only divided capital in Europe, split in half by a wall and a stretch of no-man's-land known as the Green Line. The division left deeper scars on the psyche of the Cypriots than it did on the land. You don't have to be in Nicosia for long before you tune in to the underlying fizz of resentment and anger that rattles down through the generations, as if the fighting had stopped just last week rather than over three decades ago.

My first meeting in Cyprus was at the Cypriot Ministry of Foreign Affairs. The desk officer for Commonwealth affairs met me in reception and began apologising for the state of his office as we walked through the building.

'I always apologise,' he confided, 'because it is always messy.' He showed me into a room that was more landfill than workspace. I perched myself on a tiny chair amid drifts of paperwork overhung by bundles of notices pinned to the wall and began to give him an overview of the expedition. He was enthusiastic but seemed confused about how he could help. I wanted to know if there was any opportunity of obtaining funding, but first I needed a message of support from the president of Cyprus. The desk officer explained that he would personally write the letter and that the president would sign it if he liked the expedition, but there was a problem. 'I'm not saying that I have too much work,' he started (although I suspected that what he really meant was that he had far too much work), 'and I'm not saying that it isn't important,' (although what he probably meant was that he had much more important things to do), 'but the Commonwealth isn't very high on our priority list.' I considered the irony of his statement in light of his position as the desk officer for Commonwealth affairs. He peered at me for a moment over his spectacles before sighing in resignation and began to move piles of papers from one end of his desk to another, as if looking for something. I imagined that he must spend the majority of his day moving piles of paper around his office just to make space to work. 'I'll need to know the names of the candidates you choose,' he said, still moving paper. 'Not that it will matter if they are Turkish Cypriots,' he added a little hastily (indicating that what he really meant was that it would be a big problem). 'I will do my best to get you a letter of support.' Having moved several more piles of paper he found what he was looking for – a notepad – and together we began composing what the letter from the president should say. As we constructed sentences, I felt mildly fraudulent. I hadn't expected to have this much involvement in the process. At the end of the meeting the desk officer promised to notify me if any funding became available. I couldn't really ask for more than that. He was young, busy and under pressure. 'I now have to go and talk about big ships arriving in Cyprus next week,' he said as he saw me out into a lobby full of navy captains with big hats and shiny buckles.

Feeling buoyed by such a positive meeting, I returned to the hotel and started to prepare for the interviews the following day. Media coverage of the expedition in Cyprus, although slow to start, had been substantial and and, as a result, I'd received just under 85 applications from Cypriots. In each country I planned to interview a shortlist of ten candidates, but found deciding who should be on that shortlist an agonising process. Most applicants made it clear how badly they wanted this opportunity and I hated the fact that I would have to turn most of them away. The first round of selections was made instinctively. There had to be something in the form that struck a chord with me, a sentiment that I recognised or a reflection of some aspect of my own enthusiasm and purpose. The second round of selections was more robust. I looked for people who seemed clear about their own motivations and who were driven by more than a desire for fame or a sentimental draw to Antarctica (such as a desperate craving to see penguins). I was sure that many of the applicants had the determination to ski to the South Pole but what was harder to ascertain was whether they had the tenacity to help me make the expedition happen in the first place. It is the months of training, the endless evenings of sponsorship proposals and media phone calls that take the real effort. I needed practical people that wouldn't shy away from the mundane jobs, who had the strength of mind to shrug off the inevitable rejections and keep plodding away regardless.

I was extremely grateful not to be alone in making these decisions; I had enlisted the help of a group of friends who had considerable expedition knowledge between them, so I had confidence in their opinions. The group formed mini assessment panels for each country, sharing their thoughts with me about the applications. My eventual shortlist for Cyprus included a ski champion hoping to represent Cyprus in the Winter Olympics, the leader of a volunteer group working to clean the seabeds around the island, a member of the Cyprus State Youth Orchestra and the logistics manager of the Cyprus World Rally Championships. I printed out each application form and wrote myself a checklist in capital letters on the cover of my notepad to refer to during the interviews: Were they physically capable of completing the expedition? Would they contribute to fundraising efforts before the expedition and outreach after it? Would other women be able to identify with them? Could I imagine living with them in a tent for six weeks? (This last point was known as the 'tent test', and was the most important criteria of all.) However, it had occurred to me that no matter how probing my questions, choosing a single candidate from each country on the basis of an interview would give me little idea of how all seven women would get along when they met. Instead, I'd decided to select two women from each country and to organise a training event in Norway during the coming spring. This would be a chance for me to see who worked well together in order to select the best group from among them.

The University of Cyprus had kindly agreed to let me use a conference room as the venue for the interviews. I'd arranged to meet each of the ten Cypriot candidates, one at a time, at 45-minute intervals throughout the day. It was going to be exhausting and, at the end of it, I would have to decide which two women would be the contenders to represent Cyprus on the team. As my early-morning taxi wound its way through the suburbs to the university campus, the city felt abandoned. It was a major national holiday in Cyprus and most of Nicosia had packed up to head for the beach or the cool air of the mountains. I arrived at a modern glass and steel building in a large and empty car park. The doors were locked and it looked deserted. I noticed movement in a small office to one side and knocked on the window. The guard jumped and looked at me in astonishment. He made a throat-cutting motion. Either I was facing death or the place was completely shut. The guard rushed round to the door in a fluster. 'Closed, closed!' he shouted through the glass.

'I'm here to use conference room one hundred and fourteen,' I explained.

'Closed, all closed. No one here,' insisted the guard emphatically.

He was an older man, overweight in a way that only men of a certain age can be, with a gloriously protruding belly. He wore open-toed sandals, crumpled trousers and a white vest under his blue shirt, despite the heat. It was clear that he had every intention of sending me away.

'No,' I said firmly, shaking my head. 'I have ten women arriving to be interviewed.' I wasn't sure how much English the guard understood but I hoped that the desperation I felt was clearly etched on my face. Our mutual miming pantomime went on for a while. Someone was called and I spoke to the voice on the phone. It was clear that no one was expecting me and I began to envisage being sent away to find a shady spot in the car park from which to conduct the interviews – not exactly the professional image I had hoped to project to potential team members. So it was a surprise when the voice on the phone began apologising. I handed the receiver to the guard and watched his face fall as he listened to the news that he was to play host to this troublesome English stranger who had turned up at his door on the biggest national holiday of the year.

Still surprised that I hadn't been forced to chain myself to the university building and demand a conference room, I prepared for my very first interview. Stephanie, the first candidate, arrived almost immediately. Dressed casually in a polo shirt, with her long dark hair pulled back into a hasty ponytail and not wearing any make-up or jewellery, she looked like she'd come straight from a game of hockey. Any nerves I might have had about meeting my first interviewee were totally obliterated by the sheer force of her energy and enthusiasm. She spoke with complete openness, as if we were old friends, and I soon found myself won over by her self-deprecating humour and ready laughter.

After Stephanie came Athina. She was smartly dressed and softly spoken, clearly nervous and genuinely incredulous to be shortlisted. Her application had been considered and thoughtful, one of the best. What's more, she was a satellite communications expert: an extremely useful skill to have within an expedition team. She was exactly the sort of woman I had been thinking of when putting the expedition together; someone who had so much to offer and yet couldn't see it herself. I knew that taking part in the expedition would transform her confidence; I knew it because I had seen it happen again and again when training women in the Arctic. However, her motivation was about patriotism rather than personal development. 'Listening to the news here in Cyprus,' she explained, 'you'd think that everybody knows about us, but people from other European nations don't actually know anything about the problems here. They don't even know about the occupation. This expedition will be an opportunity to tell everyone about our island, to let them know about Cyprus.'

Next to arrive was Nicky, the author of the very first application I had received. She had been the stand-out application for me, not just from Cyprus but from all the countries. Sure enough, we fell into easy conversation. She had all the right ideas about the expedition and I could picture her in my team. I could tell that she would be a great confidante and a huge support. The problem was that she had spent most of her life in New Zealand. I wasn't sure if women in Cyprus would be able to identify with someone who had grown up elsewhere. I brought up the point and her reply was that it was all about how you communicated. I agreed but couldn't get rid of the reservation. Although she was Cypriot through and through, she sounded like a New Zealander. I thought of the radio interviews – would people question if she was Cypriot enough?

Lia was the last of the ten candidates. She was a driving force behind the Cyprus Search and Rescue Team but found it difficult to convince people to volunteer. 'People in Cyprus like to lead a comfortable life,' she started. 'It is difficult to make them see beyond their house, their family, their car. Cyprus needs something like this expedition to wake them up! Young people are not very independent. They live with their parents until they are married. Some have flats of their own but they are usually paid for by their parents. Women get married, have children and look after their family. That is it!'

As I packed up to leave the university I felt incredibly weary. It had been a long day but the toughest part was still to come. I had promised everyone a decision by the end of the day, partly because I didn't want to unnecessarily prolong the uncertainty for the candidates and partly because the selection was based on gut feeling and that wouldn't change, no matter how long I left myself to mull it over. There were four clear contenders: Stephanie, Athina, Lia and Nicky. Nicky had been my favourite but I was concerned about the issue of nationality – a concern that was deepened, bizarrely, by the guard. As I left he asked if all the ladies had been Cypriots and seemed surprised when I assured him that they all were. 'New Zealand!' he said. I realised he was referring to Nicky. I tried to explain that she was a Cypriot who had simply lived in New Zealand for a while but he shook his head, wagging his finger at me like a metronome. I shrugged and let him have the point but his reaction was exactly what I feared from the general Cypriot public. I wasn't ready to admit it yet, but in my heart I knew that I couldn't choose Nicky.

Back at the hotel I sat in the evening sun enjoying a slight breeze and a cold beer as I re-read the applications of the remaining three candidates. The responsibility of the selection weighed heavily on me. The success of the project depended on choosing the right people. I had been confident about Stephanie from the moment I met her. She was a yes, leaving me with a choice between Lia and Athina. Athina was clearly conscientious, thoughtful and considered but I wondered if she lacked the determination to see the expedition through. Lia, on the other hand, had plenty of determination and I had no doubt she would ski to the pole, but I wasn't sure if she would be quite as committed to the outreach, the sponsor research and all the other less physical, less glorious, sides of the expedition. I had promised each of the interviewed candidates that I would call them to let them know my decision. As I sat with the phone in my hand, I wished I'd promised an email instead, but after the women had gone to such trouble to attend an interview, a personal phone call was the least they deserved. I did the easy ones first, calling the candidates to which I was giving good news.

Athina answered the phone tentatively; she was expecting my call. 'I think you would be an excellent teammate, so I'd really like you to come to Norway next year,' I explained. 'Would you like to?'

There was confused silence on the phone. 'Are you choosing me?' she asked, finally.

'Yes. You and one other woman from Cyprus. I'd like you both to come out to Norway and try out for the team.'

'I can't believe you are choosing me. Are you sure?'

I couldn't help laughing but I could hear the emotion in her voice. I was sure she had tears in her eyes. In contrast to Athina's quiet uncertainty, there was no hesitation in Stephanie's reaction. She nearly burst my eardrum with her squeals of excitement. She was triumphant and rang off quickly to share the moment with her family.

Now that Athina and Stephanie had both agreed to come to Norway, I had to make the calls I was dreading. As I disappointed each candidate in turn, they were all very good about it, which somehow made it worse. As I rang off from the last call I felt like a complete villain. Despite the earlier elation, at that moment I didn't feel that my project was a very positive undertaking at all.

The next day I met Stephanie and Athina at a cafe in the city. I had arranged for some press to be there and, as both girls arrived, they were interviewed by Sigma TV and photographed by a journalist from *Cyprus Weekly*, one of the island's big newspapers. I could see that all this attention had taken them by surprise and I recognised the look on their faces as they sat waiting to be interviewed. I knew how they were feeling. Media is exciting but daunting. When the camera points at you, it is suddenly a very lonely place to be. You tell yourself that there is no reason to be nervous, while simultaneously resisting the urge to run away and hide.

With the press out of the way, we sat down to talk through what would happen next. It was interesting to see how Athina and Stephanie responded to each other. It was a tough position for them to be in and I addressed the subject directly, 'You are, in effect, in competition with each other, but I hope you won't see it that way. We have a long way to go before getting to Norway and you will need each other's support in order to get there.'

Even so, I detected a slight friction between them. They were certainly very different characters and I felt that Stephanie was instantly competitive, while Athina disapproved of Stephanie's exuberance. As we waited for dinner to arrive, I told them about my meeting with the desk officer at the Ministry of Foreign Affairs. I was astonished when they said that they had both received phone calls from him that morning asking them to send him a copy of their passports and a CV in order to get the support of the president. I recalled his assurances that it wouldn't have mattered if they were Turkish Cypriots – but he obviously wasn't taking any chances.

Our discussion was interrupted by both women's mobile phones going off at once as they received a stream of incoming messages and phone calls. 'That interview must have been on the news!' said Stephanie. They read a few of the messages, both phones still bleeping without pause, and each answered one or two of the calls, babbling in rapid Greek to excited friends and relations.

'My cousin was sitting in the garden with all their family watching a big TV,' said Athina in a brief break between calls. 'Suddenly I appeared in front of them! I could hear them all in the background shouting!' The two women were so thrilled; it was a lovely moment. They were both very proud to be involved in something so exciting. It broke my heart to think that only one of them would be coming to Antarctica.

I had a lot more information to share about the expedition but it was too much for them to take in all at once, so we called it an evening. I didn't get back to the hotel until after midnight and an hour later I was sitting in a taxi on my way to the airport. The taxi driver was English and we got talking about the expedition. 'You've got two girls from here going?' he asked. 'Cypriots?' he reiterated, looking at me in the rear-view mirror as I nodded confirmation. 'I'll be surprised if they stick it,' he said. 'Cypriots like their home comforts. I shouldn't think they'll like roughing it in the cold.'

'I hope I've found the exceptions,' I answered.

Just as I got to the airport my phone beeped with a text message. It was from Nicky to send me a contact she'd promised me during her interview. I felt desperately sorry for a moment. She would have been a great teammate. And then I thought about the taxi driver's comment. He'd been so surprised that the two selected women were Cypriots; to admit that one of them had lived in New Zealand for most of her life would have somehow diminished the impact. I knew I had made the right decision but I was still sorry I would not have the opportunity to get to know Nicky better.

Ghana

Sweeping low over the roofs of seemingly endless rows of houses, we touched down on the runway under an angry red African sun. I could see clusters of cars at busy junctions and hundreds of people strolling the streets. In the taxi, driving away from the airport (windows open, music blaring), I looked out at Ghana and found myself smiling. I don't know why. It was dark and I was tired, but the air was warm and soft and everything just felt so easy. I'd been full of trepidation about Ghana, my first trip to sub-Saharan Africa. Everyone I'd spoken to about it had narrowed their eyes. 'You're going alone? To Africa?'

Those who had actually spent time in Ghana reassured me that I would love it. They turned out to be right. Already, the immigration official had shaken my hand enthusiastically and personally welcomed me to Ghana, the porter at the airport had helped me to get through the throng outside the arrivals hall and steadfastly refused payment, patting me on the back instead, and now the taxi driver was chatting to me amiably. He had 'Blood of Jesus Christ cab' written across the back window, which struck me as a little inappropriate. You don't expect to see blood of any variety in a cab, especially in a country where the driving is so bad. But at least I had avoided the one emblazoned with 'Say Your Prayers'.

My hotel was right on the beach and, as I stepped out of the taxi, I could hear the roar of the sea. The next morning I followed the sound of the waves down to the beach. A wide stretch of flat, wet sand ended in a cloud of spray. The whole place was fuzzy with a thin mist that veiled the horizon and left the view along the coast slightly hazy. Two boys came over to say hello but were soon distracted by their game in the waves. A woman balancing a tray of bread on her head sat on a washed-up tree trunk for a rest and in both directions indistinct figures wandered along the beach to or from the city. Near the watery horizon, a cluster of brightly coloured fishing boats clung to the swell. As I stood alone, taking it all in, an emotion welled up inside me. I was overwhelmed by the fact that I was in Africa.

Ghana had kept me awake during the long overnight flight. I had only six applications, two of those from Ghanaian women living in the UK (and therefore ineligible) and one from a woman who was clearly not aware of what she was applying for. I had invited the remaining three for an interview but had only heard back from one of them. It was embarrassing to have only one candidate. Maybe all those doubters had been right and the concept of this expedition was just a step too far for Ghanaians. Alternatives ran through my mind. Perhaps I should forget interviews on this visit and just use the time to drum up applications. I could return later, or try a completely different country. But I wasn't ready to give up on Ghana just yet. After breakfast, I packed my laptop, phone and notebooks and walked to the British Council in the centre of Accra.

After a short wait in a spotless reception, I was shown into a large office to meet Diana, the corporate communications manager, and Juliet, the business director. Both women were incredibly elegant and Diana, in particular, was so perfectly turned out, in every detail, that it was intimidating. I felt distinctly shabby in comparison. They both listened as I described the expedition and my attempts to find eligible women who wanted to take part. I explained that my efforts from the UK to get media coverage in Ghana had been spectacularly unsuccessful and asked for their help. Juliet was slightly incredulous, 'Do you think you will find a Ghanaian woman who will want to do this?'

Before I could respond, Diana came to my defence, 'Of course they will want to do it. I'd love to go.'

Juliet's eyes widened, 'You would?'

I must admit, looking at Diana's immaculate nails and elaborately coiffed hair, even I was a little surprised.

'Well,' she conceded. 'I'm not really a roughing-it kind of person but I love the idea. I think lots of women would want to go, if they hear about it.'

That was the key – getting news of the opportunity out there. Diana gave me a list of media contacts and sent my press release to dozens of her own personal contacts in other cultural organisations. Juliet warned me it would be hard to get their attention. 'Accra is very political right now. We have elections in two months' time and the UN climate change talks start today.'

'Perhaps they have room for a little light relief?' I countered, hopefully, but Juliet didn't seem optimistic.

The difference of opinion between Juliet and Diana was representative of the reaction I'd had everywhere. For a start, opinion on polar travel is very black and white – people either get it or think it is completely crazy. In addition, people seemed to have a strong view on whether it was something their countrywomen would be capable of. In Cyprus, everyone was surprised that I had received as many as 85 applications from Cypriot women. In Ghana they seemed equally sceptical that it was something that would interest Ghanaian women.

I started ringing the press numbers given to me by Diana but quickly discovered a big problem. It was Thursday and the interviews were due to be held in just two days' time. Even if a journalist wanted to carry my story, it wouldn't be published in time. My only hope was *The Ghanaian Times*, which was published on a Friday. It would mean convincing a journalist to write the story before their press deadline that afternoon, but it was worth a try; it was a widely read paper. After trying the newsroom number several times without getting an answer, I decided to go to the newspaper office in person.

I jumped in a taxi with a driver who knew where *The Ghanaian Times* was based. He dropped me off by a shabby front wall with a large group of intimidating men hanging around the gate. I hesitated for a second, fighting the urge to jump back in the taxi and run away from all the stares I was attracting. Instead, I walked up to the gate as confidently as I could and asked to see the editor. Expecting the guard to send me away, I had a number of arguments ready in my head but he casually called over a young boy hovering inside the compound. The boy walked me across a muddy courtyard surrounded by low concrete buildings and led me to the editor's office. The bare-walled room contained several desks piled high with folders and it was so hot that the air felt too thick to breathe. Four men in shirts sat behind their desks: one was talking loudly on the phone, another was tapping at the only computer in the office and the other two were having a heated discussion about the copy in their hands. None of them appeared to notice me. There was a line of plastic chairs against the back wall where two very bored men sat looking at me, as if waiting to see what I would do next. I approached the man on the computer and asked if I could see the editor. He nodded and indicated the row of plastic chairs, but showed no signs of fetching anyone. I felt defeated for a moment and turned to join the despondent men already in line, when one of the arguing pair broke off to ask me what I wanted. I quickly gathered that this was the editor. I introduced myself and began to explain what I wanted. He listened until I had finished. 'So you want to ask for women to join your expedition. Yes?'

'Yes,' I agreed, relieved that he had got the idea straight away.

'But surely this is advertising? This is not a story, this is an advert.'

I shook my head and quickly reeled off a number of ways in which it was an interesting story rather than an advert, feeling slightly frustrated that I had to explain the newsworthiness of an obviously newsworthy story. 'This is a sports story,' he said in a tone to suggest there was no argument. I was led back across the courtyard to a building where a very young man tapped on a computer as I described the expedition. He handed the printed copy to a boy who immediately sprinted out of the door. 'It will go in the paper this evening,' said the journalist, nodding me towards the courtyard as he turned back to his computer.

Delighted at my success, I left the compound, flagged down a taxi and confidently asked to go to Joy FM. It was all very well getting a story in the paper, but Ghana was a radio country. If I wanted to reach a large number of women in Accra, my best bet was to get on the air, and Joy FM was one of the most popular radio stations in the city. The taxi dropped me off outside a building buzzing with people coming and going. Inside, I asked for Alex, a young friendly journalist I had spoken to earlier that day on the phone. He was enthusiastic about my story and wanted to record an interview with me for the lunchtime show.

We climbed several flights of stairs to a small studio at the top of the building and recorded an interview. By now the questions I was asked in press interviews had become familiar – they usually followed a similar pattern and so my answers had become unintentionally practised. Today was different. 'Can you explain to our listeners exactly what is skiing?'

For a second or two I was at a loss at how to begin explaining skiing. 'It's a method of travelling across snow, using long, thin, pieces of wood' (I winced inside at my primitive description) 'strapped to your feet so that you don't sink into the snow with every step.' After a shaky start I didn't think I'd done too badly.

'And what is the South Pole?' continued Alex. I was ready this time, upright in my seat and concentrating; I wasn't going to be caught out twice.

I got through the interview, telling myself that I would never get nonchalant about interview questions ever again, but Alex's questions also gave me a clue as to why the application rate had been so low in Ghana. I don't think I had truly appreciated just how alien a subject this was to the average Ghanaian. In a country barely a spit from the equator where there are no mountains and no snow, why should anyone know what skiing is? If you had no idea about Antarctica, the South Pole or skiing, an advert asking you to apply to ski to the South Pole was not going to spark your imagination; it would simply be written off as nonsense. As my taxi nudged through the Accra traffic back to my hotel I felt more depressed than ever. Perhaps the sceptics were right; perhaps I had been too ambitious and a little unrealistic.

That evening I logged onto my email account with trepidation to see if the interview on Joy FM had prompted any last-minute applications. I squealed excitedly as my inbox showed 17 new messages. This brought the total number of applications from Ghana to 23. I excitedly read through the new applications and saw with relief that some of them were really great: a development worker involved in women's rights, an investment banker who had given up her affluent lifestyle to follow her dream of becoming a successful singer-songwriter, a nurse from the northern region and a chef in one of Accra's plushest hotels. I wrote to the ten strongest candidates inviting them to an interview and went to bed in a good mood. Once again, disaster had been diverted by the narrowest of margins.

On the day of the interviews I sat drinking coffee in the hotel looking out at the sea. I'd already checked my emails and been disappointed. Of the ten candidates I'd invited for interview, only six had replied. I had tried ringing the remaining four but there was no answer. I consoled myself with the thought that six candidates were better than one. My first interview that morning was with Ama, who was waiting for me when I arrived. She had been the only candidate when I'd arrived in Ghana two days previously. Ama worked for an NGO, looking after volunteers from the UK who came to Ghana to work on school building projects. She was a lovely person but had so much humility that I wondered if she would have the conviction she would need to stand up in front of halls full of people to talk with confidence about the messages of the expedition. The interview made my heart sink: could I really give this wonderful woman the training she would need in order to take part in an expedition like this? She was certainly tougher than me in many ways, but an expedition to Antarctica was so clearly beyond anything she had ever experienced or had ever thought of experiencing that the thought of it seemed almost cruel. The interview brought back all my old doubts about the sensitivity and questionable wisdom of what I was doing. These concerns had never been far from my mind, but the enormity of the responsibility now made me feel sick. Could I take a woman from rural Ghana – a woman who has never left the country, seen snow or felt freezing temperatures – to Antarctica?

My hopes weren't raised by the application form of my next candidate. Sheillah was 23 years old and, although her form was well written, it struck me as rather naive. When she arrived she was so timid that she wouldn't sit directly opposite me for the interview, but insisted on sitting across the room on a chair just inside the door. Once she had recovered from her initial shyness, I was soon struggling to interrupt her flow of dialogue and a different person altogether began to emerge. 'I was the first born,' she told me. 'So, of course, my parents wanted a boy. But because I was the first born they gave me the freedoms they would have given a son. So I am privileged to have had that freedom to do whatever it is I want to do.'

She was interrupted by a sudden flood of water gushing from an air-conditioning unit in the office we were using. I pushed a bucket underneath to catch the water but Sheillah instantly fell into business mode. She strode off into the reception area, returning quickly with a reluctant orderly who mopped while she stood over him directing. Now I could see how this 23-year-old in her business suit could cut a formidable figure at work and carry her authority. Sheillah was ambitious as well. 'After the expedition, whoever goes will have a platform,' she explained. 'I want that platform to launch my own NGO which will use peer pressure for positive things, to encourage volunteerism among young people in their holidays and other ideas that I am working on.'

Barbara arrived in the afternoon. She was a freelance writer who had recently returned from three years studying in America. She was easy company and confident, but her body language betrayed the fact that she was acutely aware that she wasn't in shape. I got the impression that she felt this would preclude her, but in fact I wasn't as worried about fitness as might have been expected. I know from personal experience how quickly you can gain physical fitness if you have the determination and motives to do it; it is the character that is more important. After Barbara came Hannah, a woman struggling to climb the professional ladder. She worked for the Ghana News Agency and seemed more insightful than the other candidates, but at the same time slightly tragic. It was clear that she worked hard but had never really been given the breaks she deserved. 'People think that to get an opportunity they must leave Ghana; that they must go to the developed world. People are even walking across the sand to Libya. Walking! But there are opportunities in Ghana if you look for them. That's what I want to tell people.'

Once again, I'd told all the candidates that I would ring them that evening with a decision. I sat on the beach outside the hotel, digging my feet into the sand, trying to weigh up the options. Sheillah had impressed me with her dynamism and conviction but, as in Cyprus, I found it difficult to choose between two remaining contenders: Barbara and Hannah. It came down to the tent test. I could see Barbara in an expedition scenario clearer than I could imagine Hannah. And so the decision was made. I rang Barbara and Sheillah to break the good news. While Barbara squealed down the phone and jumped around in excitement, Sheillah took the news as casually as if I'd told her the weather report. I knew right away that I had made a mistake.

India

I squeezed myself through the aisles of the plane cabin, found my seat and sat down with taut pains around my eyes. It hurt to focus and it even hurt when I closed my eyelids. I'd only managed a few hours' sleep during the three flights from Accra to Delhi and I could feel the tiredness wrap itself around me like an unshakable fog. I didn't feel capable of getting through the day ahead, but there wasn't a choice – there were too many people that would be let down. Thanks to a disruption in my flights, I would arrive in Delhi 24 hours late, meaning that I would miss a whole morning of interviews. As some of the candidates had travelled for days across India to attend their appointments, the decision was made to reschedule all the interviews for that afternoon. The British Council in Delhi had agreed to host the interviews, so they were able to take care of the arrangements. I would touch down at 9 a.m. and was now due to see my first applicant at midday. To make matters worse, that evening I was giving a talk in the large auditorium at the British Council to an audience of 150. The tickets had all been allocated, so there was no getting out of it.

The British Council kindly sent a car to collect me from the airport and as I walked through the door of their central Delhi building, I was presented with a toasted sandwich and a flask of hot, sweet coffee. I cast heartfelt thanks to those responsible for the incredibly thoughtful gesture and prepared for the first interview in the small glass-walled office I had been allocated. Waiting for me was Commander Dam, a mountaineer and expedition leader in the Indian Navy. He had led military expeditions to both the North and South Poles and had agreed to sit in the interviews with me. After meeting applicants in the other countries alone, I thought it would be helpful to get another perspective. The Commander was a slight man with a big smile under a neat moustache and incredibly clear skin given his occupation and his 43 years. There was no sign of any cold injury on his face, or a single wrinkle. He was stiffly formal as he introduced himself and took a severe stance next to me at the desk as the first candidate was shown in.

I could see that Smirthi was nervous but, as I began to ask her questions about her life, she calmed down and talked with passion about her work to save the pangolin. She showed me a picture of this strange armadillo-like creature, an anteater covered with large, razor-sharp scales that only survives in small pockets of rural India and is threatened with extinction. I invited questions from the Commander, who asked Smirthi several pointed queries about the climbing experience she had described on her application form. His tone was a lot tougher than mine had been. It was clear that the Commander meant business, and I felt a little unprofessional in comparison. As the candidates came and went, I began to feel like the unwilling half of a good cop, bad cop routine. We met a doctor who was very intense and talked too long after each question. I gave her the benefit of the doubt, assuming it must be nerves, but the Commander interrupted impatiently, 'Yes, yes, yes, you have told us that, but what was the most physically difficult thing you have ever done?'

Next came Lata, who was so quiet and unassuming that I couldn't see her holding her own within a team. After the interview, the Commander championed her case, emphasising her climbing competence and expedition experience, but I just didn't get that gut feeling about her. The next candidate, Aparna, had sounded great on her application form and she didn't disappoint. She had trained as a lawyer and had worked on several projects to improve conditions for female prison inmates. Clearly a very determined and focused person, she was emphatic about her commitment to all aspects of the project. The Commander wasn't convinced. Aparna was due to start a new job with the Ministry of Foreign Affairs and the Commander was adamant: 'They will not let her go. It is too much time away.'

By the end of the day I was beginning to feel a little desperate. Apart from Aparna, none of the candidates seemed to be likely team members. I could see by the Commander's expression that he was equally concerned for me. 'Do you wish now that you had seen others?' he asked. Before I had a chance to answer, Reena entered the room and filled the space with her beaming smile. She had presence, both physically and in personality. She sat down and watched us intently as we asked her our questions. She had a disconcerting way of intently holding eye contact as she thought about her answers before speaking. When she made a joke, her booming laughter was so sudden and unexpected that it made me jump. She seemed a little eccentric but the warmth of her character was endearing. Before she left the room I knew that she was my second candidate.

'Can you announce the winners in an Oscar style?' asked Vijay from the British Council, who had organised my talk that evening. I was supposed to be announcing the successful candidates at the end of my lecture, but I hadn't expected to make much of it. I looked at my watch. There were just 15 minutes to go until the audience, already gathering in the foyer, were due to file into the auditorium. I also had to get changed and talk to the press, and now I had to write Oscar-style introductions for each of the ten candidates I had interviewed. My head was spinning, but I couldn't refuse. I decided I needed to look after myself first. I got changed in the toilets, startling a woman checking her make-up as I scattered my belongings throughout the room. Another woman came in as I was adjusting my top. 'You look great,' she said conspiratorially. I threw her a look of thanks – only another woman can know the comfort of a comment like that. I retreated upstairs to the glass-walled office to write the introductions and to gather my thoughts. I felt as if I could put my head on the table and fall asleep within seconds. I could barely focus and was so anxious about the impending talk that it was making me tremble slightly. I rarely use notes or prompts during talks and I don't like to rehearse too much. Over-polished talks sound dull, so I like to rely on my wits. Unfortunately, I had had so little sleep during my series of flights from Ghana that my wits felt stretched to breaking point.

As I entered the auditorium, it was already full. I took my place on stage and felt like a condemned man as I was introduced. Then came my cue to speak. I started my talk feeling strangely detached from my own voice. I looked at the audience's faces in the gloom of the auditorium; they were all blank. I couldn't get a sense of how the talk was being received in the stony silence. Usually I hear something from the audience – agreement, shock or laughter. I told a story that was supposed to be amusing and noticed a row of faces near the back. I couldn't be sure in the near darkness, but it looked like they were laughing along with me. I focused on them for a while and it calmed me down. I began to get into my stride and was slightly taken aback when the room erupted into spontaneous applause at a key moment in the talk. I felt enormous relief; it was going well. At the end of the talk it was time for the

Oscars. There was a lot of shuffling about on stage before Vijay produced a huge cardboard congratulations poster, like a lottery winner's cheque, to hand to the selected candidates. I looked at him pleadingly for a second. This was not exactly the tone I had wished for but there was no time to argue. 'This isn't *The X Factor*,' I muttered to myself. I read out my introductions and noticed for the first time that all ten candidates were sitting in the first two rows. Vijay performed a mock drum roll on the lectern and dramatically announced the names of the selected candidates. Reena and Aparna came on stage; Aparna looked fabulous in a flowing lemon sari and Reena was equally shimmering in blue and green. I handed them the poster as instructed and couldn't help laughing as they looked completely nonplussed about what exactly they were supposed to do with it.

The evening came to a close with a raft of flashing cameras snapping the three of us. I was once given some advice about speaking: 'Be careful, it can make you feel very important.' This advice sprung to mind now as I was suddenly surrounded by a circle of faces – people who wanted to ask questions, people who had asked questions and wanted to continue the conversation, reporters, well-wishers and, somewhere among them all, the women who had been shortlisted. I tried to make a point of focusing on them rather than everyone else, but was physically pulled away. One reporter was pressing me to make a statement about climate change ('Would you say the situation in Antarctica is critical?'), while a photographer ordered me around, 'Stand there. Look relaxed.' I never take press coverage for granted and am grateful for any media attention, as I know just how important it is for sponsors and suppliers, but there were so many people that I didn't get a single complete conversation with anyone.

At the end of the evening I lay in bed at a nearby hostel. I had waited so long to sleep but now I found myself buzzing with adrenalin. I looked around the tiny room, which was more prison cell than accommodation. The hard wire bed was pushed into one corner, framed by leaky pipes, and the small window was covered by a curtain held together with years of grime. I heard a roar outside and, after a few minutes, realised it was rain. I went outside into the corridor that was open on one side, like a balcony, to see rain so torrential that I couldn't see the top of the surrounding skyscrapers. As I watched, something out of the corner of my eye caught my attention. A big brown monkey with a bright pink face sat, at head height, on the balcony a few metres away. As I stared at it, it turned its head slowly to look at me. We stared at each other for a few seconds before the monkey looked back out at the rain. I did the same and we sat there in silent company. After a long while I remembered how tired I was and went back to my room, leaving the monkey to his thoughts.

The night before I left Delhi the Commander had invited me to his house for dinner with him and his wife, Namita. He answered the door wearing a T-shirt from the research station at the South Pole. He was more relaxed than the last time we had met; all trace of formality had disappeared and been replaced by irresistible charm. We sat down to a home cooked meal of paneer and spicy vegetables in a room hung with posters of past expeditions and dominated by an elaborate trophy from the navy that commemorated the Commander's South Pole expedition. I felt an instant fondness for the Commander and his wife and after a wonderful evening in easy company I was extremely touched to be presented with a copy of the Commander's book about his Everest expedition with an inscription inside: 'From below one can't see what's above. From above one can see what's below... That's why I climb. From really high places and frozen landscapes, here's to you.'

I held the book close as I left. This expedition was my own mountain to climb and it felt like I was currently right on its bottom slopes. The Commander had given me a timely reminder of why I was doing all of this and that the view from the top of my own personal mountain would be worth it when I got there.

CHAPTER THREE

PET GIBBON

Singapore

After the sensory overload of India, Singapore was a vision of heavenly calm. I glided through a silent, glimmering and empty airport, a cathedral-like space in glass and chrome, and floated through queue-less passport control, pausing to fill in an immigration card at a conveniently placed desk with pens ready to be used. From passport control I was handed a trolley by an airport worker as my bags rolled out, immediately, onto a baggage carousel. As I passed through customs a sign pointed me to a desk where a smiling attendant sold me a ticket for a shuttle bus that was ready and waiting outside, with a driver who helped me with my bags and looked after them while I bought myself a coffee. We set off in the bus towards the city. I was the only passenger.

The early morning sun shone through the window as I sipped my coffee and looked out at highways bordered with flowering rhododendrons. The greenery was gradually replaced by tightly packed tower blocks until we arrived at the YMCA in the city centre. I met Sandra from the British Council in the lobby. She was a petite lady with dark, loose-fitting clothes and a neatly-pinned hijab. We had corresponded by email intensely in the lead-up to my journey; as well as organising a venue for the interviews, she had arranged for me to give several talks during my short stay in Singapore. It seemed that Sandra had accepted the British Council's aim to engage the young people of Singapore in the climate change debate as a personal mission and she attacked the challenge with enviable energy and efficiency. We both agreed that any excitement about the expedition could be used as a starting point to generate a wider interest in Antarctica within the context of global climate change.

We walked across the quiet roads to a nearby cafe where I tucked into a tuna baguette and a tall latte. Sandra wasn't eating because she said she was planning a big meal later but halfway through our meeting I realised that she was fasting. I had completely forgotten that it was Ramadan, the Islamic month of fasting. Sandra wouldn't have eaten anything since daybreak, not even so much as a sip of water. In the intense humidity of Singapore I couldn't imagine how difficult it must have been. I immediately apologised for eating in front of her and pushed my food to one side, feeling awful. Sandra didn't seem to mind, but I still felt guilty for not being more sensitive. She handed me an envelope of papers and a copy of the schedule she had prepared for the next five days. She ran me through what I was doing, where I should be and who I was going to meet. I didn't need to think a single thought of my own; Sandra had it all covered.

The Singapore interviews started early the next day in a classroom at the British Council. The first candidate was an army officer who had written eloquently in her application form about her belief that there was a significant need in Singapore for positive female role models. During the interview she spoke in such a soft voice that I could barely hear her. Her job involved being in charge of large groups of soldiers on a daily basis, which seemed totally at odds with this painfully timid woman struggling to keep her nerves under control.

Later followed a woman who had been a member of the Singapore Women's Everest Team, who, from the moment she sat down, gave the impression that she had already assumed I would offer her the place. She seemed to see the interview as a rather tiresome formality. She casually passed me copies of glowing references written by former expedition teammates. The references described a very different person from the one sat in front of me and I wondered if her manner was due not to arrogance but a supreme confidence that was backfiring. Unfortunately, I couldn't take the word of a reference, I had to make the decision based on what I myself had seen and in this case I had made my decision before she had even left the room. Later that evening when I called to thank her for coming to the interview, but break the news that she hadn't been selected, she was angry. 'But why?' she demanded. 'I am the perfect candidate.' I tried to respond fairly but her attitude riled me. It didn't help that I was still smarting from an email I'd received from an applicant who hadn't been asked for an interview:

> To say I am deeply disappointed is an understatement. It was a very crushing revelation for me not to be shortlisted. So I reviewed what went 'wrong'. I looked hard at your comments on the successful ladies and realised perhaps your semi-finalists weren't altogether the 'ordinary' women I was led to believe is what your expedition is looking for. I can't help but wonder if I should have just written a scripted application to yourselves and thereby given myself a better chance?

This wasn't the first critical email I'd received from an unsuccessful applicant but I was working so hard to make the expedition as open to as many people as possible that I found the suggestion that there was a conspiracy behind my choices particularly frustrating.

There certainly wasn't anything false or scripted about the two women I had selected from the Singapore interviews. The first, Sophia, carried her inner confidence as visibly as a neon sign. She was a busy mother of three with two demanding jobs and it was clear that she didn't have the time or the inclination for any nonsense. She arrived for her interview in a casual tracksuit and I got the impression that it was just another item on her to-do list that she was squeezing into a typically manic day. She was petite but wiry, with defined muscles on her arms, a physique that was explained by her part-time job as a kick-boxing and aerobics instructor. When I asked Sophia how she felt about leaving her children for two or three months, she waved the issue aside. 'When I filled in my application form my eldest daughter said to me, "Mum, it will be a miracle if you get chosen." I want to go on this expedition to show my daughter that miracles do come true and that it is OK to dream big. The important thing is that we must try.' Her face broke into a big smile and she laughed as if her story had been a joke but I could tell that she had meant every word.

The second woman was Lina, an engineer and adventure-racer who had led a team from Singapore in the 2000 Eco-Challenge (notorious as one of the most demanding adventure races in the world). She had been a strong contender from the moment I read her application form and meeting her didn't change my mind. Lina was instantly likeable. I could sense her quiet determination to succeed at whatever she put her mind to but she was also modest and good-humoured. I could easily imagine Lina as a well liked and dependable member of the team and felt lucky to have found her.

That night I was invited to a dinner party at the home of the director of the British Council. The other guests were a careful blend of adventurers, academics and community workers. Among the adventurers was a man who had led the first Singapore team to the top of Mount Everest. As soon as we started talking he began questioning me, in detail, about my plans and telling me about his own leadership experiences. As soon as he uttered the words, 'I used to be exactly like you... until one day I woke up in my tent and smelled the coffee,' I began to form a dislike which was later confirmed during dinner when he quite suddenly, from the opposite end of the table asked me, 'So, Felicity, have you ever had to sack a team member?' The question was asked in the manner of an accusation, as if, by saying that I had not, I was admitting a woeful inexperience (he controversially sacked one member of his team just before leaving for Mount Everest). He clearly felt me to be unequal to the task of leading an expedition with such a complex team and seemed to want to make sure the others present came to the same conclusion. I am not sure why, but throughout my life I have often been underestimated – perhaps because I have chosen to place myself in situations where I do not fit the expected norm. Whatever the reason, I have learned to use the frustration I feel in response as additional motivation to succeed.

At the end of the evening the guest presented me with a signed copy of his latest book and I got the distinct impression that he probably wouldn't have bothered if he hadn't already inscribed a message to me on the front cover. I kept it as a reminder to myself to be confident in my own abilities, regardless of the scepticism of others. However, months later, I would have cause to think back on his question at dinner that evening and laugh ruefully at how similar our expedition leadership experiences were about to become.

Brunei

Within hours of landing in Brunei I started to realise the difficulty involved in doing any kind of business in a Muslim country during the month of Ramadan. Wandering into the city centre to find a local SIM card for my mobile phone I found that all the shops had been shut since early afternoon. The early closing didn't just apply to shops; offices, museums, visitor centres and ferries were all the same. As the mid-afternoon heat approached 40°C, most people were understandably drowsy and had gone home to rest until they could break their fast at nightfall. With everyone at home, the streets were left empty and quiet.

Bandar Seri Begawan is the capital of Brunei but it's not a big city. Downtown is little more than a shopping mall and a mosque, while across the river there is a sprawling settlement of wooden buildings on stilts connected to each other by a maze of narrow bridges and raised walkways. Most of the buildings are houses but there are also shops, mosques, schools – even a police station with white and blue police boats moored up beneath the stilts and a fire department painted red.

As arranged, Karen met me in the lobby of my hotel. She was the director of a well-established educational charity in Brunei and had kindly offered me the use of her offices to interview the Bruneian applicants. As we drove, we talked about her life in Brunei. 'It has been a happy place to bring up children but the best thing about living here is having an *ama*,' she said. An *ama* is a cross between a maid and a nanny who helps with the housework and looks after children. Karen sighed; in just a few weeks she was returning to the UK after 20 years in Brunei. 'Without an *ama*, I'm going to have to learn how to iron again.'

The charity's offices were bright and airy, lined with shelves of children's books and educational toys, the walls crowded with drawings and posters of dancing cartoon words. I was introduced to the receptionist, Siti, who was so excited about the expedition interviews that she had obviously gone to a lot of effort to prepare for the day. She had stuck a large poster on a board outside the office that read, 'Volunteer Women's Commonwealth Arctic Expedition interviews' and methodically asked me questions about each of the candidates that would be coming along. I'd had more than fifty applications from Brunei and the shortlist included an interpreter, a sports reporter, a midwife and a businesswoman – but my first interview was with a Bruneian celebrity. Norhayati had just been named 'Brunei's First Lady Explorer' in a ceremony a few weeks before as a result of a ten-month overland journey she'd made from Africa to Brunei with her husband. Her trip had been broadcast on Bruneian TV and written about in the newspapers. When I first contacted the Bruneian authorities about my expedition, they had immediately put Norhayati forward as a candidate with a heavy hint that she should be my choice. I was keen to interview Norhayati but her fame didn't work in her favour. I wanted to prove that anybody could achieve their dreams – Norhayati had already achieved hers. She arrived wearing a long Malay-style dress but with her head uncovered. It was clear from the outset that she had not come to be interviewed; she had come to tell me about her experiences. I knew almost immediately that she was unsuitable for the team but enjoyed meeting her all the same. She had overcome many prejudices, on grounds of gender and religion, to be a jungle guide. 'Many people turn up to go on my trips, particularly the men, and assume that I am helping them prepare for the trip but that their guide will be a man,' she told me. 'It is only when we set off with packs on our backs that they realise I am the guide, the only guide. That's when they get worried and start asking questions. After a few days, when they are exhausted and I am still strong, they accept that I am the guide.'

By mid afternoon I was anxious that I still hadn't met any realistic potential team members but then Aniza arrived, a softly spoken air hostess with large almond-shaped eyes and a dazzling smile. She eloquently described her wish to be part of something that could present Brunei positively as a nation, to show other Bruneians that they need to engage in international matters and to generate greater national pride. Her views were so considered that I was surprised when she revealed that she was only 19 years old. I had been doubtful whether someone so young would be able to carry the burden of returning home as a role model but Aniza's quiet confidence was reassuring. 'How would you convince me that you have the mental toughness required to get you to the South Pole?' I asked. Aniza didn't hesitate with her reply. 'I would tell you about my pet gibbon.' She pulled up the sleeves of her top to show me her forearms, which were criss-crossed with long scars. 'Every morning I have to feed him and every morning he scratches me. But I don't give up.' We both laughed, but it was a persuasive answer.

Shortly after my interview with Aniza, I met Era. I wasn't hopeful as she entered the room. Physically tiny, she seemed timid and unsure of herself but she answered my questions with conviction and passion. 'I would use my experiences on the expedition to motivate the youth of Brunei to do great things,' she told me. 'We have a privileged life in Brunei but many young people are lazy and fall onto the wrong path.' Having married her husband less than a year before and spent the last three years as a mathematics teacher in a secondary school, Era had a clear idea of what she wanted from life and seemed to have it all planned out. 'Being a good Muslim is important to me and I want to keep learning how to be a better Muslim,' she explained. Even so, Era described the culture shock of returning to her own country after spending a number of years overseas with her family. 'Brunei has become more conservative while I was away and at first that was hard.' She hesitated before continuing, as if unsure how much to reveal. 'I like to play soccer but now it has been banned for girls to play. It's annoying.' Despite the fact that I was a good five years older than Era, her emotional maturity made me feel like a rash teenager in comparison. I could see that Era had the self-belief to keep her motivated and already I sensed that I was going to be able to depend on her.

I met with Era and Aniza at my hotel the following day and was really pleased to notice that they seemed to get on well with each other. As we discussed plans for Norway and the expedition, Era talked about consulting with her religious leaders about what rules she would need to follow while she was away and what exceptions would apply to her regarding prayer and fasting. Islam requires time for prayer five times a day but there are dispensations when travelling and missed observances can be made up later. As Era tried to explain some of the intricacies of her obligations, it all seemed so complicated. I was brought up as a Roman Catholic but the idea of consulting a religious authority about the smallest details of personal life decisions seemed so alien to me. I left them both in the lobby, talking excitedly about raising money and discussing who they could approach for support. Seeing them so focused on the road ahead gave me a sudden boost of euphoria. The team that had been a figment of my optimism for so long was now forming in front of my eyes. I was no longer alone and would soon have a worldwide network of women as determined as me to make the dream of an international polar expedition a reality. Stepping into the hotel lift, I filled my lungs with air and let it out again slowly. For a moment I allowed myself to wallow in a feeling of triumph and excitement.

New Zealand

Wellington was sunny but bitterly cold. September is winter-time in New Zealand and as I stepped out onto the street, a grit-filled wind blew into my face. After a while my nose began to run and my eyes started to water in the cold wind but it didn't take me long to find Turnbull House, a historic red-brick building that sits like an obstinate intruder amidst the modern concrete and glass skyscrapers in the heart of the city. The caretaker showed me the room I had hired for the interviews, gave me a set of keys and introduced me to the complexities of the alarm system. I headed back to the youth hostel and went to bed, exhausted.

I woke up knowing something was wrong. Blinking at my compact room, I knew what it was. I felt really well rested. I'd had a good long sleep. I must have overslept. I threw back the covers and leapt out of bed, grabbing the clock. It was already 10 a.m. – I was an hour late. I quickly plucked the sheaf of application forms from my bag and found the number of my first interviewee. She was already waiting outside Turnbull House wondering what to do. I gushed an explanation and asked her to find a coffee shop to wait in while I got there as soon as I could. Within the hour I arrived at Turnbull House to find Melanie, another candidate, pushing at the locked doors of Turnbull house looking confused. I felt terrible; applicants had come from the furthest reaches of New Zealand but it was me who was late. With Melanie in tow I quickly set up the meeting room and wrote new times for the interviews on a whiteboard outside the door. By limiting each interview to 30 minutes rather than 45, I could still see everyone.

Thankfully, Melanie was very laid-back. She had arrived home from a long stint abroad just the day before and had only applied at the last minute thanks to her sudden decision to return – it all seemed like it was meant to be. As a nurse and former ski patroller, she would be immensely useful as a team member and a calming influence in a crisis. I could visualise her as someone that the less experienced team members could look to for reassurance. The next candidate, Helen, arrived with a coffee for me – I could have hugged her. In my hurry that morning I hadn't had time for breakfast. As I gratefully wrapped my hands around the warm paper cup, we chatted casually. Helen had been trying to get to Antarctica for years. She would clearly be determined and passionate about the project. Next was Charmaine. I liked her instantly. She was a doctor in the army and, as with Melanie, I could see that other less experienced team members would respond well to her calm confidence. She was also a specialist in nutrition and physical training, knowledge that would be very helpful in our preparations for Antarctica. When the next candidate arrived and was yet another wonderful and competent lady with many strong abilities of clear benefit to the expedition, I started to realise that selecting the candidates from New Zealand was going to be extremely tough. I wanted to include everyone, and choosing was going to be heartbreaking for me, as well as for the candidates.

After the last interview I walked back to the hostel very slowly, thinking about each of the candidates I had met. I chose Melanie almost straight away, but it took me longer to decide on Lani, a young film-maker and committed community worker, over Charmaine the army doctor. Lani was the sort of person I would love to be – active, confident, creative and highly principled – but as I rang her number I noticed something on her application form that I had inexplicably missed beforehand; she had given her nationality as 'New Zealand/Australian'.

'Ah, I wondered if this would be a problem,' she said when I asked. Lani explained that she was still an Australian citizen even though she was a permanent resident in New Zealand. My heart sank. I had to discount Lani for the same reason I'd had to decide against Nicky in Cyprus. I could imagine the controversy if the New Zealand media discovered that the first New Zealand woman to ski to the South Pole was actually an Australian citizen. Lani was upset. 'I do so much for my community and yet when it counts I'm not Kiwi enough?' she demanded. There was nothing I could say. During my journey I had seen for myself how strongly people feel about nationality. I rang off and stared at the wall for a bit before bursting into tears. Maybe it was just the cumulative exhaustion of travelling for two months but the New Zealand selection had hit me hard. I had spent the day with women who had been full of enthusiasm but who were now bitter with disappointment. My tense conversation with Lani replayed in my head. An inspirational woman who cared about her community had been plunged into anger and frustration because of me and my rules. Combined with my experiences in Singapore it appeared that the expedition had done more damage than good.

As I waited for Charmaine and Melanie to arrive for our meeting the next day, I felt a familiar churn of nerves, worried that they might not be the people I remembered and that I would be faced with the realisation that I had made a mistake. Melanie arrived first, a big grin framed by blonde curls. Charmaine arrived shortly afterwards and was, in many ways, the complete opposite to Melanie. Petite with cropped dark hair, she was reserved but I thought I sensed a kindred spirit in her. As I sat down with them both I noticed each looking at the other in appraisal, as if trying to work out why they themselves had been selected. It was clear that they were very different characters but, like the Bruneian candidates, they seemed to get along with each other easily. When I had worked my way through the usual avalanche of information, I left them both in the cafe to digest what had been said. I walked back to the hostel along the waterfront, battling the wind as usual, and tried to imagine what kind of team would emerge from the group of candidates I had selected so far. I was sure that either Melanie or Charmaine would be a huge asset as I tried to form a single unit from this band of strangers but I wasn't confident that this would be enough to cope with the level of inexperience in all the other women. I had already come so far but there was still an awfully long way to go.

Jamaica

A documentary about violent gangs in Kingston probably isn't the best in-flight entertainment choice when flying to Jamaica. People had given me more warnings about travelling in Jamaica than any other destination on my trip. My dad, who had watched me set off for all sorts of places over the years, was unusually anxious when I rang home. 'Be careful won't you? Watch your back. It's dangerous,' he said in a low voice full of concern. It made me nervous.

The customs official studied my passport carefully as I arrived in Montego Bay. 'Where are you staying?'

'Knightwick bed and breakfast,' I replied.

He looked at me oddly. 'Bed and breakfast?'

He thought for a while before disappearing to confer with his colleagues. He came back smiling. 'Knightwick House is what we would call a villa,' he explained. 'A bed and breakfast is somewhere a man might take his girlfriend,' he paused before adding, 'just for an hour or two.'

Outside I collected my hire car and minutes later was heading into the town. I was navigating using the map in a guidebook but there was not a single road sign anywhere to help me find Knightwick House. Eventually I stopped to get a better look at the map. A man with dreadlocks rushed up to the car. I locked all the doors – jumpy from all the warnings I'd been given – but rolled down the window. 'You lost, sister?' he asked. I told him the name of the road I was looking for but he didn't know it. We waved goodbye then he added, 'You want any smoke?' He dipped his fingers towards his mouth to illustrate that he wasn't talking about cigarettes. I drove away leaving him disappointed. I'd been in Jamaica less than an hour and had already been offered marijuana.

The next morning I set off around the coast. I had five days to make it across the island to Kingston for the interviews but along the way I had a lot of phone calls to make. As in Ghana, I arrived in Jamaica with just a handful of applications. I needed to get the word out about the expedition – and quickly. I felt like I was holding my breath. It would be a shame to only have a few applicants; Jamaica deserved better than that. I emailed the press attaché at the Jamaican High Commission in London, who sent out an update through the Jamaica Information Service. The British Council in Kingston had offered to host the interviews, so I rang the director, Pauline, who sent me a long list of radio stations to call as well as the names of a couple of newspaper editors. The big paper in Jamaica is *The Gleaner* and I was determined to get some coverage from them. I called the editor and, although he was friendly, he wasn't willing to run a story on the expedition. 'This is an advert?' he asked me repeatedly. I tried to convince him that this was in fact a story, not an advert, but it became clear that he had already made up his mind. I listened to the local radio stations in my car as I drove around the island and noticed that talk shows seemed to be really popular, so I arranged to be the first caller on a national evening talk show. I had been warned by the producer beforehand that they could only give me three minutes on air but it was long enough to mention the expedition website and all the main information. The panel of presenters discussed the merits of such an outlandish plan for the next seven minutes – which in radio terms is an epoch.

My persistence with the media paid off; by the time I reached Kingston, five days after arriving in Jamaica, I had over thirty applications and could breathe again. My first stop in Kingston was to meet with the deputy high commissioner at the British High

Commission, who gave me a fascinating insight into Jamaican society. 'Everything that is being done at a grass roots level, at a community level, is being done by women,' he explained. 'Women are the organisers, the go-getters, the improvers and yet Jamaica is a very macho society. You will never see women involved in the violence; that is all down to the macho side of the culture. And yet, you get to a certain level and the women disappear. For example, there are very few women ministers.' He and his press officer were very enthusiastic about the expedition and gave me several leads for sponsorship as well as offering to help with the media.

I crossed the compound to speak to Pauline at the British Council. I had arrived at lunchtime and her team in the office sat eating, eyes wide, as I told them about the expedition. They were incredulous, but excited, and I felt instantly welcome. Pauline had already helped enormously with the media and now she generously agreed to give up her Saturday to open the office for the interviews. She was already there when I arrived the following morning but she greeted me with disappointing news. Out of the ten candidates that I had worked so hard to find, two had already called the office to cancel. One had damaged her car and the other had forgotten about the appointment and now found herself too far away to make it in time. As the remaining eight candidates came and went, Pauline chatted to them in reception while they waited for their turn. She wasn't able to join me in the interviews but when I had seen the last candidate, I sat at her desk and we talked through our opinions on each woman. I enjoyed having someone to compare my notes with, particularly someone with such good insight, and while Pauline locked up for the day, we both agreed on who my selected candidates should be.

My first candidate was Kim-Marie, who had cut an imposing figure, power-dressed in a black skirt suit complete with matching handbag. She had an impressive cascade of dreadlocks that fell to her shoulders and a laugh that rang loudly through the office. It didn't take much prompting to get her talking about herself and her views and I was soon finding it difficult to interrupt her. It didn't matter; as she spoke I was fascinated and impressed. Kim was clearly not someone who intended to sit around and wait for others to give her opportunities; she was actively seeking them out and had already spent time with a tribal people in India and worked for a group in Palestine protecting women's rights. She didn't have any expedition experience but she was very active, regularly running long distances, and dynamic enough to make me feel confident that she would play her part in the organisation of the expedition. One thing was certain: if there was money to be had in Jamaica to support the expedition, this was the woman who would find it.

Equally disarming was Alecia. She threw me slightly at the start of the interview by presenting me with a range of paperwork to support her application, ranging from a CV and education certificates to letters of recommendation. The paperwork was unnecessary but I was impressed by her thoroughness. Looking for sponsorship and preparing for the expedition would need a professional approach and Alecia had shown she was up to it despite her young age; she was a newly graduated 21-year-old.

Alecia and Kim had a lot in common but there was an obvious friction between them when they met. Kim was excited, which accentuated her garrulous tendency, and I could see Alecia becoming increasingly frustrated at not being able to speak. Kim seemed completely oblivious to the tension and gave Alecia a huge hug as we parted, stressing numerous times that they were in this together. As I walked away I wondered whether or not to be concerned about potential antagonism between them but realised there was little I could do. I would have to watch, and wait, and hope that they would work it out themselves.

The UK

Waking up in my own bed for the first time in three months, I didn't want to move. It felt as if I had no energy left. I knew there was an infinite list of things to be done but I couldn't seem to get my mind to focus on exactly what they were. I sat up in bed with a coffee to write a to-do list, but thinking about it all was too exhausting. I finished my coffee and slept for most of the rest of the day.

In the post that morning was a letter from the Winston Churchill Memorial Trust welcoming me home. I was incredibly grateful to them for their belief in the project and the letter prompted me to start the report they had requested about my journey. I sat in bed with my laptop and focused completely on the report for the next three or four days. As I typed, the route ahead seemed to solidify itself into a plan of action. By the time the report was finished my enthusiasm to attack the growing to-do list had returned.

In the meantime, applications for the UK reserve position had closed. I was going to be the UK representative on the team but we also needed a reserve in case someone had to drop out at the last minute due to illness or injury. The original plan was to ask the unselected candidate from each country to be a reserve but it would be impossible to train so many people to the required standard. I decided on one reserve and, as the involvement of the UK was so critical to our funding, I resolved that the reserve should be from the UK. I'd received more than fifty applications from women in the UK, most of whom had a lot of previous experience. The reserve role was a difficult position to fill, requiring someone who would invest significant time and energy into a project that they might not, ultimately, take part in. Critical to the interviews would be to establish what their motivation would be.

I invited ten of the applicants for an interview but shortly afterwards received emails from two unselected applicants asking for reconsideration. After battling such requests in Singapore and New Zealand I gave in this time and added their names to the shortlist. I arranged to meet all the applicants in a cafe bar in a street alongside Charing Cross station in London. It was a place I had used to conduct team interviews for a previous all-female expedition three years before. Back then, the staff had thought I was on some kind of lesbian speed-date but this time they twigged straight away. 'What are you holding interviews for?' the waitress asked as she served me a large latte. When I explained the details of the expedition, the bar staff became curious in the women that turned up, even pointing me out to those that arrived early. It was like having my own team of PAs. As I refilled my coffee from the bar they'd pass their judgement. 'She didn't look up to it to me,' said one barman about one applicant.

'Really? Why not?'

'The way she came in,' he continued. 'She seemed a bit hesitant and hung around the door. All the others have come right in straight away.'

I wasn't sure on the reliability of his selection technique but in this case he was probably right. The candidate had seemed a bit lukewarm about the whole expedition.

My last interview was with Helen, one of the women that I'd included at the last minute. She had an infectious good humour and the interview soon felt more like a gossipy natter with an old friend. She had already completed three guided polar expeditions but was eager for more. I took care to explain the limitations of the reserve role and the uncertainty involved. Her motivation, she said, was to gain more experience in the mechanics of putting an expedition together. Much later than I had intended, I left Helen and caught a train home. There had been two other main contenders but by the time the train pulled into my station, I knew that the choice had been obvious from the moment Helen walked into the cafe. I would be an idiot to turn her down.

In choosing Helen, my shortlist of 15 international candidates (two from each of the seven countries plus the reserve from the UK) was complete, and with it, the first stage of the selection. In total I had received applications from more than 800 women and had interviewed 72 of them, face to face, over the last 76 days. As I scanned through the list of selected candidates I was pleased with the variety of women represented. They ranged in age from 19-year-old Aniza to 43-year-old Helen. Among them were a teacher, a doctor, a satellite communications specialist, an engineer, an air hostess, an aerobics instructor, a civil servant, a personal assistant, a journalist and a mother of three. Some were single, some were married; some had significant outdoor experience, some had none whatsoever. All wanted to prove what they were capable of, not just as individuals, but as women. They all had different reasons for wanting to be a part of the team, from Reena who wanted to encourage more Indian women to seek a career in the outdoor industry, to Sophia who wanted to prove a miracle to her teenage daughter; but the immediate goal was the same for everyone: getting ourselves to the South Pole.

CHAPTER FOUR

THE PASSPORT PROBLEM

I could hear my mobile ringing. By the time I had swum through the fog of unconsciousness and forced myself awake, my mobile had stopped and the house phone was ringing instead. It was Era from Brunei. I blinked at the clock; it was 2 a.m. 'But what time should I have rung you?' she asked impatiently down the phone as I reported the time to her.

'You said ten o'clock in the morning GMT.'

'This is ten o'clock your time, not GMT. Brunei is eight hours ahead of GMT,' I attempted to explain, rubbing my eyes blearily.

'So what time should I call? Ten o'clock GMT or ten my time?'

My head was still thick with sleep and the numbers swirled around my head without meaning. I couldn't concentrate. 'Era, it's two in the morning for me. I can't talk about this now. This is definitely the wrong time. I will Skype you in roughly eight hours.'

It had been more than three months since I set off on my selection journey and the eclectic group of women I had chosen, but who had never met each other, were already socialising through messages on Facebook and the expedition website – but today was our first attempt at a conference call through the Internet. Spread over six different time zones, we couldn't find a time between us that would suit everyone, so instead I was due to speak to each country, one at a time, starting with New Zealand at 8 a.m. and ending with Jamaica at 10 p.m. I asked the group to work in GMT to make organising times easier but it wasn't a natural concept for everyone and we were having teething problems. The girls from New Zealand appeared online at 8 a.m. but there was nothing from the Singaporeans at 9 a.m. Aniza from Brunei popped up early but was cut off by one of the Indians. I spoke to one Cypriot but not the other and we were joined halfway through by Barbara from Ghana, who was early. By the time I had finished speaking to the Jamaicans at nearly midnight my brain was dribbling from my ears. It had been a big day and a complete shambles but I wasn't disheartened. This was the first attempt, and I was sure that we would get better at it. In fact it took us three or four attempts before we were able to have a complete conference call with everyone but at least I eventually stopped getting phone calls in the middle of the night.

Since returning from the selection journey, I had been busy planning the next phase; a two-week selection and training event in Norway for all 15 candidates. Many of the women had very little experience of subzero temperatures, and one or two had never even seen snow before, so my worry was that it was impossible for the majority of the team to have any real understanding of what an Antarctic expedition would be like. The journey to the South Pole would be a 900-kilometre ski across some of the most hostile terrain in the world and would take at least 40 days. It was one thing for the candidates to sit in an office in Ghana or Brunei telling me how keen they were to experience the challenges of

Antarctica, but quite another to do it for real. I needed the women to be tired, cold and a little bit scared for a few days to truly appreciate what the expedition would involve. Luckily, I knew just the place to make this happen. The Hardangervidda is a high mountainous plateau in the heart of southern Norway. During the winter it's a rolling plain of snow, notorious for harsh weather and challenging conditions. It was the most Antarctic-like place I had ever seen outside of the polar circle. It had the same vastness that I remembered in Antarctica, vastness that would make even hardened polar travellers feel vulnerable. The Hardangervidda is almost completely uninhabited except for a few remote huts. My plan was to find a base on the Hardangervidda and to assemble a group of experienced volunteers to train the candidates. The training team would teach them everything they would need to know in Antarctica, from skiing and avoiding cold-weather injuries, to pitching tents and using a liquid-fuel stove.

Taking on so many new skills in a such a short time and sleeping out in tents in temperatures of around −20°C would put the women under enormous pressure but this would give me a better idea of how they would cope as individuals in Antarctica and how they got on with each other. It was the relationships that worked well amongst the group that would ultimately determine who would be selected for the final team. This all-important selection would be made at the end of the first week, meaning that seven women would have to leave, while the remaining eight stayed behind for another week of training. I knew, even as I planned it, that splitting the group would be painful. I didn't want it to turn into a talent contest and I didn't want to be cruel but I comforted myself with a vow that I would ensure the selection was conducted as sensitively as possible.

One of my first priorities was to put together a budget. As well as the cost of the candidates' travel to the Hardangervidda, we would need food, accommodation and equipment. I estimated that I would need at least eight experienced volunteers to help me train the candidates and although they would give their time for free, it seemed only fair to pay for their travel and costs. I was confident that I could reduce many of the costs through sponsorship and perhaps by applying for some grant money but it was clear that, with all the money I had received from the Winston Churchill Memorial Trust gone, we were going to need additional funds.

Right from the start I had stressed to the candidates that I would need their help raising money and so far they had thrown themselves at the task with enthusiasm. The Indian candidates elicited financial support from the Indian Mountaineering Foundation (IMF), while the Singaporean candidates received similar funding from the Singapore Sports Council (SSC). In contrast, the Jamaicans decided to hold a big party, called The Cold Front, to raise money through ticket sales. I warned about the danger of relying so completely on one event but they were so confident that I allowed myself to be won over. 'The whole island will be there,' Kim reassured me. 'This is Jamaica; everyone likes to party.'

When it was time for an update from the Ghanaians I wasn't surprised that it was only Barbara that answered the call. 'Is Sheillah with you?' I asked.

'I phoned her a minute ago,' said Barbara flatly. 'She is on a bus on her way back from work, or something like that, and trying to get to an Internet cafe.' There was a pause before Barbara put into words what I had read between the lines for a while. 'I'm afraid that I'm not getting the support I would like from Sheillah.'

It had been a problem almost from the start. Sheillah rarely joined a conference call with the team and hadn't once offered an explanation for her lack of communication. I understood that it might be difficult to be available but after the last missed call

I had written her an email explaining that she had to keep in regular contact with the expedition so that I knew how she was progressing and so that she could interact with the rest of the team. I received a message back that was full of apologies and promises to be more active. That was the last I'd heard from her and I was running out of patience.

Barbara, on the other hand, had been working really hard but had been struck by two major setbacks. For the past six months the presidential elections in Ghana had paralysed the country; no one was interested in anything but politics. More ominously, several companies had accused her of being part of a big scam. They were suspicious that the expedition was a fraudulent way to extort money. 'Even when I showed them the letters from you and the quotes from the Commonwealth secretary-general they said, "So what? Anyone can write a letter." I don't know what I can do to convince them that this is genuine.'

Barbara seemed to be losing heart but I did my best to rally her morale. 'Barbara, one way or another, I will get you to Norway.' What I didn't say was that I didn't have a clue how I was going to do it.

One of the Cypriot candidates, Stephanie, sent me to secure support from a family friend who had offices in London. He was a Cypriot oil baron and a geologist so I had packed several maps of Antarctica, hoping that, like most geologists, he would get excited at the first whiff of chart paper. 'I'm here to see Dr Simonian,' I told the receptionist in the glass-fronted building. She looked puzzled. 'Oh, you mean Kapo!' she exclaimed in sudden comprehension and smiled knowingly as she led me up to an office. I was introduced to a man who looked more like an indulgent uncle than a wealthy oil baron. He shook my hand warmly and we sat down at a large round table to talk. I launched into a presentation about the expedition but after a few minutes

Kapo interrupted politely, 'Do you have any maps of your route in Antarctica?' I felt triumphant as I pulled the folds of paper from my bag and spread them across the table. We spent the rest of the meeting poring over annotated nunataks and ice streams. The next day I got a call from Stephanie. Kapo and his company, Comtrack Services, had offered the expedition $10,000, the majority of the money we needed for Norway.

At least now we could guarantee that Norway would go ahead. It was my job to make sure it was a success and for that, we needed a lot of equipment. I needed to provide 15 people with everything from clothing to skis, sledges to first aid kits. Day after day I would sit at my desk with a huge list and ring suppliers asking them to help.

I wouldn't have had the courage to ask for free products without the genuine belief that the project had something tangible to offer in return. Even so, making these calls grated against every fibre in my body. I hated it and would spend a minute or two steeling myself before dialling each new number. The rejections were often brutal and each one made making the next call even harder. I was fully aware that all of the companies I contacted probably received dozens of similar requests and I was under no illusion that for many small specialist suppliers, providing free products would be a significant investment. I wasn't frustrated by the negative replies but what did get annoying was the wavering. It seemed to be that the smaller the value of the product asked for, the harder I had to work to secure it. In return for 16 pairs of socks from a very large, mainstream company I spent days providing reams of information that the marketing team had requested about every aspect of the expedition, agreed to dozens of demands in return for the product and spent hours on the phone with them talking through each detail of the deal – and still the eventual answer was negative. It was exhausting.

One marketing lady I spoke to was under so much pressure that her imminent breakdown was audible. She screeched down the phone at me, 'I have no budget! I have no budget!' I decided not to try approaching her again, for fear of pushing her over the edge.

The Christmas holidays arrived but I found it hard to switch off. Norway had been scheduled to start during the last week in February, barely two months away, and there was still so much to be done. I reminded myself to celebrate all the successes we had had so far and to think about all the positives, but it felt like I was presiding over a house of cards; everything was dependent on something else, nothing was definite. If one piece fell, the whole thing would collapse. As a result I veered between wild excitement at the prospect of pulling everything together and a deep stomach-gripping dread at the spectre of it all falling apart. On New Year's Eve I sat watching other people's fireworks from the balcony of my flat, wrapped in a blanket, eating Stilton and drinking fizzy wine. I tried to think ahead to New Year's Day 2010. Would I be standing at the South Pole with seven others as planned? The thought died in my head. Something inside me wouldn't allow myself to look that far into the future. Instead it was focused on Norway. If I could just make Norway happen, then and only then, would I allow myself to look towards Antarctica.

I'd recently met with two ex-marines I had known for a number of years. They had decades of training in Arctic warfare and had seen dozens of hard men from tropical countries like Trinidad and Jamaica go through the process. 'We are talking about tough guys, but they had real problems in the Arctic,' one explained. 'It's not that they just didn't like the cold, they physically couldn't acclimatise. Some people have an allergic reaction to the cold and there is nothing you can do.' I'd heard opinions like this before and had dismissed them all as urban myth but these men knew what they were talking about and it made me pause. What if the girls simply couldn't acclimatise? I was creating a schedule for Norway that would provide a slow and gradual introduction to the climate – as gradual as it could be within the short week we had – but there was a real possibility that it wouldn't be enough. I myself had seen very strong, fit and experienced men from the UK arrive in the high Arctic after months of preparation and fundraising, only to ask to go home within days. It wasn't that they weren't able to cope physically but something in their brain was switching off, telling them they couldn't cope. The effect was known privately as Arctic Shock and it only seemed to happen in the first few days. I reasoned with myself that you didn't need to come from a tropical country to find -20°C demanding; even those from temperate regions like the UK would find it hard. The need to acclimatise would be essential wherever you came from. However, if I was wrong, it could be terminal for my project. If I wanted to get anywhere near Antarctica, Norway would need to be the proof that the women could acclimatise to the cold and learn the skills they would need to stay safe.

Our first team conference call of 2009 wasn't as promising as I would have liked. Money was the biggest problem. The media was full of frenzied reports about credit crunches, global banking meltdowns, recession and tightening economies. It had to be the worst time in 20 years to be looking for sponsorship and the entire team seemed demoralised. Era from Brunei was concerned about a letter that she had sent to the Bruneian authorities back in November asking for permission to fundraise for the expedition. The Ministry of Culture, Youth and Sport had told her that the letter had been lost. 'I have a copy but the ministry won't accept a copy, it has to be the original,' she explained.

'Can you send another letter?' I asked.

'No. They say it has to be the original.'

'So, you can't do any fundraising until the ministry find the original letter that they have lost?'

'Yes,' Era confirmed.

It just seemed barmy. 'So, is anyone looking for it?' I asked.

'I don't know. They say they are looking.'

I was looking forward to speaking to the Jamaicans. They had held their big fundraising event, The Cold Front, a few days before and I was keen to know how much money it had raised for them. As soon as I heard Kim's voice I could tell something was wrong. 'We made nothing,' she said miserably, 'in fact I think I may owe money.' Silently I rested my forehead on my desk. This was a disaster. Apparently the event had been a sell-out and lots of local artists had turned out to perform but at the last minute the lighting crew had demanded money. Kim had no option but to pay them but when the band heard about it, they also demanded money. There was still some ticket money to collect but it looked as if they would struggle to break even. Kim didn't sound like herself. She sounded like she had given up. 'I'm feeling very sorry for myself right now,' she admitted.

Part of me was irritated by her news. I had, after all, warned her about relying too heavily on one event. But what she needed right now was motivation and a clear route forward. 'Forget The Cold Front, you haven't got time to analyse what went wrong because you need to concentrate on finding the seven hundred dollars you each need. What ideas have you got?'

'A bake sale!' said Alecia with instant enthusiasm. 'We can sell them on the university campus.'

I paused in order to pose my question tactfully, 'Can you realistically sell fourteen hundred dollars worth of cakes?'

Alecia thought about it. 'Me and my mom can bake a *lot* of cake.'

I quietly placed my forehead back on my desk.

The news from Ghana was equally glum. Sheillah had continued to be elusive. In response to my latest email she had replied, 'God will provide.'

'But you've got to give God a fighting chance!' I exploded at the computer screen as I read her email. Divine intervention is a risky fundraising strategy even if you provide an outlet or two for the miracle but as far as I could see Sheillah hadn't written a single letter, made a single approach to a sponsor or come up with one decent idea. My patience was spent. It was to be expected that Sheillah and Barbara might not be able to find sponsorship; Ghana was by far the poorest country involved in the expedition and so subsidising the Ghanaian participants had been factored into the budget. It didn't really matter what amounts were raised by candidates in each country as long as everyone was putting in equal effort. This is where Sheillah had failed and I now felt that to fund her trip would be to give her a free ride and that would be an insult to all the other women that were working so hard to win financial support. It would be a shame to have only one Ghanaian in Norway but there seemed little point in Sheillah attending as I already knew that her attitude was completely wrong – there was no way I could have her on my team for Antarctica.

Barbara's situation was different. She had worked really hard and been unfairly thwarted at every turn, but the money wasn't her only problem. Despite my incessant nagging for months, Barbara still hadn't applied for a visa. I got the impression that there was something stopping Barbara applying but, for whatever reason, she didn't want to tell me. 'I go to the embassy but the guard on the gate turns me away,' she finally admitted. 'He looks at my papers and tells me they are not complete.' Barbara had been too embarrassed about the fact that she had been turned away to tell me about the problem. Barbara wasn't the only one with visa issues. Alecia and Kim in Jamaica had also left it until the last minute to apply for their visas and were almost out of time.

I woke up early the next morning after yet another bad night's sleep and sat on the edge of my bed staring at the wall. With just a few weeks left before we were due to depart for Norway, my brain swirled with everything that I knew I had to do but I felt empty; I couldn't find the energy to move, never mind think clearly. I hadn't been able to sleep or relax properly for weeks. There wasn't a moment when I wasn't thinking or working on the expedition. The stress was beginning to show in the size of the bags under my eyes and the paleness of my face. I looked ill. It was more than lack of sleep: it was mental exhaustion. I just wanted it all to stop. I wanted to be able to pause time so that I could crawl into the darkness somewhere and rest. But I knew I couldn't stop. So many people were relying on me to find the answers. The only thing keeping me going was the knowledge that there was no other option. I had to find those answers. I had to make this work.

My first call was to the Commonwealth Foundation, a grant-giving branch of the Commonwealth dedicated to supporting civil society organisations. I had spoken to the Commonwealth Foundation before regarding grant-funding but the expedition didn't fall within any of the foundation's criteria; we were too unusual and unwieldy to be categorised. Undaunted (and driven by a rapidly dwindling pool of alternative options), I explained our current problem and asked if the foundation would be able to fund the cost of flights for the Jamaicans and Ghanaian, making it possible for them to take part in the Norway training. 'The central purpose of the foundation is to bring together people from all over the Commonwealth,' my contact explained. 'This is essentially what you are trying to do, even if, strictly speaking, you fall outside our remit.' I held my breath as the voice on the line paused to think. 'Let me see what I can do.' I crossed my fingers as I put down the phone.

My next move was to contact High Commissioner Burchell Whiteman at the Jamaican High Commission in London, whom I had met the previous summer and who had been so supportive. I wasn't sure how he could help Kim and Alecia but decided to simply explain our problem and see if he could suggest anything. It turned out he was in Jamaica at the time and emailed a reply almost instantly. 'I can help. I just need to know the dates the applications were made.' I let out a long sigh of relief. This was incredible news. I was so grateful.

I rang the embassy in Ghana handling Barbara's visa to Norway and spoke to the consul, explaining what Barbara had told me. 'I'm sorry,' said the consul, 'but I think your team member is lying. We've got a great team on the gate. They have no right to ask for this lady's documents and there is absolutely no way that could happen.' I was stunned. To assume Barbara was lying seemed to be a very quick and callous assumption to make. Despite her accusation, the consul allowed me to arrange a time for Barbara to come and see her personally. I gave Barbara the details and strict instructions to stand her ground at the gate. 'Barbara, if anyone tries to send you away demand to see the consul. You have her name – use it. Do not leave until you have seen her. If you have any problems, call me.' I was on standby all day, preparing myself for an argument with the consul, but when Barbara called it was good news. She had received an apology, a letter of support and the promise of a visa within a few days.

My positive mood at our great progress was ruined by an email from Kim. 'Couldn't make it to the embassy to submit my papers today. Traffic too bad,' she wrote. I yelled at the computer screen. With a week to go before she was due to depart for Norway, not to mention the hard work I had put in and the strings that had been pulled on her behalf by an incredibly generous high commissioner, I couldn't believe the lack of urgency on her part. If I had been in her position I would have made sure I got to the embassy. I would have walked if necessary. My frustration was turning to despair.

Another shock arrived the next day. Sitting in bed I decided to answer a few more emails before going to sleep. Peter, already half asleep himself, sat up next to me as he heard me groan at the computer screen. 'What is it? What's wrong?' he asked. It was an email from Barbara that had been sent to all the candidates. I read it aloud to him:

> Dear all,
> Due to the fact that I'm not able to secure any sponsorship to be able to join you in Norway, I am forced to opt out.
>
> I have withdrawn my applications from both Norway and UK embassies, as I will not be able to use them to travel. It's a catch-22 situation; I could get the visa, and have no money, or I could get the money and not get the visa in time.
>
> It has been very tough preparing for this event, and I blame myself for any poor planning that resulted in this unfortunate result. I wish that Sheillah would have contributed more, in terms of finding sponsorship, writing and distributing letters, training, etc. Two heads are always better than one; maybe, in the areas that I lacked, she could have filled in the blanks. Ah well, shoulda, coulda, woulda.
>
> Not attending Norway obviously means that we don't get to be part of the selection process which determines the final team. I don't want to give up this chance, but it's out of my hands right now.
> Regards,
> Barbara

The email felt like a body blow. I wanted to cry with frustration but I was so tired I was numb. It felt like the whole project was falling on my head. Peter tried to console me, 'This isn't the end of the world, you still have a great project even if the Jamaicans and Ghanaians don't come.' But for me it changed the whole fabric of the expedition. I tried to get around it in my head, to get used to the idea of them not being there but it didn't feel the same. After the frustration came the anger. I was livid that the email had been sent to the entire team. Why hadn't Barbara talked to me first? Hadn't I deserved even that tiny courtesy? This email would do enormous damage to the fragile confidence of an already jittery team. I returned an email to Barbara immediately and was talking to her first thing the following morning, 'You should have told me first, Barbara.'

'I think I just had a panic moment,' she explained.

I could see that a lecture was not what Barbara needed so I swallowed my anger and gave her some reassurance. 'We all have moments like that, Barbara, but you have to see them for what they are. You can't write emails like this on a whim.'

I asked her to write an explanation to the team which she did immediately. 'Felicity has given me a verbal back rub and I feel a lot better,' she wrote.

I was also able to give Barbara some good news. The Commonwealth Foundation had been in touch. They were going to fund her flight, as well as the Jamaicans'. She was coming to Norway. All she had to do was get her visa.

For now I felt I had done what I could for Kim, Alecia and Barbara. I needed to turn my attention elsewhere. There were just three days to go until I was due to fly out to Norway myself, and I still needed socks, thermos flasks, ski poles, ski boots, sledges and food for 24 people for up to a fortnight. I was overdue on several press releases and needed to supply the journalists who were due to join us in Norway with their travel information and joining instructions. I had to drive to Cirencester to collect the skis we were borrowing and to Sheffield to collect the sleeping bags and down jackets for everyone. I also needed to find time to print out safety documents, update the website and perhaps, if I was lucky, pack my own bags.

Every morning brought a fresh avalanche of emails and it seemed that every single message required a time-consuming action to be taken immediately. The phone didn't stop ringing either. It wasn't uncommon to be speaking on Skype while my mobile and house phone were both ringing simultaneously. The situation was approaching farcical proportions. So many people were doing so much to help and yet there was no one but me to pull it all together. Everyone needed something yesterday and suddenly it seemed that the world was a pack of snarling dogs all tearing away at me piece by piece. As it was I was working from 6 a.m. until midnight every day and still it wasn't enough. There were other stresses, too. I had been working full-time on the expedition for six months without pay and I was broke.

I had never felt quite this low before and it worried me. My emotions were completely bipolar. I swung from feeling really excited and proud, to feeling despairingly depressed and just a little bit angry. People expected so much and were so ready to criticise, giving me little credit for the fact that I was creating the expedition out of nothing.

Just as I was leaving to meet Peter, who had volunteered to drive all our equipment to Norway in a borrowed Land Rover, Paul Deegan called. I vented my frustrations at him for a full hour. He told me about a famous swim coach who said, 'Once you're stood on that starting block, you're standing with what you've got.' He meant that at the moment you start the race it doesn't matter what training you haven't done, or the drag-reducing suit you didn't choose; what matters is that you get on with the race. The advice calmed me down as we loaded the Land Rover and trailer. My dad had come to the rescue by providing the trailer at the last minute. He had been struck by inspiration and converted an old trailer tent. It looked like an old-fashioned caravan with the top half sliced off, still complete with cabinets, carpet and a functioning door. It was hard not to laugh at it but I was thrilled; it was ours. Dad had even put stickers along the side proudly displaying the expedition website address in big red letters. The gesture was perfect.

The Land Rover finally trundled off towards the ferry and I dragged myself home. There was a message waiting for me from Charmaine in New Zealand to let me know she was about to get on the plane that would eventually bring her to Norway. It was strange to think that some of the women were already on their way. It felt like putting a coin in an old-fashioned arcade game – once you let go of the coin, the mechanisms are given momentum that can't be stopped. The end results are out of your control and all you can do is watch. I felt like I had just let go of the coin. I wasn't sure who, exactly, I would be meeting off the train in Norway in a few days. Would Barbara be there? Would Kim get her visa in time? It was up to them now.

Arriving at Stansted airport it wasn't difficult to spot the photographer, Rob, and the film crew, Al and Elliott; they were standing next to a conspicuous mountain of luggage that I noted with anxiety. I had known Al for a while. He and his business partner, Elliott, were both climbers and had made filming in tough locations their speciality. Rob was a photographer who had worked with me on previous expeditions. With a theatrical background he could be alarmingly flamboyant at times but he was dependable, accommodating and took great photographs. As we greeted each other I made a mental effort to bite my lip about the luggage. They were here as a favour, taking time out of running their business to help me, so I was in no position to be annoyed.

Next to arrive was Helen, who had made the long journey down from her home in Derbyshire, closely followed by two of my volunteer trainers, Sarah and Mark. I had met Sarah during my very first overseas expedition. She was an expert on Greenland and now ran her own travel company, which specialised in polar holidays. Mark is one of those people that you feel you have known for years within minutes of meeting. He had been part of a team I had trained the year before when he had been a competitor in a race across the Canadian Arctic. This would be the first time Mark had taken on the role of instructor and although I knew he would be brilliant, I suspected that he was a little nervous.

The normal check-in procedure at the airport had broken down and instead, a young girl in a short skirt and heels stood on an airline counter using a handheld megaphone to yell out the next plane to leave from a list on her clipboard.

As we waited, I tried to reduce the weight of our luggage and condense the number of bags as much as possible. I threw heavy snow boots in front of the team and convinced them to wear them on the aircraft, putting their lighter footwear in the hold luggage instead. The snow boots were like oversized wellies with felt liners and thick rubber soles. Each boot weighed a kilogram.

With our plane already boarding, we were finally called forward to check in, with no time to argue over the excess baggage fee. It came to over £500. I handed over my credit card with tears in my eyes. It was money that the expedition didn't have and we were so short of cash that this kind of mistake would be crippling. We dashed through security as our gate was closing, Rob and Elliott removing the cumbersome snow boots to run in their socks. Red faced and gasping for breath, we reached the gate and handed over our boarding cards. Last in line was Elliott, and when he didn't arrive on the gangway I went back to the gate to look for him. Elliott was standing by the boarding desk, boots in hand. 'It's my passport,' he stammered, looking as if he was about to burst into tears. 'It expired in January.'

'Sorry,' said the gate attendant, handing back the passport. 'You can't travel and your bags will have to come off the plane too.'

Elliott and I looked at each other in panic. I had condensed lots of bags into just two or three while we waited to check in and as a result neither of us could remember exactly what kit had ended up in his bags. It was bad enough that we would be without Elliott, but now it looked unlikely that Al would have enough kit with him to do any filming at all on his own.

This was the first hour of the first day of our trip and already I'd had two major disasters; the excess baggage and Elliott's passport. Neither was my fault and yet somehow both threw my confidence. Was I completely incompetent after all?

Boarding the plane, I broke the news to Al just as Elliott rang his mobile. Elliott was on his way into London to try to get a new passport in time to get to Norway before it was all over. He'd had to buy a pair of shoes in the airport as the snow boots were the only footwear he had been left with. More seriously, the bag that had been returned from the plane contained most of the sound kit, leaving Al seriously depleted but he could still film using the sound from the camera. It wouldn't be great but it would be better than nothing.

Filming the expedition wasn't critical to the project, whereas the £500 sitting on my credit card to pay for the excess baggage made me feel physically sick. Where would I find the money to pay off the bill? I decided not to allow myself to dwell on it. This was only the first day of a complicated and pivotal training event and I had to focus completely on the fortnight ahead.

CHAPTER FIVE

HANDBAGS AND SNOW BOOTS

I arrived in Norway with the training team and film crew a day before the rest of the women. Peter, who had spent two days driving the Land Rover and trailer full of equipment all the way from the UK, collected us from the train station in the tiny village of Haugastøl on the edge of the Hardangervidda long after nightfall. With the entire training team crammed into the Land Rover we made the slow and twisting climb up onto the plateau. The headlights picked out deep drifts of snow piled up on either side of the narrow road but we could see little else in the darkness. After a long hour we pulled up next to a darkened hut, half buried in snow. This was Dyranut Fjellstova, a family-run hostel perched on the highest point of the plateau. The hut was usually closed for the winter months but the owner had been persuaded to let us use the place for a fortnight. We hadn't expected any special treatment but the owners had clearly taken the effort to prepare the place for us. The windows were unboarded, snowdrifts had been cleared from the doorways and, the ultimate of thoughtful gestures, a simple meal had been left out. We fell on the food gratefully before pulling out our sleeping bags and finding somewhere in the hut to sleep.

The following morning I was the first to wake. I had been too tired to explore the building before going to bed but now, pulling on a thick jumper, I padded through the grey light of early morning to have a good look around. The hut was lined in pine to make it cosy and hung with stuffed animals and painted scenes of a green Hardangervidda that looked very different to the landscape visible through the windows. As well as a central dining room heated by a large, stone fireplace there was a fully equipped kitchen, a small office which became a meeting room for the training team, a bathroom and several bedrooms. Al took over the largest bedroom as a temporary editing studio.

The candidates would be staying in a long accommodation block with its own bathroom that was separated from the main hut by a few hundred metres of drifted snow. I grinned to myself in satisfaction; the size and layout of the hut couldn't have been more perfect if it had been built specifically with our group in mind.

The fire in the dining area still glowed from the previous evening. I pushed some extra logs into the grate and drew close as I wrapped my hands around a hot mug of coffee, gazing out of the wide windows at the monochrome landscape that surrounded us. The Hardangervidda was as wild as I remembered it. Apart from a 6-metre-high wooden troll perched on the hill opposite the hut (a whim of the owner), there was no other sign of civilisation as far as the eye could see. Clouds of snow blotted out the horizon so that it was impossible in places to tell where the heavy sky ended and the snow-covered hills began. Like a bowl of cream-covered fruit, the snow flowed seamlessly over every undulation and as the day went on, the light shifted over the smooth, flawless surface so that the brain had to work hard to get a sense of perspective. With no trees or buildings to give an inkling of scale, a small clump of snow a few metres away could look like a mountain in the distance and a tiny drift of snow could seem as tall as a neck-breaking escarpment.

I heard the others stir one by one and soon everyone was sitting around one of the long tables in the dining area with hot cups of tea, allocating themselves jobs for the day to prepare for the arrival of the candidates. By late afternoon I was in the Land Rover on my way to meet the group off the train from Oslo. Two more trainers, Jim and Jo, had met the women as they arrived at Oslo airport and accompanied them on the train. Jo had been a part of an all-woman team that I had put together to cross Greenland two years before. She was also a secondary school teacher and so was very good at herding temperamental groups and preparing for the unexpected. Jim was Sarah's husband: I had known him since we had both worked for the British Antarctic Survey nearly a decade earlier. Jim had sent a text to say that they had met the women and caught the right train but he hadn't given any information about how many women were with them. So as I nervously waited on the station platform with Peter, Rob and Al, I still didn't know exactly who would be getting off the train. Had Kim got her visa in time? Would Barbara be there? I paced up and down the platform, more impatient with each passing minute. I thought about how often I'd imagined this moment and how impossibly unattainable it had seemed at times as we had faced setback after setback. I squinted down the tracks, searching for the lights of an oncoming train. I couldn't stand still, partly due to the cold that was seeping through my jacket and partly through excitement.

The tracks began to fizz and I took a step back from the edge of the platform watching the approaching headlights. The train slid along the station, slowing down enough for me to glance into the windows of each carriage as it passed. I searched for a cluster of women, for a face that was familiar, but spotted nothing. The train stopped and people spilled out of the doors. I looked up and down the platform, looking for anyone I knew, but there was no sign of them. I started walking alongside the train, feeling the concern in my stomach. There was a flash of cameras behind me and I turned to see a gaggle of well-wrapped bodies huddled by a doorway at the far end of the train. They were here! I ran over to the girls and began hugging my way through the group.

At first it was hard to recognise who was who; all I could see were broad smiles under big hats, fur-lined hoods and woolly scarves. There was Lina and Mel, now Alecia and Athina. Kim, she had made it! And Barbara! Everyone was here. The group looked hopelessly out of place as they began dragging wheeled suitcases across the snow-covered platform, handbags still firmly in place in the crooks of their arms. As the suitcases were manhandled onto the roof of the Land Rover, I hung back from the group and took a minute to soak in the moment. Here they were, a group of women from all over the world come together in a remote corner of Norway in the dead of winter. It wasn't the South Pole, but right then it felt like an equal achievement.

'They are an awesome bunch of ladies,' Jo muttered, coming to join me. 'You've chosen well.' I couldn't help smiling in agreement. Barbara looked great after four months of training while Aniza from Brunei and Reena from India chatted animatedly to each other and Charmaine jumped onto the roof of the Land Rover to help secure all the luggage. All of them looked completely at ease, as if they had already known each other for years.

The Hardangervidda had prepared its own very special welcome for the women. A storm was brewing up on the plateau and so the only road that snaked up to our hut from the valley was closed. Peter disappeared to talk to the snowplough drivers who make regular journeys across the Hardangervidda to keep the road clear of snowdrifts. They agreed to take us as far as the hut in convoy but some of the women would have to ride in the cabs of the snowploughs. One snowplough with three of the women in the cab led the way, the Land Rover followed and a second snowplough brought up the rear with another three women in the cab; the Norwegian drivers looked surprised but delighted as these exotic women and their handbags made themselves comfortable. The snowploughs are huge machines the size of a large lorry; squat and powerful with vicious-looking blades taller than a man welded to the front. The blades cut through the snowdrifts that were already forming on the road, flinging plumes of snow into the darkness. We followed in the Land Rover a few metres behind the lead plough, but even so it wasn't long before the blizzard had completely obscured it from view. All we could see were the flashing lights on the snowplough staining the snow orange so that, from the front of the Land Rover, it looked like we were driving into a broiling ball of fire. It was a dramatic sight and I realised an anxious silence had fallen over everyone inside the vehicle. I turned to look at the faces in the back. Aniza was closest to me, her eyes wide in horror and her mouth hanging open in shock. It was the first time she had ever seen snow.

Arriving at the hut we ushered the group inside quickly, helping them as they stumbled in the deep drifts and fought to keep the blowing snow out of their faces. Even the training team were pleased to finally shut the door against the blizzard outside and enjoy the warmth of the fire. As the candidates tucked into the casual meal Sarah and Mark had prepared I gave them all a brief overview of the week ahead. We had a lot to cover so I warned them all about early starts and late nights but stressed that the trainers would support them every step of the way. I knew how scary the Hardangervidda could be and I was slightly worried about how the women would react when the morning revealed exactly how isolated we were. The short journey from Land Rover to hut had been enough to make one or two women a little nervous but I suspected that, more than the conditions, it was the selection that everyone knew was coming at the end of the week that was the most daunting. 'This is a selection but it is not a competition,' I told the group. 'It's not about who is the fittest or the fastest, it's about creating the best mix of people, so the best thing you can do is just to be yourself. I know it's hard but try to forget about the selection and just enjoy being here.'

The next morning I couldn't help laughing as we watched the candidates emerge from the accommodation block and struggle through the snowdrifts to the hut. They all wore the big down jackets and snow boots they had been issued the night before but several still clutched their handbags as they fought against the wind-driven snow. A few stopped midway to gape at their surroundings, incredulous, before putting their heads down in grim determination to continue. I think for some, the 50-metre walk to the hut that first morning was a mini-expedition in itself. After breakfast we gathered everyone in the lecture room with a comforting fire blazing. The very first lecture was about cold weather injuries. Having this lecture so early on risked scaring the women but I couldn't chance the group spending any significant length of time outside without them first being aware of how dangerous the cold can be. We drew on the experiences of all the trainers to explain injuries such as frostbite, hypothermia and snow blindness, as well as the less obvious – but more common – dangers of blisters, bad hygiene and dehydration. It is ironic that one of the greatest dangers in the cold is to overheat. Sweating through exertion or wearing too many layers leaves skin and clothing damp. The moisture freezes in the cold, which can lead to potentially serious frostbite or hypothermia. The candidates had to learn to fight the natural instinct, when faced with subzero temperatures, to wear excessive layers. They also needed to realise the importance of keeping their socks and gloves dry to protect their fingers and toes from injury. The trainers would be making sure the girls had spare gloves and socks, checking the ones they were wearing were dry and that the group were drying their kit properly every evening but the trainers wouldn't be able to see everything. The girls needed to learn to be responsible for keeping themselves safe if they were going to go to Antarctica.

Lecture over, the chairs were pushed to one side and the men ordered to leave as the girls were issued the rest of the clothing they would need for the training. The room was soon full of half-naked women squirming into thermal long johns and windproof salopettes. I had tried to match the sizes of the clothing with the measurements the candidates had sent me by email but women very rarely fall into clear categories of small, medium and large – and this group was no exception.

With everyone dressed in their new kit, complete with goggles, gloves and snow boots, we all trouped outside into the snow. Two of the candidates had not seen snow before arriving in Norway; most of the others had had no more than brief glimpses on holidays to the States or a freak snowfall that hadn't settled – certainly nothing like the amount of snow that smothered the Hardangervidda around us and continued to fall from the sky in big fat flakes. I got them all building snowmen in groups and had to laugh as I overheard Alecia from Jamaica getting frustrated. 'The snow won't stick together!' she ranted as yet another fistful of white powder fell from her hands. She noticed me watching her. 'I'm trying to make a head for the snowman but it keeps falling apart,' she told me. 'This is surprisingly difficult.'

After snowmen came the art of snow angels. Many of the girls paused before falling backward into the snow as instructed, unsure that purposely floundering in ice-cold powder could possibly provide any semblance of fun but, one by one, the whole group was soon flapping in the snowdrifts, pointing and laughing like children at the angel-like impressions they left behind. Finally, the training session erupted into the inevitable snowball fight, the women throwing snow into each other's faces and making unsuccessful chases, their getaways hampered by heavy snow boots and deep snow. Eventually the group were ushered back into the hut, red-faced with exertion and so overheated that steam rose from them like warm breath on a cold morning. They had learnt their first lesson about how easy it was to get too hot, even at −20°C.

Later that evening Elliott arrived, having made a miraculous last-minute dash from London with his new passport. He looked a bit dazed as he entered a hut full of more than 20 excitable, noisy women but soon settled in, disappearing with Al to fill their makeshift editing studio with more wires and boxes of magic.

The next day it was time to get the candidates on skis. After a quick lecture in the hut from Jim about bindings and the theory of how to ski, we all went outside to put theory into practice. We were using cross-country skis, which are narrower than typical downhill versions. Cross-country skis are designed for walking, so although the toe of the foot is fixed, the heel is left free. The bindings on the skis were simple plastic affairs designed to be used with the well-insulated snow boots that the girls were wearing. The problem was that most of the candidates had tiny feet, whereas the boots were larger sizes. Many of the girls found their feet swimming in excess space, which made it even harder when they came to strap on the skis. In Alecia's case, I saw her feet come out of the boots completely a couple of times so that she was standing in the snow in her socks – clearly not ideal.

In many respects cross-country skiing is a lot easier to learn than downhill skiing as it is basically walking (the motion is a bit like sliding along a polished floor in socks) but the skis do take some getting used to and require balance, particularly when going up or down slopes. Despite the difficulties and the fact that, for many, this was their first time on skis, the candidates did extremely well. The concentration and determination was clear on their faces and although there were tumbles there wasn't nearly as much falling over as I had expected. However, Kim, in particular, found it tough. Her spectacular dreadlocks were already caked in snow from her numerous tumbles and her woolly hat clung precariously to the top of her head, threatening to fall off with every fall. 'My legs won't do what I want them to!' she complained. As I commiserated with her, Barbara fell heavily right next to me. I helped her up and had to laugh as she sighed in resignation. 'I thought there would be some kind of instant thing where the skis and snow move together as soon as you put them on,' she admitted. 'But it's not like that. I've got to be in control.' She nodded grimly in agreement with her own statement and pushed off into another glide, landing in a heap a few metres away.

We kept the first ski session short but returned to it throughout the day, alternating lectures inside with increasing periods of time outside. Gradually, the girls learnt to wear fewer clothes as they went outside, even when the wind was blowing snow horizontally through the air, and it was great to see the periods between falls getting longer. By our third day on the Hardangervidda the trainers were able to lead small groups on their skis on short routes around the hut, skiing up nearby hills and finding long slopes to practise on.

That afternoon the sky closed in again and as the air filled with blowing snow our world gradually shrank until we could barely see the accommodation block from the hut. The candidates needed to learn how to pitch the expedition tents and there was no better time to learn than in the middle of a Norwegian blizzard. The tents were a make and model that I had used on all my previous expeditions, and we planned to take the same tents to Antarctica. They were four-man tunnel tents with four poles that could be left *in situ* when the tent was packed away. They were well thought out in design, with a large enclosed compartment inside for sleeping and big areas at the front and back that could be used for cooking or storage.

In Antarctica these tents would be our only shelter, making them a vital lifeline. Without them we wouldn't last very long in the harsh conditions and would risk injury or death from exposure. The ability to get them up quickly was critical: it would be too cold in Antarctica to stand around in discussion and often the noise of the wind, combined with layers of face-covering, would make it difficult to communicate anyway – so developing a tent routine beforehand was important to make sure everyone on the team worked simultaneously and as efficiently as possible. Jo had been in my team that crossed Greenland and so together we demonstrated our tent routine to the candidates. The girls watched carefully before splitting into groups of four to try pitching the tents for themselves. All the trainers were on hand to help as the group struggled in the growing wind but they were determined to get it right, particularly as they all knew that tonight they would be sleeping outside in the tents for the first time.

As darkness fell and the wind continued, the temperature dropped noticeably and the thermometer outside the hut fell to –27°C. All through dinner the girls were quieter than normal, nervous about the night ahead in the tents. We had prepared them with a lecture about keeping warm at night, sharing tricks that the trainers had learnt through experience as well as warnings about mistakes we had all learnt to avoid the hard way. Armed with sugary snacks, hot water bottles, head torches and warm hats, they reluctantly took the plunge after dinner, leaving the hut in small groups to face their sleeping bags, which were already laid out in the tents.

With all the candidates outside it was a quiet evening in the hut and a good chance to plan the next few days. I wanted to take them on a mini-expedition away from the hut so that they could get the feel of what a real expedition might be like. I spread out a map of the local area and took a good look with Jim and Peter. Each evening we wanted to camp near the road, just in case we had problems, but during the day we would send the candidates deeper into the Hardangervidda around the local valleys and hilltops. Each trainer would be in charge of a group of three or four women, so that the groups could ski separately, even though we would all follow the same route. The girls would also take turns to haul a sledge that would contain everything their little group would need for the three days, including fuel, food, sleeping bags and tent. The sledge wouldn't weigh very much but skiing while dragging a sledge can be tricky (I'd been run over by my own sledge enough times to know) and considering that the candidates had only been skiing for two days, it would be challenging enough. In the tents, the girls would be using liquid-fuel stoves, as we would in Antarctica. We had practised outside with the stoves until everyone was confident with them but any mistake when using the stoves inside the tents could be costly – I had seen how quickly tents could burn. I was uncomfortable with it, but I had to let the women try for themselves. They would all need to be competent with stoves in Antarctica and so it would be silly not to trust them with the stoves now.

I stayed up late in the little office at the back of the hut to catch up on the publicity work that needed to be done. Media in each of the eight countries were following the progress of the candidates, eager to know how they were doing. I was tired but it felt good to spend some time alone. The office with its single light hanging in the window felt cosy and Sarah had magically produced a chocolate pudding which she had left for me on the desk. I tucked in with a big spoon in between bursts of writing on the expedition blog. I'd asked all the girls to write about their impressions of each day and I transcribed some of their writing onto the website. 'It felt like I was kayaking,' wrote Lina from Singapore about her first day on skis. 'Although the snow was blowing relentlessly into my face when I was skiing, once you focus and get that rhythm going, you just shut everything off, it felt so free.'

The website was receiving well over 22,000 hits a day and it was incredible to think that so many people were following our progress. It wasn't long before the Norwegian media also showed an interest. As the group prepared to leave on our mini-expedition the next day, a film crew from the Norwegian national network TV 2 arrived, as well as reporters from two local newspapers. Having spent a successful night in the tents the candidates were all eager to try an expedition for real. Sledges were packed and well strapped, candidates stood ready on skis or made short practice runs up and down in front of the hut; we were ready to move out. With each trainer leading their small group we set off north from the hut, one group at a time. We soon met our first obstacle: a long but gentle downward slope. The slope was no more serious than others the candidates had trained on but in their haste to get going, plus the added pressure of the cameras and the new challenge of being attached to a sledge for the first time, there was carnage. Within minutes bodies and upturned sledges littered the slope. Candidates floundered in the deep snow to get back on their skis; others had collided and now struggled to disentangle limbs and skis. I winced as I glanced at the film crew busily filming the disaster. Too late I realised that I should have asked them to come back another day. The candidates didn't mind though: they were so busy laughing at their undignified falls that they were oblivious to the cameras. No one had been hurt and once the group had tumbled to the bottom of the hill everyone picked themselves up and carried on.

It was a gloomy day with a strong wind blowing clouds of snow along the surface, encrusting everything in ice and limiting our views. The groups drifted away from each other until they were just hazy figures in the distance, all moving in the same direction. Each group, under the direction of their trainer, stopped regularly for breaks, ensuring that no one had overheated while skiing or got too cold while they stopped. Progress was naturally slow and it took us three hours to reach our planned campground just 4 kilometres from the hut. The weather had deteriorated during the afternoon so that the girls struggled to get the tents up as the wind tugged at the material and cold wet snow slapped into their faces. They were grateful to finally get inside, get the stoves on and cook some dinner.

The next morning I took a walk around camp as the girls were finishing up their breakfast and getting ready to set off. I met Athina from Cyprus walking back from the camp's makeshift loo dug into the snow. 'If someone had asked me a week ago if I would be doing something like this, I'd have said, "Are you nuts?"' she laughed, shaking her head in disbelief. Subzero living was a completely new experience for Athina. Half the time she wore an expression midway between terror and awe, while the rest of the time she literally beamed with the excitement of it all. This wasn't Athina's world but I could see that she was proud of herself for seeing it through and not giving up.

I ducked my head into one of the tents and spoke to Aparna from India. She was full of stories from the night. 'When I woke up my nose was against the tent wall with the snow right outside!' she laughed. 'I thought I'd lost my nose as it was freezing cold! But it's fine,' she added with a shrug. I was only in the tent a few minutes but it was long enough to notice that Aparna didn't seem to be helping much as her team busied themselves around her. I decided to ski with her team that day so that I would have a chance to see what was going on.

We were the last group to move out. As Stephanie from Cyprus and Aniza from Brunei led off, with Aparna and me following a little way behind, the other groups were strung along the route ahead of us, already quite a way ahead. Aparna took the first turn at pulling the sledge and chatted happily as I skied alongside her. 'The sledge is not a problem,' she confided. 'I am happy that this is my strength; this is the way I can contribute to the team because I am not so good at all that other stuff.' She waved a hand vaguely in the direction of our recently vacated camp.

'Working out strengths and weaknesses is important,' I agreed. 'But I don't think you can limit yourself to just one role, you need to pitch in wherever. For example, say you have someone in the team who is so confident with the stoves that everyone leaves that job to them. Imagine if that person gets injured and the others need to light the stoves but they've forgotten how to do it. You can have a specialism but you still need to be able to do everything else if you need to.'

We skied in silence for a few minutes as we both thought it over. 'I am very strong-willed,' Aparna replied eventually. 'This is often a blessing but now it makes things difficult for me here. But I will listen. I will try, Felicity.'

The insight and the honesty of her answer took me by surprise. It reminded me of why I liked her so much and I hoped that my comments, while necessary, hadn't offended her. We skied under a blue sky streaked with wispy clouds, the sunlight radiating from every surface so that it sparkled. Gentle slopes gradually rose on either side of us, creating a wide valley with overhanging rocks encrusted in ice and huge boulders topped with thick hats of fresh snow. The valley ended abruptly at a steep drop so that we could look down into a huge bowl that flattened out and stretched for miles. We could see the other groups making their way across the landscape, now so far away that they were just tiny multi-coloured dots. Since leaving the camp I had tried to close the gap between our group of stragglers and the other teams but our progress had been slow thanks to numerous stops to adjust clothing or to secure the sledges. I tried to impose a routine of stopping only once every 40 minutes – but five minutes later we were halted once again by an urgent ski-binding adjustment. I repeated my lecture. 'I know it's hard but we need to reduce the stops. If something is wrong, don't stop immediately to sort it out if you can wait instead until our next break. We only need to keep going for 40 minutes at a time. If you plan ahead so that you are wearing the right clothing, there shouldn't be any need to stop between breaks.'

Aparna was the worst culprit, having stopped half a dozen times to remove and then replace layers of clothing. Despite our frank conversation earlier she snapped at me testily, 'But what should I do? You say I cannot sweat, so I need to change my clothes. I cannot do that and ski.' I tried to explain about thinking ahead at each break, to wear less at the start so that she wouldn't sweat but it made little difference and we continued to stop as and when she felt the need. I got firm with the trio, refusing to allow them to stop between breaks and making them adjust clothing while on the move. Aparna fell over in the process and glared at me from the ground as if to say, 'See what you have done?' but I refused to relent. This was a skill anyone wanting to go to Antarctica would need to be willing to master.

As we made our way across the bowl the sky filled with smooth, globular clouds, turning the snow a uniform grey and making it hard to pick out any features. The wind started to chase streams of powder snow across the surface and I helped the women cover their faces to protect their skin from the cold. We started to climb a gentle slope at the far side of the bowl, imperceptibly gaining height until suddenly a view opened up behind us, revealing how far we'd come. We met some of the other groups having a break on the broad summit of the hill and followed them on the soft descent. Stephanie had taken over pulling the sledge and valiantly brought it down the hill, repeatedly picking herself up after every fall. The sun reappeared to pick out the ripples in the snow with a golden yellow light before sinking once again into the now pastel-pink mass of cloud. The snow that had been running past our feet occasionally rose into squalls, floating across the landscape like ghostly spectres.

Alone once more, the four of us skied on between two gnarled peaks before looking down a long slope. We could already see some of the other groups down below, too small to be distinct, setting up their tents. It was getting dark and we were all cold and tired. The slope should have been an easy glide to get us home quickly but as the four of us set off down the hill I noticed Aparna falling back. She was having trouble keeping her skis in a V-shape as she glided downhill meaning that she couldn't control her speed. After a slow start she would begin speeding up until the tips of her skis crossed over and she came crashing down into the snow. I skied alongside her to offer some advice but as she fell again she decided she was going to sidestep down the hill. I could understand her trepidation but the slope was so gentle that side-stepping was unnecessary and would take an awfully long time. I tried to coax her into giving the snowplough another shot but she resolutely refused. 'Aparna, you will only get better if you keep trying.' But it made no difference. The others began to get cold waiting for her, so I let them go ahead. I watched as they reached camp and started putting up the tent in the distance; we were still a long way off. As Aparna continued to refuse any other techniques to get her down the hill quicker, I gave up trying to persuade her.

Later that evening I found Stephanie stomping around camp digging snow viciously to pile around the already well-anchored tent. 'She is impossible!' Stephanie fumed as we took a walk. 'We have been doing everything for her and she just sits there!' She was referring to Aparna. I understood her frustration but the outburst alarmed me. In Antarctica the team were all likely to get on each other's nerves from time to time and we'd have to learn just to get on with it. I asked myself if Stephanie would be able to do that.

Kim from Jamaica was also a worry. The trainers, myself included, spent most of our time trying to reign in her inherent chaos. I'd spoken to her several times about the importance of keeping track of her kit and taking responsibility for looking after her equipment. She'd got a lot better but the days still usually started and ended with a general camp-wide search for her lost clothing. 'I thought the hardest thing out here would be the skiing,' she tried to explain, 'but actually the hardest thing is keeping track of three layers of clothing. At home I'm used to wearing one layer and I can't lose that because I'm wearing it. Out here I have three pairs of everything.' That night she couldn't find her hat. Next morning, as her group packed away their tent, it appeared in the snow underneath; they'd been sleeping on it.

The last day of the mini-expedition had a celebratory feel to it. The wind had dropped completely and the sun came out, transforming the moody world of white we had come to know into a pristine landscape of sparkling crystals. The route back to the hut took us over a wide frozen lake and we halted halfway across it to put up the tents and have some lunch. I marked out a racecourse nearby and split the group into two for a sledge relay race. The candidates took it in turns to pull a sledge around the course with Mark and Jim as the load. Instantly competitive, the girls cheered for their team as they belted around the track. It was very close until it came to Alecia from Jamaica. There was no doubting her determination, her face was creased with serious willpower, but she wasn't able to pull the weight of the sledge. She wasn't the smallest woman in the group (Era from Brunei was smaller); the problem seemed to be that she was too flexible. Every time she took up the strain and prepared to push forward, she'd bend at the hips like a straw folding in half, and the sledge wouldn't move. We slowed down the opposing team to give her a chance but even so she was painfully slow. Her problem came as a surprise as she had been strong on her skis. I had initially been more worried about Era. As the smallest in the group I wondered if she would be able to pull the same weight as the others but throughout the mini-expedition she had made a point of being right at the front of the group, powering uphill with the biggest loads. She had obviously anticipated my concern and set out to show me what she could do. The other trainers had noticed too and commented on how impressed they were with her stamina.

By late afternoon we were approaching the hut. The sun had dipped in the sky and was staining the snow with blushes of soft pink and purple. The group slowed to almost a dawdle as if no one wanted the trip to end. The selection had never been far from anyone's mind but as the candidates unstrapped their skis at the door of the hut, the thought closed around everyone: who would be leaving tomorrow?

After dinner I ushered all the candidates out of the hut into their separate accommodation so that I could speak to the trainers about the selection in private. The trainers had all spent as much time as I had with the girls and so I was interested in their opinions about who was working well within the group. We sat around the open fire, enjoying a bottle of whisky that had been produced from somewhere. I looked around at the faces of the trainers; they all looked destroyed. The week had taken its toll and I felt a wave of gratitude for these wonderful friends who had worked so hard: Peter who had driven the Land Rover up and down the treacherous road several times a day running errands; Al and Elliott who had yomped through knee-deep snow with their heavy cameras and equipment to film the group; Rob who had braved blizzards with his camera and spent long hours with me in the office updating the website; Sarah who had produced endless cakes and biscuits from our scanty stores; Mark, Jim and Jo who had spent long days in the cold coaxing and encouraging the candidates. Norway wouldn't have been possible without their enthusiasm.

We all agreed that the candidates had shown impressive guts in taking on everything we had thrown at them in such a short space of time. Each day as we had added an extra layer of complexity I had wondered if today was the day we would push it too far and see the girls crack, if today would be the day that someone wanted to go home. Despite the fact that some of the candidates had clearly struggled, no one had come close to giving in or had shown signs of Arctic Shock, and they were all genuinely still enjoying themselves. In the past I'd led far more experienced groups of people in the Arctic who hadn't shown nearly as much resilience. I talked through each selection with the trainers. They were as sorry as I was to be sending anyone home: all the candidates had worked so hard that it seemed cruel.

We talked about Cyprus first. The trainers confirmed my own instinct that Stephanie was the right choice but losing Athina was going to be a huge wrench. All through the training she had shown such courage but the hard truth was that she still didn't have the confidence she would need for Antarctica. If she was part of the team she would need a lot of reassurance which would be an unfair demand on the other team members.

The New Zealand selection was unanimous. Although we all liked both Melanie and Charmaine, Charmaine was the stronger candidate. Out of the two Bruneians, Era had impressed everyone with her show of endurance and her practical common sense. Equally clear was the Singaporean selection. Sophia had been a calm and efficient influence in every group she had worked with, whereas Lina had remained noticeably aloof. None of the trainers had any worries about Barbara being automatically selected for the team. She had been strong physically as well as a great team player, always at the centre of the laughter, always the first to encourage others who were having difficulty. She was a natural.

The Jamaican selection had been decided conclusively by Alecia's performance in the sledge race. Her inability to pull a sledge put her out of the running and yet, until that point she had been the clear favourite. The discussion turned to whether we felt Kim would be a suitable team member. At the start of the week most of the trainers would have said no. She was a very dominant character within a group and so talkative that it suppressed everyone else. On top of that she had found the skiing difficult and was struggling to get herself organised. But over the week we had noticed a significant change. She had worked hard at the skiing and mellowed out within the group. Perhaps her over-dominance was down to nerves and as she became more comfortable within the group she would fit in better. We decided that Kim should be offered a place on the team but that I needed to make clear to her the points she needed to work on.

Most difficult of all was the Indian selection. Neither Reena nor Aparna had struck anyone as particularly suitable. Aparna was great fun and had been good at pulling the sledges as well as being a powerhouse at the pre-expedition admin but, in several instances, she had caused friction within her tent groups There were reservations about Reena, too. She was strong but surprisingly out of shape considering she led treks in the Himalaya for much of the year. Everyone expressed the feeling that she hadn't contributed much to the team. I thought about going back to India to interview other applicants, or starting a completely new search but it only seemed fair I should give Reena a chance. If I made it clear how close she had come to not being selected and how much she needed to work on engaging with the rest of the team, perhaps we would see a difference.

It was early morning by the time we had finished talking. As the training team drifted off to bed I was reluctant to sleep. The next day was going to be tough. I remembered how I had felt ringing unsuccessful candidates after the interviews. If I had felt like a villain then, tomorrow was going to be much, much worse.

I gathered the candidates together in the morning after breakfast and told them how impressed the trainers had been with their performance. 'Today I have to make a horrible choice and seven of you will be leaving us. I will be speaking to all of you one by one this morning but I hope that whatever happens today you will all leave Norway with good memories.' The candidates were asked to stay in the accommodation block until they were called over individually. Once they had seen me in a small anteroom, the trainers were ready to accompany the girls over to the hut where they could wait for the others. I didn't want those that had been selected to break the news to their country partner. It would be better for them to hear it from me.

I asked for Athina first as she was the one I was dreading telling most of all. I knew she would be devastated. She was nervous as she came in and sat opposite me. I suddenly felt embarrassed and didn't know where to begin but this was one of those moments where I needed to push my own feelings aside and be 'Felicity the expedition leader' that the candidates needed and deserved to see. This wasn't about my feelings, this was about Athina. As I told her the news I saw her face change. I could see that my choice wasn't a surprise to her but that she hadn't given up hope. As we talked it over she started to cry, trying to wipe her tears away, angry with herself for letting them come. I couldn't bear seeing her so heartbroken and gave her a big hug. She sobbed on my shoulder, 'Thank you for the experience. I have had such a good time.' Jo came to give her a hug and, with Athina still sobbing, guided her over to the hut. I let out a long sigh as I fought back tears of my own. I had expected this to be hard but it was far worse than I'd imagined.

I was crying again as I broke the news to Stephanie, this time in response to her emotional reaction to being selected. She looked at me wide-eyed for a second before jumping round the room, hugging everyone in sight, tears flowing. Before she left I cautioned her that Athina was upset and to tread lightly. Stephanie understood, and I knew I could rely on her to be sensitive.

Alecia's reaction was also heartbreaking. I explained that, in the end, it had just come down to the sledge-pulling. She pleaded with me to reconsider, promising to go away and train so that she would be able to pull the sledge. She valiantly tried to hold back the tears but they came eventually and I couldn't stop myself welling up with her. When she could see that the decision had been made, she wiped her eyes with a smile and stood to leave. 'Well, I have learnt a lot and I will always be grateful for that.' We hugged and she left.

Kim came in shortly after and in many ways this was a tougher interview. I was giving her good news but I also needed to make sure that she knew her place was dependent on her getting organised and showing that she was able to look after herself. 'The Kim we saw at the beginning of the week wouldn't be on this team,' I explained to her. 'But we can tell that you've really been trying this week. The skiing got better and you are listening more and getting some systems in place. You are still a long way off but I believe you'll get there if you work at the fitness and at getting organised.'

Kim listened quietly. I was worried that she would be offended at such blunt feedback but instead she nodded her head seriously. 'I will do whatever it takes,' she said solemnly. I believed her.

Sophia took the news that she had been selected so casually that at first I wondered if she had understood my meaning. Her reaction puzzled me. I knew that she perceived herself as the underdog of the Singaporean candidates and had assumed from the start that Lina would be chosen, but she didn't show any sign of surprise or delight. I began to wonder if I had made a mistake but before she left she said something that explained her subdued response. 'I must talk to my husband and my kids. There will be a lot of pressure in Singapore for me to succeed.' More than any of the other candidates Sophia had appreciated, even at this early stage, the responsibility they were taking on in terms of national expectations. Her mind had not paused at celebration and triumph; it had fast-forwarded to the months of hard work ahead and the challenges she would face.

Lina was the only candidate that took the rejection badly. It was clear that she had assumed she would be chosen and I wondered if perhaps this was why she hadn't engaged with the group, thinking that she had plenty of time to get to know them later. She demanded an explanation. 'You are very fit, very focussed and very methodical which are all great qualities and I've no doubt that you would get to the pole,' I began, 'but I think you see the challenge as you against the conditions rather than seeing the challenge as creating a team that will succeed.' Lina nodded in silence, stood abruptly and left, leaving the door open behind her.

I had been worried about breaking the news to Aparna but she was actually extremely gracious, so much so that I wondered if she had already known in her heart that she wouldn't be selected. She brushed aside the rejection and chatted instead about all the things she had enjoyed. I found myself feeling very sorry that we would be saying goodbye to Aparna; she had been a very good sport.

Reena was emotional about her selection but more so as I explained gently how close she had come to leaving with Aparna. She was genuinely mortified that we thought she wasn't contributing enough to the group and that we had concerns about her fitness. She listened intently as I suggested several areas she needed to work on. 'I will work really hard, Felicity,' she reassured me. 'I will not let you down and you will all be proud of me, I promise you.' As she left I felt a wave of guilt. It wasn't my intention to make her feel bad but I also needed all the team members to be realistic and to know what they needed to do. I could just give them all big hugs and tell them they were brilliant but it wouldn't help us in the end. They *were* brilliant but we also had a long way to go before we were ready to take on Antarctica.

With the last interview done I walked slowly over to the hut where all the candidates were now gathered. It was a strange atmosphere inside. There were lots of tears but there was excitement, too. Lina remained noticeably apart from the group, unwilling to talk to anyone, while Alecia and Athina, still in tears, were receiving plenty of hugs. Everyone seemed very supportive of everyone else but still I was pleased that we had arranged for the Land Rover to transport the seven that were leaving pretty much immediately in order to catch the next train to Oslo. Those that were staying needed time to celebrate without feeling guilty and I needed to concentrate on consolidating the new team. There were endless rounds of goodbyes and more tears before finally everyone who was leaving was in the Land Rover.

My new team stood in the snow outside the hut waving at the Land Rover until we couldn't see it any more. We stood subdued for a moment and I knew I had to say something. I pulled the group together, our heads bent forward as if in a rugby huddle. 'This has been a really tough day but now we need to look forward. Take a good look around you at these faces because these are the faces you will be skiing to the South Pole with. This is your team now and whether it succeeds or fails is up to us.' I could feel the excitement radiating outward from the beaming smiles. The girls looked around at each other. This was it. This was my team: Era (24), a civil servant from Brunei; Steph (26), an IT worker from Cyprus; Barbara (29), a journalist from Ghana; Reena (38), a trekking guide from India; Kim (30), a political adviser from Jamaica; Charmaine (36), a military doctor from New Zealand; Sophia (36), a mother of three from Singapore; myself (31), representing the UK and our reserve, Helen (43), an outdoor activity instructor from Derbyshire.

CHAPTER SIX

THE NINTH TEAM MEMBER

Walking into Westminster Abbey, shivers worked their way down my spine and I felt euphoric. Organ music echoed from the walls and my eyes swept upwards, past the flags and flowers, to the webs of stone and glass high above. Imposing and majestic, the abbey radiated stately ceremony and my skin tingled as I thought of the weight of ages that surrounded us. I walked behind my new team, each of them transformed in their national outfits: Barbara looked stunning in her figure-hugging Ghanaian dress, the colourful woven material falling to the floor; Reena had wrapped herself in a magnificent crimson and gold sari that floated behind her as she walked; while Era was pink and floral in a silk headscarf, carefully pinned to tightly frame her face.

We'd been invited to Westminster Abbey in central London to attend the Commonwealth Day celebrations and to be presented to the Queen at a reception later that day in Marlborough House, the headquarters of the Commonwealth Secretariat. It had been hard work and a tough wrangle to get all seven women from the training in Norway to London (including a last-minute interview at the British Consulate in Norway to get Barbara a visa), but watching the faces of the team as we waited in a small anteroom at Marlborough House for the Queen to arrive, I was sure that all the trouble had been worth it. The women waited in an expectant hush, all eyes on the open doorway. The Queen arrived, accompanied by the Duke of Edinburgh, and shook hands with each member of the team. The Duke listened as we explained our plans before giving his judgement. 'You're all mad,' he announced, before moving on to the next guest waiting in line beside us.

As the women flew home, it was clear that we would need to meet again as a team before we travelled to Antarctica. I decided to arrange another training meet for September, which would be a few months before our planned departure for Antarctica. It seemed to make sense that we should head for New Zealand because Charmaine was confident that she would be able to use her military connections there to help us – and it was one of the few places we could find snow at that time of year. Apart from myself, Charmaine was by far the most experienced member of the team. I liked her enormously and I hoped that she would play a second-in-command role within the team, someone that I could confide in about team issues and could trust to back me up when tricky decisions had to be made. I usually spoke to the team, as a whole, as I would speak to the least experienced among them and I was worried that, because of this, Charmaine might feel undervalued, so I made a point of speaking to her before we left Norway to encourage her input. 'It's really reassuring to have you on the team and I hope that you know a lot of what I say to the team is intended for others. I have no intention of teaching you to suck eggs.'

Charmaine laughed before becoming serious, 'If ever you need a sounding board, someone to talk to, I'm happy to listen.' I appreciated her offer and was secretly relieved that she had taken on the responsibility of arranging the New Zealand training. It meant that I was able to concentrate on getting the rest of the team fit in time.

The team had left Norway under no illusion about how much effort they needed to put into their fitness training in preparation for Antarctica. Training for a polar expedition can be counter-intuitive in many ways; it is more about increasing stamina and endurance rather than general cardiovascular fitness. I spent a morning with the team putting a training plan together. We split the training into three main areas. The first was strength, using resistance training with weights to build up key muscle areas. The second was interval training, increasing cardiovascular fitness through short bursts of energy. The third, and most important, was endurance training through low impact exercise over increasing lengths of time. The team made reams of notes and once they got home it was great to see the email chatter flying back and forth as they started to put what they had learned into practice. I was relieved that they were taking it seriously and pleased that each of them quickly found a suitable trainer to help them put together a specific programme. Barbara continued to work with the terrifying Prince Agbemble in Ghana who had got her in shape for Norway. He ran a gym ominously called the Body Snatcher Boot Camp and insisted on being called 'The General' during training sessions. In Jamaica, Kim had been offered support from the Jamaica Defence Force in the form of her very own officer who would help her with some motivating endurance training. Era in Brunei had teamed up with the wonderfully named Dr Danish of the Sport and Research Centre at the National Gym. In addition, she was keen to do as much expedition-specific training as she could. You often see polar adventurers training by pulling car tyres around to simulate pulling a sledge but Era went one better: she took the wheel off an old wheelbarrow and pulled it along the sandy beaches of Brunei to almost exactly mimic pulling a sledge on snow. Sophia was also training with a sledge. Under the guidance of Dr Ben Tan, head of Changi Sports Medicine Centre in Singapore, Sophia was pulling a sledge full of weights around what looked – judging from the pictures she posted on the expedition website – like a disused car park. Sophia religiously recorded the results of each training session on our team website and within a few months was training with terrifying weights, hauling 180 kilograms (at least three times her body weight) in her makeshift sledge. I started to get worried that she was overdoing it. 'There is no need for you to be pulling more than 100 kilograms,' I wrote, 'as we won't be pulling this kind of weight on the expedition. You really can't risk injuring yourself. This would be the biggest disaster of all.'

Reena had perhaps the best training ground. Returning from Norway her work took her back into the Himalaya where she spent day after day trekking at high altitude with heavy loads. This was great for endurance but she still needed to get into a gym to increase her strength and cardiovascular fitness. A dull morning in my office was brightened by an email from Reena describing her first ever visit to a gym. Whereas most people are ready with at least a dozen different reasons why they never go near a gym if they can help it, Reena had an almost evangelical conversion. 'It was like going to a disco with the loud music and all the beautiful people,' she enthused.

With training programmes and support in place I was confident that the team would be prepared physically for Antarctica and that after our training meet in New Zealand they would also have the skills. Financially, on the other hand, our prospects were dismal. Antarctica is possibly the most expensive place to reach on the planet. Flying anywhere in Antarctica isn't simply a matter of buying a ticket for a seat on a flight; it involves hiring the whole plane, complete with crew, and buying the fuel to go in the tanks. We needed over $400,000 just to cover our flights and essential rescue cover. It was a daunting amount of money to find.

In India Reena had succeeded in making an appointment to see a senior minister who had access to sport funding. She arrived expecting to meet the minister but was instead given a ticket and asked to wait along with dozens of other petitioners. When it was finally her turn, Reena was shown into a room where she assumed she would meet the minister in person but in fact found only a phone on a desk. The minister's PA was on the line. Reena told him about the expedition and later related the conversation to me. 'He was very enthusiastic and was sure the minister could provide some funding and he said that only a small commission would be necessary.'

'Commission?' I repeated suspiciously.

'Yes. In India, if you want a national award, you pay a commission and you get it.'

It took me a moment to realise that we were talking about bribery. Despite Reena insisting that 'commissions' were inevitable in India, I was adamant that we would find another way.

Meanwhile, Era in Brunei had finally received the precious letter from the Ministry of Culture, Youth and Sport giving her permission to raise funds for the expedition but – as if the financial crisis wasn't enough of a handicap – now the world was gripped by the H1N1 virus scare. Some 66 people in Brunei had fallen ill, and the authorities responded by stopping all gatherings including sporting events and fundraisers. Era's planned sports tournament fundraisers would be cancelled on both counts. Even worse, no one was sure how long the ban on public gatherings would last.

Kim in Jamaica had decided to hold another fundraiser called Frozen. After the disastrous Cold Front event in which Kim had actually lost money, I was cautious as she talked through her plans but she assured me that this time it was going to be a success. I wasn't convinced but it was clear that she wasn't going to change her mind.

In order to secure aircraft support for the expedition we had to pay the logistics company, Antarctic Logistics and Expeditions (ALE), by a deadline that was fast approaching. We planned to depart for Antarctica in November and it was already August when I received a promising call from Sophia. A distributor of computer software in Singapore had mentioned that his parent company, Kaspersky Lab, were looking for interesting projects to sponsor. Kaspersky Lab is an Internet security firm led by Eugene Kaspersky, an expert pioneer in anti-virus software. It is now the largest privately owned company in the world and trades all over the globe, from the Americas to Japan. Our contact worked within Kaspersky Lab Asia. With India, Singapore, Brunei and New Zealand all falling within their sales region and represented on the expedition team, we had a lot to offer them in return for financial support.

Within a week of submitting a sponsorship proposal I received a call from a woman called Suk Ling in Malaysia. As she explained that she was the director of South East Asia for Kaspersky Lab I could feel my heart starting to thud in my chest. The fact that someone so senior had personally called the expedition indicated that they were taking our proposal seriously and I realised that this could be the most critical phone call of the entire project. This was my chance to sell the expedition, to make sure that Suk Ling would report back that we were the ideal venture for Kaspersky Lab. My heart thumped louder as she explained that Kaspersky Lab was only interested in being an exclusive title sponsor. I felt the pressure of the hopes and dreams of eight women, my team, all hanging on my performance at that very moment. This was it, every word had to count. We talked about departure dates and logistics, media coverage and our planned training in New Zealand. Suk Ling asked if the team could travel to Singapore for a press conference (I agreed immediately, visas permitting). As the questions became more detailed my hopes rose even higher. Suk Ling asked me to prepare payment schedules and draft contracts for her and finally we spoke about the name. Could the expedition be renamed to include Kaspersky Lab in the title? I agreed immediately and we played around with some options on the phone, such as the Kaspersky Lab Commonwealth Expedition or the Kaspersky Lab Women's Antarctic Expedition. After an hour or so Suk Ling seemed satisfied that she had the information she needed. 'We will revert to you the final decision by this Friday,' she promised.

I put down the phone and pressed my hands onto on the table. My heart was still thumping and I was so full of excitement that I wanted to leap around the room, to yell from the rooftops but no, not yet: until I had a signature on a contract I would not allow myself to believe it was real. The conversation with Suk Ling had been so positive and so specific that it was almost impossible to think that Kaspersky Lab would decline to be our sponsor but still, I had been to the brink of sponsorship with other companies and other expeditions in the past, only to be let down way past the last minute. I could not, and would not, let myself get caught out like that again.

Waiting for the decision from Kaspersky Lab, I sat in my office hardly daring to breathe. I tried to get on with other work but ended up literally staring at my computer screen waiting for a response to arrive. As the week passed I received several emails from Suk Ling to clarify minor details. Replying to each email was agony. I felt as if each of my replies was a potential deal-breaker, as if one misplaced word, one badly phrased sentiment could ruin everything. This had been our best lead and it was also our last chance. The probability of getting this close to full sponsorship again before our payment deadline in a fortnight was less than zero. Everything depended on securing sponsorship from Kaspersky Lab.

Friday arrived and I was nearly sick with anxiety when I opened up my mailbox to find an email from Suk Ling. It said simply, 'Great news. My management has approved the sponsorship.'

I wrote to the girls immediately. I could imagine the yelps and sighs of relief around the world as one by one the girls opened the email and replied – each with more imaginative use of exclamation marks than the last.

'YIPPPEEEEE!!!!!! Finally, I can breathe a little easier now!' wrote Sophia.

'Absolutely UNBELIEVABLE news!!!!!!!!!!!!!!' emailed Steph.

'WOW WOW WOW!!!!!!!!!!!!' typed Reena, 'I am so happy!!!'

'All right, now I know my Lord God is faithful to his children! Our tears, sweat, hard work and perseverance will not be in vain,' wrote Barbara to the team. She added, 'Present status: being kicked out of Internet cafe for uncontrollable screaming!'

True to form, it was a few days later before Kim picked up the email, 'I am still jumping around,' she said. 'Have to digest it.'

Once the celebrations were over there wasn't a lot of time to dwell on our triumph. In three weeks' time we were all due to meet in New Zealand. Charmaine had taken the lead on the arrangements but hadn't provided many details. As much as I trusted her to do a good job, I needed to know where we would be staying and what kit she had managed to source locally. I was surprised at her lack of communication; it was almost as if she was deliberately keeping me in the dark. I sensed trouble but consigned the problem to my subconscious to mull over. Barbara was a more pressing priority. For the past month I had been nagging her daily about her visa for New Zealand in an attempt to avoid a repeat of the fiasco before Norway but communication was scarce. She avoided talking to me on Skype and her emails were vague. I started to recognise the signs: something was wrong. Sure enough, three weeks before our departure I received an email from Barbara informing me that she wouldn't be coming to New Zealand.

> I may not be able to attend the NZ training event as planned, because I won't be able to afford to at the time... but I'm trying to look at the bigger picture. I NEED to make it to Antarctica, even if it means sacrificing an important event such as New Zealand. I just feel that with the time left, I would be better off continuing to fight for the money to get to Antarctica... whatever it takes...

I had explained to Barbara so many times that we were raising funds as a team, that she didn't have to find all the money herself. I understood her pride and the fact that she didn't want to be subsidised but the truth was that we were all being subsidised one way or another. As long as she was working as hard as everyone else to find support (which I believe she was), the expedition funds were there for her to use. The expedition could buy her ticket to New Zealand but the expedition couldn't magic up a visa – that was down to Barbara and yet again she had left it too late.

Skipping the training in New Zealand wasn't an option. Barbara had taken on all the new skills in Norway easily but all the women still needed to work on a number of routines before they were ready for Antarctica. I wondered if perhaps I had been too gentle with the team; perhaps I hadn't imparted properly the dangers of the South. The team needed to be well trained, otherwise they would get injured. Frostbite can happen in a second and if our drills were bad we would end up spending more time than necessary exposed to the cold.

Once again I found myself on the phone to various embassies and high commissions sorting out Barbara's visa. As I listened to holding music on expensive overseas calls I wondered despairingly how I had allowed myself to get in this position again. Had I learnt nothing? Sometimes I worried that I treated the girls like children, while at other times I kicked myself for not holding their hands tighter, for assuming levels of responsibility and understanding that simply weren't there. I didn't blame the team; I was the one who had told them they were capable of this and so I was the one who had to accept the consequences of that belief.

I arrived in New Zealand in September expecting winter, but Christchurch looked suspiciously spring-like as I walked towards the main square. The team were due to fly in at various times throughout the day but Barbara, who had just received her visa, now needed a flight. I walked into a big, empty travel agent and explained my problem to the two women sitting in front of their computers. They looked increasingly intrigued the more I explained about my problem and they were soon tapping away furiously at their keyboards, occasionally pausing to talk to each other in strange flight-code language. The first available flight had Barbara arriving just two days before we were all due to leave New Zealand. There was no point asking her to travel halfway across the world, at great expense, for two days. The two travel agents refused to give up but after three hours I called a halt to the search. I had to go and meet the rest of the team in the airport and couldn't leave it any longer.

We drove south in a convoy of three vehicles from Christchurch to our new base, which Charmaine had arranged for us in a small hamlet called Twizel. The girls were all thrilled to see each other again and as they filled the car with excited chatter I stared out of the window at the passing landscape and thought about Barbara and the consequences of this latest twist. Barbara would not be coming to New Zealand and without this additional training there was no way she could come to Antarctica. That left me with two options; to accept that we would have no Ghanaian on the team, or to find a way to get Barbara the training she needed.

I thought about a team without Barbara. Without her we still had a multi-cultural commonwealth team but it was the fact that we would lose Barbara herself that seemed wrong. She and I had both worked so hard to get this far that I felt a stubborn refusal to let her go and I think this was because, in many ways, Barbara represented exactly the sort of person that this expedition was all about: a woman who was capable of great things but who had never really been given a chance to prove herself. In Norway she had shown that she would not have a problem getting to the South Pole given the right training and preparation but now it seemed that she would not get the opportunity, due to money and pride. Despite the bleak outlook and the fact that all my common sense screamed at me to draw a line underneath the issue, I wasn't ready to give up on her yet.

Then there was Helen to consider. She had been dealing admirably with the awkward reserve role but I knew she was finding the uncertainty hard. Helen had fulfilled her side of the bargain: she had trained as hard as the others; she had spent as much time, if not more, as the others helping me with the logistics and planning; and she had shown just as much commitment. All of this was in return for the genuine possibility that she might be called on to come to Antarctica. Was it unfair that I was going to such great lengths to ensure that the original members of the team made it to Antarctica and, in doing so, preventing her from coming?

Our base in Twizel was a small wooden cottage painted pastel pink that belonged to a friend of Charmaine's. We spread out over the long, grassy yard at the back of the cottage to take a look at all our gear. A British clothing company, Montane, had agreed to provide all the layers we would need for Antarctica and they had sent sample clothing to New Zealand for our training so that we could decide what we wanted and let them know which sizes we would need. Helen and I had brought all the clothing out with us as luggage on the flight from the UK and had managed – through well-practised subterfuge – to avoid any excess baggage charges. Now that I saw it all laid out, it seemed incredible that we had got away with it.

As well as trying out the clothing, we also needed to try out the food. During the expedition our main feed of the day would be a dehydrated meal prepared by adding boiling water to a bag and allowing the contents to stew. As a Muslim, Era could only eat halal meat (meat from animals that have been slaughtered in a way prescribed by her religion) but I hadn't been able to find a supplier of expedition meals that were halal. To avoid one team member having separate food from everyone else (which would be a logistical nightmare) our only option was to be a vegetarian expedition, despite the impact this would have on our nutritional intake. I prepared a sample of each vegetarian variety of the expedition meals I had sourced so that the team could try them. The response was generally underwhelming. 'It looks like the contents of a baby's nappy,' Kim commented.

'Mine *smells* like a baby's nappy,' Steph replied.

'Well, it's better than the green one that looks like snot,' said Helen.

'I think it's supposed to be fish,' remarked Sophia.

As the meals were discarded, unfinished, it was clear that I was going to have to find an alternative.

The plan for the next week was to leave the cottage and drive even further south to the Pisa Range near Wanaka for a training expedition. The range was home to New Zealand's one and only cross-country ski park which would make an ideal base to use as a start and end point for our mini-expedition. It was a relief as we zigzagged up the steep mountain road toward the park to finally see some snow – the first we'd found since arriving. It was the end of the winter season and the snow had retreated to the very tops of the ranges but even up here it was patchy, revealing large areas of rock and soil. I looked over the maps with Charmaine. Considering the snow conditions we would have to make our way up onto the higher reaches of the range along one of several wide ridges that led onto a narrow plateau at the top. We agreed on the plan but Charmaine was cagey, as she had been since I'd arrived. She seemed to be drawing away from the team, always doing her own thing rather than joining in with everyone else. During our time at the cottage Charmaine was repeatedly the last to arrive at team meetings, excusing herself to attend to something else or typing away on a laptop during team discussions. There was something more that was harder to define, something I found uncomfortable about her comments to the team, particularly about decisions I had made on anything from gear choices to aspects of our sponsorship. I wondered if I was being paranoid but it increasingly felt like an insidious, perhaps even unintentional, undermining of my role as leader.

As the team set up our first camp in a snow-filled gully just out of sight of the cross-country ski lodge I took the opportunity to talk to Charmaine. We wandered away from the tents, plodding through the deep snow, until we were out of earshot. I got to the point quickly. 'Charmaine, the girls look up to you and it's a huge boost for me to have someone with your experience on the team but we need to work together – otherwise it just causes confusion. This team needs clear and uncomplicated leadership; it gives them confidence.'

Charmaine listened seriously but answered casually, 'Felicity, you are the leader. I understand that and have absolutely no problem with you being the leader. But you don't include anyone in your decisions. The team aren't stupid, their opinions count.'

Her feedback surprised me. I felt that I had gone out of my way to elicit opinions from the others and one of my biggest frustrations was the fact that no one seemed to respond. I listened carefully to Charmaine's comments but couldn't help thinking that she was talking more about her own feelings than those of anyone else on the team. Despite my efforts to make her feel valued, Charmaine clearly felt that she wasn't being included in the decision-making process. I promised to change that but still needed her to see that she needed to change too – she needed to communicate with me better.

'I'm not on an ego trip, Charmaine. If you don't like the way I'm doing something you need to talk to me – but privately rather than bringing it up in front of the team.'

Despite the awkwardness of what was said, it was a friendly conversation and as we walked back to the tents I felt like the air had been cleared. It was only as I felt the relief that I realised how much the friction had been bothering me.

It was a tough first day. We spent the morning doing small local circuits to get re-acquainted with the skis before adding sledges to the mix. Each member of the team pulled their own sledge, just as they would in Antarctica. The sledges weren't heavy but the terrain was more challenging than I would have liked for our first day, forcing the girls to sidestep up icy slopes, traverse around awkward hills and make some memorable descents. Eventually we reached the foot of the ridge that would take us up onto the plateau and we camped for the night with an incredible view across the Southern Alps.

Starting early in the morning the route forward looked deceptively simple but by midday we found ourselves halfway up an increasingly icy and treacherous slope. The gradient to our right had become gradually steeper and I was worried that if someone fell they would fall all the way to the valley floor. However, the consequence of turning around would be that we were confined to the valleys below for the rest of our training. Remembering Charmaine's comments the previous evening, I gathered the group together on a rare flat patch on the icy slope and outlined our situation, as I saw it, asking the group for their opinion on what we should do. There was an awkward silence. I resisted the urge to fill the gap and waited.

Finally Sophia said, 'I don't think it is really worth the risk to continue. We should go back.' Everyone agreed. I was pleased with the decision; in truth, we didn't really have much of a choice but the hesitation of the women to suggest our next action spoke volumes. The girls were certainly not stupid and I greatly respected their opinion but neither, when it came to it, did they have the experience to make certain decisions. There would be times when I would have to make decisions based on my own experience, and in those cases the women would have to trust my judgement. I wasn't sure if Charmaine would be able to do that, and the realisation worried me. If Charmaine disagreed with me on the ice, it could split the group and that could be dangerous. I had seen it happen in other teams and knew how disruptive it could be. More expeditions fail thanks to bad team dynamics than for any other reason.

As the light dimmed we found a spot to camp away from the ski trails and pitched the tents. The snow was wet and soggy, making it damp and miserable inside. I had put a lot of thought into how to divide the team between our two four-man tents. Kim was working really hard on her skiing and general organisation but she was still the least confident team member and required the greatest input. To help, I placed her in a tent with the three most experienced members of the team; Helen, Charmaine and Reena. I shared a tent with Steph, Era and Sophia who were all novices but who seemed to be coping well.

Charmaine and Kim had formed what at first appeared to be a very unlikely friendship. Charmaine was impressively organised, with a brisk no-nonsense attitude and strong self-discipline, whereas Kim was hopelessly disorganised, chronically whimsical and easily distracted. Nevertheless, they formed a connection with each other and Charmaine was able to persuade Kim to listen to her advice in a way I had failed to do and as a result Kim was making great progress. It was good to see them getting on so well but as I sat in their tent that evening I noticed a clear division within the tent group. Charmaine took control of the small 'kitchen' at one end of the tent and Kim sat next to her, both of them with their backs to Helen and Reena who sat together dejectedly at the opposite end of the tent. Kim and Charmaine chatted quietly to each other laughing at private jokes, while Reena sat in silence. As I talked with Helen and Reena about the day ahead, I tried repeatedly to pull Charmaine and Kim into our conversation but when I left the tent the divide re-established itself immediately. The pattern repeated itself the following day as we skied. Kim increasingly depended on Charmaine to help her, to the point that Kim was refusing help from anyone else. As Steph stooped to help Kim re-strap bags onto her sledge I overheard Kim stop her, 'No, no, no. Charmaine does that for me.' Alarm bells started to ring in my head.

The day, generally, was pretty miserable. Confined to the valley our only option was to ski back and forth along a 2-kilometre stretch of lonely ski trail that snaked alongside a partially frozen river. The surroundings were extremely pretty but after the first half dozen repetitions it got a little boring. The sky that had been leaden since morning started producing sheets of soggy sleet that soaked through our clothing and equipment. Polar environments are usually very dry, so polar equipment is aimed at keeping out the cold rather than the wet. As a result, a downpour can be the most miserable experience possible. We pressed on through the sleet and I cheered myself with the thought that in many respects this was the best training we could have. It was monotonous, as Antarctica would be, and there was little opportunity to talk to each other. The team quickly felt cold, miserable and dejected – just as they were likely to do in Antarctica. The training became a preparation of mind as well as body in a way that I couldn't have designed in advance.

I secretly hoped that we would be able to make the journey to the South Pole unsupported, meaning that we would set off with everything in our sledges that we would need for the entire journey. To do this, I estimated that the team would each need to be able to pull around 80 kilograms in their sledge. If we couldn't manage this, I would have to arrange for a resupply to be placed by aircraft on the ice at a designated point about halfway through our journey. In order to gain a clear idea of how much weight each member of the team could realistically expect to haul in their sledge, we gradually increased our loads throughout the day. We used bags of snow as well as equipment to increase the weight in each sledge to 80 kilograms. We even used Rob (who had accompanied us to New Zealand to take pictures) as ballast, dragging him around the trails in a sledge like royalty. We had two slightly smaller sledges which were strung together, one behind the other, so that the weight was a total of 80 kilograms. Kim opted to tow the contraption but the 'articulated sledge' became a particular burden. As the team glided around a descending corner of the trail I glanced behind to see Kim, near the back of the line, lose a sledge over the edge of the bank. The weight of the sledge falling towards the river below dragged her backwards until she was left gripping hold of the side of the trail with both sledges dangling from the harness around her waist. She cried out in alarm, halfway between a scream and a shout. Steph was first to reach Kim but was unable to stop her own sledge disappearing over the same bank. Both were finally man-handled back onto the trail and lay on the snow for a moment, out of breath but laughing at their ridiculous predicament.

At the end of a full ten-hour day I asked everyone to write on a slip of paper whether they felt they could manage to haul a similarly laden sledge all the way to the South Pole, bearing in mind that we had only tried it for a day – we would need to repeat the same effort every day for around forty days. The slips were anonymous to encourage honesty but in reality I couldn't help but recognise the handwriting as I read them later that evening. Era, the smallest member of our team, had written just one word: 'Easy.' Others weren't so sure, quite rightly doubtful that they could possibly imagine what it would be like to pull such a load for so many days – even if it did get lighter each day as we used the food and fuel. The team seemed strong but I knew the toll that repeated exertion takes on the body; how hard it is to strap on a harness when every muscle aches; how every jolt seems to add a few kilograms to the weight of your sledge. I thought of Steve Jones, my contact at ALE. I have known Steve for a number of years and greatly value his advice, which has been amassed from leading dozens of polar expeditions himself. His guidance had been that leading novices to the South Pole, 5-foot-tall novices from tropical countries at that, was challenging enough without demanding that they be unsupported as well. I could see his point and yet I couldn't help toying with the temptation of allowing the team to really show what they could do.

On the last night of our mini-expedition we camped close to the ski lodge in preparation for our early departure the next morning. During the evening I took the opportunity to talk to Helen, Reena, Kim and Charmaine individually about the dynamics I had seen within their tent. I had sensed tension between Helen and Charmaine, overhearing the strain in their voices as they spoke to each other. 'Everything has to be done Charmaine's way,' Helen told me. 'She's very protective of her own personal space in the tent. There's not a lot of teamwork.'

Reena, on the other hand, expressed surprise at my concern. 'Charmaine is really helping Kim. We are all very happy,' she said. I had been really impressed with Reena over the week. She had clearly taken everything we had said in Norway on board and had arrived in New Zealand looking fit and strong. Never one to be conspicuously in the centre of things, she had nevertheless taken on an important role within the team. She was incredibly giving, saw nothing but the good in people, and was always ready with well-timed praise or encouragement. I came to see Reena as the quiet but steadfast heart of the team, radiating enough goodwill to bind the rest of the group together. The one downside to Reena's constantly positive attitude was that I wasn't sure if she would tell me if there were problems, so it was hard to ascertain whether Kim and Charmaine's close friendship was making her feel excluded or not. Despite Reena's comments to the contrary, I couldn't ignore what I had seen in the tent.

I spoke to Kim and congratulated her on her progress; she really had worked hard to be self-disciplined. There were still problems but watching her performance in New Zealand my confidence grew that, with the support of the rest of the team, she would make it to the South Pole. Without mentioning names, I gently warned Kim about the dangers of relying too much on one person and suggested that an overly close relationship within the team might make others feel excluded. 'I hadn't thought of it like that before,' she said. 'I would hate to be making anyone else feel bad.' She went back to the tent looking thoughtful.

Later I caught up with Charmaine. It was pitch-black and we both stood looking up at the stars that glimmered in a perfectly clear sky. I had made a conscious effort to open up to her over the last few days, sharing my thoughts about the logistical issues that lay ahead and seeking her opinion on decisions that had to be made. I genuinely liked Charmaine a great deal and so it wasn't difficult to chat and share a joke with her as we skied, but there was still evident tension between us. Whether intentionally or not, in front of the team she was often openly disapproving of my actions and decisions in a way that was almost patronising and ultimately infuriating. I could see that the rest of the team had noticed the rift and while some swept it aside, others (as I had feared) found it unsettling. I mentioned my worries about Kim's growing dependence. Charmaine wasn't anxious. 'I think it's just that Kim needs reassurance. This week has given her a lot of confidence so I think she'll be fine on the ice.' She was more concerned about Helen. 'She's not very open to new ways of doing things,' she said.

Changing the subject slightly, I reiterated what I had said at the beginning of the week, 'Charmaine, I know you don't always agree with the way I do things but we need to work closely together because the team are going to need that reassurance in Antarctica.'

'Well, I hope you know you can rely on me,' she replied. I smiled in thanks but as we went back to watching the stars in silence, I wondered: when it came to it, would Charmaine work with me, or against me?

At the end of the New Zealand training not everyone was able to continue onto Singapore for the scheduled meeting with Kaspersky Lab. Reena, Steph, Era, Sophia and I nervously made our way to the hotel where we would meet our title sponsors for the first time. Suk Ling was an impeccably elegant woman who greeted us all like old friends, but the stack of folders and notebooks that she carried with her everywhere hinted at the relentless taskmaster we would come to know. She introduced us to her team and finally to her boss, Harry, the man who had given the critical final approval to the expedition's sponsorship. Harry was extremely influential. As well as being managing director of Kaspersky Lab Asia and a member of the board of directors, he had a reputation as a marketing genius. Given such an intimidating CV, it was a surprise to find him an extremely relaxed character. He said very little and smiled a lot but it was clear that Harry was a very astute and exacting businessman, and I was determined that the expedition would exceed his expectations in terms of a return on his investment in us.

Suk Ling had arranged a press conference at the National Geographic Store in Singapore to launch Kaspersky Lab's sponsorship of the expedition. We arrived at the store to find it had been transformed into a representation of the South Pole. In front of a large screen displaying an Antarctic scene was a tiered stage covered in polystyrene snow, crowned with a replica of the barber's pole and silver sphere that mark the real South Pole. We were to sit on the stage with Harry in front of an audience of journalists and would be interviewed by a presenter posing as a famous polar explorer. (There was some discussion about whether the presenter should be Robert Falcon Scott or Roald Amundsen. Although Amundsen was the first person to reach the South Pole, Scott of the Antarctic was considered more famous. When asked my opinion I pointed out that Scott had actually died, along with

The group of possible team members, selected from over 800 applicants, arrive in Norway for their first taste of extreme winter conditions. (Robert Hollingworth)

Barbara from Ghana enjoys her first Norwegian blizzard after camping overnight in temperatures below −20°C. (Robert Hollingworth)

Felicity (standing, far right) teaches the candidates how to pitch a tent in a blizzard. (Robert Hollingworth)

The team in front of Westminster Abbey on Commonwealth Day. From left: Era, Reena, Felicity, Barbara, Kim-Marie, Charmaine, Sophia and Steph.

Pitching the tents for the first time in Antarctica, at what became known as Camp Kaspersky. (Robert Hollingworth)

Kim-Marie before finding the blister that would turn out to be frostbite. Note the oversized plaster covering the chilblain on her face.

Sophia looking thoughtful on our way to the expedition start point on the coast of Antarctica.

Our two tents were the only splash of colour and life in the vast emptiness of Antarctica. We were truly alone.

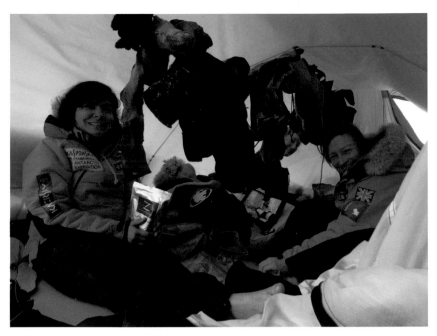

Our home on the ice. From left: Reena, Kylie and Helen.

Era having goggle trouble.

Team photograph on arrival at our resupply. You can just see the red material of our supply bags buried in the snow. From left: Reena, Sophia, Kylie, Felicity, Steph, Helen and Era.

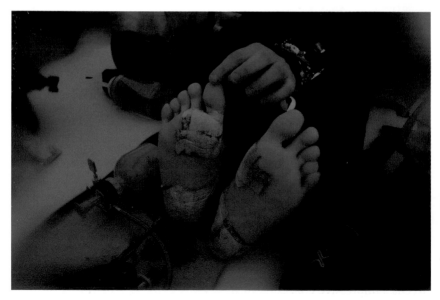

Steph warming her plastered feet by the stove inside the tent.

Sastrugi Land.

Reena's impressive collection of icicles that had built up during the day from her frozen breath.

Making the last few steps to the South Pole together, but forgetting to detach ourselves from the sledges first!

The largest and most international team of women ever to ski to the South Pole. From left: Sophia, Kylie, Era, Felicity, Helen, Reena, Steph.

his men, during his expedition to the South Pole, which might not be the best omen for the expedition. It was decided to go with Amundsen.)

Finally, the journalists began to arrive and the five of us representing the team took our places on stage with Harry. As the presenter, dressed up in a polar jacket borrowed from the store, introduced himself as Roald Amundsen I wondered how many journalists in the audience would leave the event under the false impression they had seen the real Roald Amundsen. (Judging by the write-ups afterward, quite a few.)

After the event, Suk Ling seemed pleased with the coverage but was troubled that the subject of money had dominated the question and answer session. I make a point of never talking about exact figures with journalists and had asked the team to do the same. Inevitably numbers would get misreported or old information recycled and it could lead to all sorts of misunderstandings; so saying nothing precise about budgets and funding seemed the safest option. However, the difficulty came when we were asked if we had all the money we needed. The truthful answer was no. The money from Kaspersky Lab would cover logistical costs but we still needed equipment. Kaspersky Lab was our exclusive title sponsor, so we couldn't look for other sponsors to cover these additional expenses. Instead we hoped to raise money through fundraising events or to persuade suppliers to donate the equipment to the expedition. This troubled Suk Ling and she took Harry to one side to discuss it with him. I couldn't be precise about why, but the situation worried me. I felt vaguely anxious.

That afternoon we had another press conference, this time in the form of a video conference call to four countries at once: Malaysia, the Philippines, Hong Kong and Taiwan. There were a lot of journalists and a lot of interest but again, the subject of money dominated the interviews. Harry answered all the financial questions but Suk Ling looked uncomfortable. After the press conference, the team were asked to wait outside while Harry and Suk Ling spoke with each other. We were called back into the office and, although I couldn't see that we had done anything wrong, I prepared to defend myself and the expedition. I was in for a surprise. 'Kaspersky Lab really admire your adventure and you adventurous ladies. We have put a lot of money into the expedition but we really want to see you and your team succeed – we want you to think of us as your ninth team member. But for us, because it is such a big investment, we don't want to share that with any other companies. That is why we want to be your exclusive sponsors.' I nodded and smiled enthusiastically. Suk Ling continued, 'It's not good for us that you are still looking for money.' There was a pause. I looked at Harry who sat quietly, looking at the space in front of him. 'That is why,' she continued, 'Harry has decided to cover the rest of your expenses.' All eyes fell on Harry in astonished silence. 'Harry will give you another fifty thousand dollars, even if it has to come out of his own pocket.'

I knew I should say something but I didn't know where to start. My eyes stung with tears at the overwhelming relief and as the news sunk in, I felt the financial stress that I had been carrying for the last year slide from my shoulders. It was, quite literally, a dream come true. All our money worries had quite unexpectedly disappeared. Harry was our unexpected knight in shining armour. Steph was the first to react, whooping with joy and rushing across the room to hug Harry. The rest of us followed and Harry laughed, clearly astonished that he had caused such joy. Harry and the Kaspersky Lab team had to leave shortly afterwards. We said our goodbyes and watched them leave before slumping into the cool leather sofas in reception.

No one said anything for a long minute. Reena hesitantly broke the silence, 'So, does that mean that we don't need any more money?'

'We have everything we need,' I replied. 'We're going to Antarctica.'

CHAPTER SEVEN

THE EXAM

The meeting with Kaspersky Lab in Singapore had been more successful than I could have hoped but with the sponsorship came a lot of responsibility. Returning to the UK in mid September there were just six weeks until the team departed. I was soon receiving at least a dozen emails a day from the Kaspersky Lab team and it became obvious that they expected results – fast. Not only did I have to arrange the rebranding of clothing and equipment but there was now urgent need for a new branded expedition website; departure and return events to be organised; a detailed media plan to be put in place and press releases to be written for all eight countries. The Kaspersky Lab team also had to be brought up to speed on every aspect of the expedition, particularly the details of our expected arrival at the South Pole. I threw myself willingly into the work – this was, after all, what sponsorship was all about – but it was overwhelming. Suk Ling had a team of five or six people working on the expedition at Kaspersky Lab but there was only one me to answer all their queries and requests; I was soon swamped.

THE EXAM

Feeling my stress levels reaching new heights I relished a well-timed excuse to escape for a few days. I had been commissioned by a UK magazine to write about some walking routes in the north-east of England, and I couldn't afford to pass up the work. I set out early into the mountains, as the blue-tinged haze of morning was still clearing from the valleys, and weaved upwards towards the rounded summits of the Cheviot Hills through a spectacular rock-lined gorge, scrambling along boulder-lined streams and secluded waterfalls. It was invigorating to be striding alone across the high moors on a perfect autumn day. Feeling the sun warm my back as I climbed, luxuriating in the silence and the isolation, my mind mulled over the problems I had left at home. I was surprised that out of all the issues and difficulties faced by the expedition, there was one situation that caused me more worry and angst than all the others. It wasn't the sponsorship or the logistics; it wasn't the crevasses or the cold; it was Charmaine.

The concerns I'd had in New Zealand refused to go away. The bottom line was that she didn't agree with the way I was running the expedition and I suspected that she thought she could do a better job. Her frustration seemed to be vented, consciously or not, by being increasingly awkward. In just the previous week Charmaine had informed me that she would arrive a week late at our departure point for Antarctica and had complained about several critical arrangements. I had visions of making tough decisions on the ice, only to have my actions questioned by Charmaine. The last thing I wanted was to have to deal with a confrontation in the middle of a crisis. I remembered Robert Swan's book and the trouble he'd had with a team member who wanted to run everything his own way. I didn't want to have the same experience.

It would be easy to ignore the situation with Charmaine and tell myself that it would all sort itself out once we got to Antarctica –

but in my heart I knew it wouldn't go away. If the team isn't right before you leave, it's never going to be right once you are on the ice and under pressure.

I thought about ways to improve the situation. I considered talking to her about the problem but felt that I had already tried this in New Zealand with little effect. With only a month to go until departure, there wasn't enough time to mend the faulty dynamics between us. That left me with only one option: to ask Charmaine to leave the team. The thought scared me a little. Without Charmaine, I would need to find an alternative New Zealand team member. It would be a risk to involve someone new so late in our preparations, but it seemed to be a greater risk going to Antarctica knowing that there was a problem. Already the issue was draining my energy and taking my focus away from other aspects of the expedition.

I couldn't take the gamble: I had to ask her to step down.

I thought ruefully about the question I had been asked at the dinner party in Singapore, 'Have you ever had to sack a team member?' It had seemed like such an impossible scenario back then, but now it was very real.

Charmaine would be devastated. I also wondered how the rest of the team would take the news, particularly Kim. It was going to be awful for everyone, including myself. How could I begin to tell someone that I was taking away their dream? I resolutely packed away my budding reluctance: however hard it was, it had to be done. This is when being the leader really counts, I told myself, when there are tough, unpleasant and possibly unpopular decisions to be made. I would not allow myself to hide from them.

Despite my resolve it still felt slightly unreal as I dialled Charmaine's number at the arranged time. She had been reluctant to talk but I had told her it was urgent. I was sure that what I had to say would be a shock.

'Charmaine, this isn't a happy phone call,' I paused, taking a long breath. 'I need to talk to you about your involvement in the expedition and your place on the team.'

'All right,' she replied. She sounded intrigued but nothing more. She clearly had no idea what was coming.

'I'm ringing to ask you to step down from the team.'

There was silence on the line.

'When you joined the team I hoped you'd be a confidante, a kind of second-in-command, because of your experience, but it doesn't seem to have worked out like that. There isn't the trust between us that I think is necessary and I know that it's going to cause problems when we are in Antarctica. It may seem dramatic but I have seen situations like this that have been ignored and caused serious problems. I just can't take that risk.'

I stopped talking and waited for a response. There was a long pause.

'If you have issues with me we can work them out. I honestly don't have a problem with you being the leader, I'm fine with that. Everything will be fine when we get to Antarctica, just give me a chance.'

'I'm sorry, Charmaine, but we don't have the time to work this out. We tried in New Zealand and it didn't work. I can't just cross my fingers and hope everything will be OK in Antarctica. I can't take the risk.'

'But you didn't mention anything in New Zealand. You could have at least given me the opportunity to put things right.'

I thought about the conversations we'd had during the training expedition and couldn't see how she could have missed my concerns. The fact that she seemed oblivious to any problem just confirmed all my worries that talking wouldn't make any difference – not in the time that we had left before the expedition.

I stared out of my office window at the greenery of the trees being buffeted by the wind. I felt slightly dreamlike, as if I was acting in a film and none of this was real. In a way I *was* acting – I had to be more obstinate and unkind than I'd ever had to be in my life.

'Charmaine, I've made up my mind and I'm afraid my decision is final.'

I pressed on with the practical details, letting her know when and how the team would be told. As the phone call came to an end she said simply, 'Please, Felicity. Don't do this.'

She sounded wretched and as I rang off the sound of her voice wrung all my resolve. This was not the reason I had started this project and this was not where I had ever expected to be. Despite my guilt, I didn't regret the decision. I knew that it had been the right thing to do.

Hello everyone,

I'm afraid I have some unhappy news.

I have just spoken to Charmaine and asked her to leave the expedition team.

This may come as a shock to some of you but there have been several issues, particularly since New Zealand, that I have been unable to resolve and so, after much consideration and careful thought, this was my decision.

We are travelling to a place that is dangerous. In the event of a crisis I need to have confidence and trust in the people around me and that is the reason that I have taken this action.

I am available over the next few days to speak directly to anyone who would like to talk this through – but my decision is final.

The intention is to find a new team member from New Zealand.

I know that this will hit some of you hard but the important

thing now is to focus on what is ahead and to pull together as
a team.

I have faith in you all.

Felicity

I needn't have been worried about the team reaction. They had
sympathy for Charmaine but were strangely quiet. Perhaps they
wrote to each other privately, or maybe there was simply too
much going on at the time for them to share their thoughts on
the matter.

My own thoughts turned to finding a new team member. I had
received some 200 applications from women in New Zealand
to join the expedition and the vast majority of them had been
experienced skiers or mountaineers, many of whom had already
spent a season or two in Antarctica. I needed someone who not only
already had the training and experience to take on the expedition
with minimal training, and who was available immediately, but
also someone who would fit into our team quickly and effortlessly.
I looked through my shortlist of New Zealand candidates that I
had prepared almost exactly a year previously; one name stood
out. I had met Kylie Wakelin in 2001 when she had spent a
summer working at the same Antarctic research base I had been
posted to. As two women in a very male environment we had
become friends and had stayed vaguely in touch ever since, even
though we hadn't met again since Kylie had left Antarctica.

During the original selection the fact that I knew Kylie personally
had counted against her as I worried that the objectivity of the
interview process would be questioned. Now, that same concern
had turned into a positive bonus. With very little time available
to get to know a complete stranger and very aware of the risk of
inviting someone who could turn out to be unsuitable, I could ask
Kylie to join the team safe in the knowledge that she was reliable,

fun and used to fitting in. As an avid climber and skier, she was experienced in the outdoors and, having been to Antarctica, she at least knew what to expect. For ten years Kylie had run her own company in the Mount Cook National Park, offering tourist boat tours around the glacial, ice-filled lakes but had recently sold the company to start a career as a pilot. She had just gained a Commercial Pilot License and was due to start her first job when my email arrived.

We spoke on the phone and I talked about the team she would be joining and what we were up against. She was keen to accept right away but I urged her to think about it and to send me an email when she had made her decision. I received her reply the very next morning. 'I feel like I am waiting for the camera crew and presenter to walk through the door and say, "Ha ha, only kidding, had you going!" I am writing to let you know that I am still as keen as mustard.'

As I ran through the details with Kylie, sending her paperwork and schedules and flight information, my thoughts turned to Helen. As the team reserve, she still held onto the hope that she would be asked to join the expedition as a team member and yet I had denied her an opportunity by replacing Charmaine with another New Zealander. However, I didn't want to use up my reserve because there was still another unresolved situation developing within the team. Barbara hadn't made it to the training in New Zealand, leaving me with the challenge of finding a way to get her some additional training before Antarctica. I had lots of ideas but had been stumped by complete silence from Barbara since we'd returned. No one had heard anything from her for a fortnight despite a barrage of emails and messages from increasingly concerned teammates. I had tried her mobile phone a few times but there was no connection. When an email finally arrived from Barbara, it wasn't good news. She had spent the last three weeks in bed battling malaria. 'I can't say for sure whether I'll be fit enough to prepare for, let alone participate in, the upcoming expedition.' She wrote. 'I'm sorry for disappointing you and the team, but I will be praying for you and watching every step you ladies take to and from the South Pole.' She signed off, 'Thank you for everything. I love you all and God bless you.'

I was devastated but surprisingly calm. This wasn't a situation that I could do anything about. This time it wasn't a matter of making frantic phone calls and pulling off a miracle. There was nothing Barbara, or anyone else, could do. Malaria is an incredibly debilitating illness and, even though she would eventually make a full recovery, it would take her weeks to recover full fitness. Even if she did manage to get fit in time to travel to Antarctica, driving her body to the edge by skiing to the South Pole might provoke a dangerous slide into exhaustion. I was sorry for Barbara and sorry that the expedition wouldn't now have an African representative but unlike New Zealand, I didn't feel finding an alternative Ghanaian at this late stage would be possible.

I wrote to Helen to ask if she would take up Barbara's place on the team. Having given up hope of being asked to join the expedition she had accepted a place on a month-long expedition to walk along a stretch of the skeleton coast in Namibia. She would finish the trek over a week before the expedition was due to depart but wouldn't be able to return to the UK until just the day before. I had been worried when she had told me her plans a few months previously, but without a place to offer her on the team at the time I didn't feel that I had any right to advise her against it. Now, as I wrote Helen an email, I trusted her own judgement and experience to tell me whether she felt fit and able to come to Antarctica so soon after returning from Namibia. The response was emphatic, she accepted without hesitation.

Although I was crushed that Barbara couldn't come with us, I was pleased that Helen would be on the team. Knowing that Helen would now be in the second tent gave me some extra reassurance; I hoped that she would be able to keep an eye on things when I wasn't there.

I was worried that the last-minute team turmoil might make our sponsors nervous but was relieved (and grateful) that Suk Ling was willing to trust me without concern as I explained events to her. For Kaspersky Lab the new expedition website was a more pressing issue. The website would be the team's main platform for communicating our experiences to a global audience while in Antarctica. We didn't have a limitless budget but I was determined to use exciting and economical technology to make the most of what we had. We would be carrying two satellite telephones with us on the expedition, which would enable us to call anywhere in the world, just like a mobile, but we discovered we could do much more with them than that. By ringing a voicemail number we could record podcasts that could be uploaded onto our website so that anyone could listen to us talking to them direct from Antarctica; we could write SMS messages from the satellite phone to a Twitter account that would display our microblogs on our website in real time (quite literally tweeting to the South Pole, which, as far as we are aware, hadn't been tried before); and most exciting of all, I was sure that we could give a live lecture to an audience in London while sitting in a tent in Antarctica (which certainly hadn't been done before). By sharing our experience so immediately and vividly, we could engage more people and have a greater opportunity to spread our message, to motivate and inspire, and to provoke thought.

By the end of October, I was waiting for the team to arrive in the UK. The plan was for the team to be together for three or four days before we all travelled to Punta Arenas in Chile, where we would spend a week preparing and checking our equipment in readiness for our scheduled flight to Antarctica on 12 November. Kylie was the first to arrive. It had been six years since I'd last seen her but the time vanished in an instant. She hadn't changed at all but I felt like a completely different person to the young, idealistic girl she had known in Antarctica. As we hugged I wondered if she would notice the difference in me.

My modest flat wasn't big enough to accommodate the entire team plus all our kit. Instead, my parents had offered to host us at Crofton, my childhood home in West Kent. A few months before I was born, my parents and grandparents moved into this big house with large bay windows and they have lived there ever since. It was an idyllic place to grow up. Surrounded by 9 acres of woodland I spent endless summers building camps in the trees and bossing around my younger sister. Crofton has always been a busy place: my parents are natural hosts, so the house is usually full of friends and extended family. I drove there with Kylie and began sorting through the growing mountain of boxes and parcels that had been arriving all through the previous week and which were quickly filling my parents' front room to capacity. We burrowed our way in, ripping open boxes to check what was inside.

Reena and Sophia arrived early the next morning, quickly followed by Era and Steph. I introduced them all to Kylie and left them to get to know each other as I went to greet a lorry that had arrived with a delivery of enormous boxes – it was the branded clothing from Montane. I pulled out a jacket from one of the boxes and felt a wave of pride. The bright red insulated smocks were stamped with the expedition logo which stood out in prominent white and green. Kaspersky Lab logos ran along the sleeves and the hood was framed with thick wolverine trim. It looked like a jacket that real polar explorers would wear, the kind of jacket imagined in childish daydreams of adventure. Now I knew we were going on an expedition and the scale of what we had achieved in getting this far finally sank in. Two years ago the expedition had been just a dream; now it had a uniform.

Crofton was full to bursting. As well as the team, Rob the photographer had arrived, and a constant stream of local media, from TV crews to radio cars with extendable masts, came and went. My good friend Guy arrived to give us some last-minute first aid training. He showed the team how to look after a blister and ensure it didn't get infected; how to strap up a sprain with gaffer tape; how to look after a broken bone; and how to stop major bleeding. Going through all the drugs in our first aid kits he asked each of us if we had any allergies. Sophia thought that she might be allergic to ibuprofen but wasn't sure.

'Well, there's only one way to find out,' said Guy, holding out a small white pill in the flat of his palm. Sophia looked uncertain.

'Is this a good idea?' I asked Guy. The last thing I needed was the hospitalisation of a team member the day before our departure.

Guy looked at me seriously, 'If it goes wrong here, Sophia can get immediate medical help. Would you rather she found out she was allergic in the middle of Antarctica?' He had a point.

Sophia took the pill and her eye promptly swelled up with a nasty blister just beneath her lower lashes. 'Well, at least now I know,' she said shrugging it off. Within hours her eye was back to normal.

Guy taught us the recovery position but didn't bother with CPR. 'If your heart stops you are going to need serious medical help very quickly,' he explained. 'In Antarctica you are not going to get that help so, I hate to say it, but if your heart stops, you are dead and nothing I can teach you will change that.' He was right but it was a sobering thought.

His words made me think of a conversation I'd had with Kylie the day before. She had asked about the risk of crevasses during the expedition. Crevasses are deep cracks in the ice that can occur anywhere in Antarctica. Often covered by a layer of snow, and therefore invisible on the surface, they can be wide enough for a person to fall into and deep enough for that person to never be seen again. The thought of them made me cold with fear and I had discussed the risks exhaustively with those that had skied to the South Pole before. Crevasses usually occur where the ice is disturbed by a sudden change in topography, such as a mountain range or an ice stream. By avoiding features like this, the risk of coming across crevasse fields is reduced. We would be on skis which spread our weight, making it less likely that we would fall through any snow covered crevasses, and we were going early in the season when the snow layer over the crevasses would be strongest. We could have opted to wear harnesses and rope ourselves together so that if someone fell, the rest could, theoretically, stop them but it was impractical to ski roped together. Our only protection was to ski in single file and to be extremely observant so that if we spotted anything suspicious we could take action to avoid it.

The decision was logical and justified but whereas months ago the danger had been hypothetical and distant, it now seemed real and immediate. I couldn't shake off a feeling of dread, almost a sense of premonition. My fear, which had been mitigated by objective reasoning, now became emotionally driven. Saying goodbye to my parents as we prepared to leave reignited the fears that I had tried to rationalise out of my head. Dad is usually very matter of fact in his goodbyes but this time I noticed him staying close, putting his arm around me as we stood for photos and hugging me extra tight as he said farewell. He even blew a kiss as we drove off to the airport, in a way that he hasn't done since I was little. Both parents told me they were proud but they seemed scared in a way that they hadn't been for other trips – perhaps it was simply my own fear being reflected.

As we took off in the plane bound for Punta Arenas in Chile, I could see the white and red lights of the M25 stream away into the darkness. I pushed one fingertip against the glass of the window tracing the line of lights which I knew led back home to those I love. In that moment I wanted to be in one of those cars more than anything else in the world. Usually when I leave on a long expedition, the sadness of goodbye is tempered by the excitement of the adventure to come. This time it was different. Every fibre of my body seemed to be screaming at me to stay, to run home, not to leave – as if I was being pulled by a magnet. I told myself that the excitement would come – that as I threw myself into the plans and preparations this horrid homesickness would be squeezed out. In all other respects I felt ridiculously calm. Perhaps the reason crevasses filled my mind was because there was little else left that I could worry about; everything else had already been set in motion and there was nothing I could change, even if I'd wanted to.

Punta Arenas is a city with a population of over 150,000 but it retains the feel of a frontier town. Sandwiched between the coast and a sprawling hillside, it looks out towards the Strait of Magellan, providing a clear view of incoming storms that gather on the steely horizon. I had visited Punta once before, on my way out of Antarctica nearly a decade ago, and I remembered two things about it: the constant wind and the packs of stray dogs. As a face-full of dust was blown into my eyes and I warded a pack of dogs away from our stack of luggage on the street outside the hostel, I realised that nothing much had changed.

The hostel was a rundown backpacker haunt just like hundreds of others all over the city but it had a shabby homeliness about it and we had the place pretty much to ourselves. It was perfect. The hostel manager looked slightly bewildered as the team took over his kitchen, made themselves at home in the meeting room and filled the upstairs landing with clothing and equipment. I gathered the team together and between us we came up with an action plan for the following six days. Our biggest job was to prepare all the expedition rations. To save the cost of shipping large, weighty volumes of food from the UK we had decided to source what we could in Punta. In addition, any food we had brought with us was still in its original packaging to satisfy the Chilean customs regulations. This meant that the job of sorting the expedition food into individual daily rations had to be started from scratch in our hostel.

I had spent a long time over the previous months planning the rations in minute detail, right down to the last gram. There is a formula used by sports scientists that determines the amount of carbohydrates and protein a person will need, just from their body weight. Unfortunately, the size and shape of the members of our team varied widely from tiny Era, who weighed barely 50 kilograms, to Reena, who weighed over 70 kilograms. I was the heaviest in the team by far (as well as the tallest – I often felt like a freakish giant next to my teammates), so I decided to use my weight for all the calculations. This would mean that some of the girls would get at a least a third more carbohydrates and protein than they needed but, I reasoned, too much was better than too little.

As well as carbohydrates and proteins, I had to take into consideration our fat and calorie intake. With the weight in our sledges always my primary consideration, I had set a target of no more than 1 kilogram of food, per person, per day. The task of getting the necessary amounts of carbohydrate, protein, fat and calories into just 1 kilogram of food was time-consuming and frustrating. Trawling through the nutritional information on packets of hundreds of different foodstuffs, I'd find something that was extremely high in carbohydrates but had no fat or protein; or something that was high in protein and fat but which was extremely heavy. To make matters more complicated, I had to take into account the likes and dislikes of eight women who all ate very different food at home. Kim wanted banana chips and dried mango, Reena wouldn't eat prawn crackers, Sophia didn't want too much sweet food and, of course, I also had to make sure that nothing contained alcohol or meat products (unless I was sure they were halal) and especially not products from a cow (Reena's request as a Hindu) or a pig (Era and Kim's request).

After days of trial and error, I finally had a combination I was happy with that would fit all the requirements. For breakfast we would eat porridge with sugar and fortified milk powder and a hot chocolate. During the day we would each have a bag of snacks to munch on during our breaks. The bags would contain peanuts, sesame snaps, toffee popcorn, banana chips, chocolate and boiled sweets, and we had two sachets of high-carbohydrate sports drink to add to our water bottles. In the evening we would have a dehydrated meal, a protein drink, a hot chocolate, a soup and a packet of noodles to add to our meal.

Armed with lists of the foodstuffs we had not brought with us from the UK, the team split up and scouted the shops in the city, quickly clearing shelves of chocolate, peanuts and boiled sweets as if we were on a deranged trolley dash. Powdered soup presented a problem. The people of Punta, it appears, only like asparagus soup, as it was the only flavour we could find. Forty days of asparagus soup wasn't ideal but at least everyone liked the flavour. The most elusive item was banana chips and we had all but given up when we were directed to a tiny, brightly painted shop opposite the large supermarket in town. The shop's glass counters were divided into big bins of dried fruit, from figs to papayas, and every conceivable type of nut. Not only did the shop have banana chips but they had two varieties, sweet and salty. This sparked perhaps the most heated team discussion of the entire expedition. 'What foolishness creates salty banana chips?' exclaimed Kim. 'It's not a banana chip if it isn't sweet.'

'No,' insisted Sophia. 'We want salty. We have too much sweet stuff. Banana chips are salty.'

We were all called upon to give our verdict in the Great Banana Chip Debate, each team member tasting both varieties and stating their preference. It was clear that the only compromise was to have a mix of both but the exact proportion of sweet versus salty was haggled over with all the finesse of an international territorial dispute.

Back at the hostel, we had started a production line to prepare some 460 ration bags. Each of us took control of one ingredient. I was in charge of toffee popcorn along with Kim; Steph and Reena dealt with the peanuts, Kylie added boiled sweets, Helen took control of chocolate and Sophia the hotly debated banana chips. At first it was difficult not to eat as we worked but as the sickly smell of confectionary filled the hostel, sugar was the last thing we were craving.

While we worked, the ALE doctor called on us. I'd first met him at Santiago airport when he'd come over to introduce himself (dressed in our polar clothing we were easily spotted). The first thing he'd said to me was, 'We see teams come down year after year and we watch them all make the same mistakes.' He went on to list some of the most common errors and I was pleased that none of them applied to us, but his comment had put me on the defensive. I'd worked tirelessly for two years to get as much advice as I could, including from ALE, to make sure we were as prepared as possible and yet the doctor seemed to have already decided that we were just like all the others and that there was little hope for us. I realised that from ALE's point of view our team represented something of a risk. Antarctica is a dangerous place and I was bringing a team of novices with less than a year's training to complete a journey that teams much more experienced and physically stronger than us had failed to complete safely. ALE were not responsible for us on the ice – we were a private expedition for which they were providing logistical support – but if we came to harm they would inevitably be called to account. For this reason they are stringent about which expeditions they transport to Antarctica and would be well within their right to refuse to take an expedition that they felt was unsafe or unprepared. I didn't want to give ALE any reason to doubt us.

The doctor had called on us at the hostel to go through our first aid kits. Before he left he looked through the nutritional breakdown of our rations and was concerned. It is a standard rule of thumb that someone on a demanding polar expedition will need at least 4,500 calories a day, increasing to around 5,000 calories by the end of the journey. Our rations provided 4,300 calories at the start, increasing to around 4,600 calories for the second half of the expedition. I knew this was less than usual but then our team was significantly smaller, physically, than average. During our training in Norway and New Zealand it was clear that some team members were incapable of ingesting any more than this. Once the doctor had left I thought hard about our rations and whether they needed to be changed. I am always careful not to let my own ego or pride get in the way of making good decisions. In this case, even after objectively re-examining my calculations, I was still confident that our rations were the best they could be for our team.

The team was to go to the ALE office the next day to talk about our expedition. Steve Jones, my main contact at ALE, would be running the meeting and, although he had been a very supportive friend over the last year, I knew that he was now wearing his ALE hat. He would need to know every detail of our preparations, from kit to rations, in order to satisfy himself that we were ready. As I gathered papers and documents for the meeting, I couldn't help but feel as if I was preparing for an exam. Steve would be exacting and thorough, and I needed to prove that my team was prepared.

We filed into the ALE office and were shown into a bright and airy lounge. The girls rapidly planted themselves on the inviting sofas lining the room, sprawling like teenagers, while Steve sat on a chair in the middle. He talked through every aspect of our expedition, from our expectations and training to the make and model of our stoves and satellite phones. Steve's main area of concern seemed to be our plans to remove our human waste throughout the expedition. ALE already insisted that expeditions remove their human waste from within the last degree of latitude surrounding the South Pole, as this is where there is the greatest concentration of activity. No one had yet tried doing the same for the duration of an entire expedition from the edge of the continent to the pole. Steve expressed his doubts. 'This is already a huge challenge, so I don't see the sense in making it unnecessarily harder for yourselves.' We had no idea how much waste we would accumulate and therefore how much extra weight this decision would add to our loads.

I tried to reassure Steve with the same logic I had used on myself. 'If it gets too heavy we'll just stop collecting it. If we only manage to remove our waste for part of the way before it gets too heavy, then surely that's better than nothing and at least we will have learnt about the sort of weights involved. At the moment no one knows.' Steve looked unimpressed. He clearly thought it was an act of foolishness on my part.

Seeing that I wasn't willing to back down, he moved on to another area of concern. As a result of the team's training in New Zealand, we had opted for one resupply of food and fuel to be left on the ice for us by plane. We would also be able to leave rubbish at this depot to be collected later in the season. ALE's own guided expeditions have a second, additional resupply closer to the South Pole and Steve was keen for us to do the same. The decision to have any support at all had been difficult for me but a second resupply seemed like a step too far. We wouldn't need it, I was sure of it. The discussions with Steve went on long into the afternoon. ALE warned me about the difficulties of travelling with a larger group, about the likelihood of the women spreading out. I listened carefully to their advice but as much as I was wary of being over-confident I couldn't help but feel frustrated. I didn't feel that I was being given much credit for knowing what I was doing. We had trained as a team and put systems in place to avoid such dangers. Separation was one of my worst fears and so we always travelled ski-tip to sledge-back, leaving no possibility for the team to spread out. I was confident in our team's preparation and any departure from the accepted wisdom had been deliberate and careful.

With just days to go until our scheduled departure, we laid out all the equipment that was coming with us to Antarctica in the garage behind the hostel and streamlined wherever we could to reduce weight. I was determined that we would be as lightweight as possible and went through our equipment repeatedly to root out any unnecessary spares or luxury items. Rather than each team member having their own penknife, journal, pencil, GPS, compass, camera, moisturiser, supply of wet wipes and toothpaste, we shared these items as a team. Personal luxuries such as books, good luck mascots and Christmas paraphernalia were banned as were any well-meaning 'surprise' gifts for the team. Most of the women were happy to go along with my weight-saving rules but there was some resistance as I sifted through each team member's personal items. Sophia and Reena had each packed two hats and were reluctant to leave one behind; Steph grumbled as I made her remove the wet wipes that were included with each of her sanitary towels and Kylie was disappointed when I asked her not to take the small Christmas presents that she had secretly brought for everyone. I felt like a killjoy but if I allowed Kylie to bring gifts then everyone would bring something for Christmas and before we knew it we'd have fake Christmas trees and frozen turkey slices being tucked away in our baggage, adding considerably to our loads.

I knew that the girls all thought I was unnecessarily obsessed with weight and didn't understand my seemingly pedantic, minimalist approach but I knew what it was like to pull a sledge for six weeks; I knew we would spend day after day thinking about what was in the sledge and agonise over whether every item was strictly necessary; to be desperate to identify anything, however small, that could be left behind just to reduce the weight, even if only infinitesimally. I knew that by the end of the expedition, they would understand my obsession.

Each evening, we spent a lot of time sewing. The upstairs landing resembled a sewing circle as we made ourselves comfortable round the electric fire surrounded by spare material, boxes of needles and rolls of thread. We each had almost identical clothing that needed to be colour-coded so that we knew which was ours and also had to be adapted for our own personal needs and preferences. Some cut extra holes in the balaclavas we used to cover our faces so that they could breathe more easily while others sewed pleats in the fabric so that it was a closer fit. Some made thumb-holes in the sleeves of their thermal tops to keep their wrists warm while others made 'wristies' from fleece scraps or old socks. We chatted as we sewed and although it was often the early hours before we all turned in, the sewing circle was the most relaxing part of our day.

I tried to make sure that we didn't work ourselves into the ground, that everybody got enough sleep and enough to eat so that they arrived in Antarctica fit and rested rather than stressed and exhausted, but there was a nervous energy in the team that caused mistakes to be made, mistakes that we couldn't afford. Kim came to see me in the hostel with a broken stove pump in her hand. She had been a little overenthusiastic when testing a stove and snapped part of the plastic pump, rendering our spare stove useless. I was exasperated at her carelessness but calmed myself with the thought that we could probably find a replacement in Punta. Shortly afterward Steph went into Punta wearing her windproof expedition smock and – within 100 yards of the hostel – had lost it.

'I'm sorry, Felicity. I've looked everywhere but it's gone,' she apologised.

I was furious. There was no way she could ski to the South Pole without her windproof and we didn't have spares. Each team member wore the same branded equipment so, even if we found a similar jacket in Punta, it would impact the branding of the team and our precious sponsorship. 'Well, you can't come to Antarctica without it,' I snapped. 'So you'd better get out there and find it.'

She spent the rest of the day despondently pacing the streets around the hostel looking for any sign of her bright red jacket. She asked in cafes and shops if anyone had seen it and found a man who thought he'd seen something red blowing towards the sea. I noticed the look of sympathy in the eyes of the rest of the team. They thought I was being unnecessarily harsh. Steph was clearly devastated and losing the smock had been a genuine mistake – but I saw it as a symptom of a worrying trend within the team.

Each member undoubtedly cared about our expedition and was undeniably trying hard, but something was missing. The team didn't quite appreciate the seriousness of what we were about to do. To them it was still a game; it wasn't real. I felt partly responsible for this attitude because in Norway we had looked after everyone as if it was a school trip. If someone lost an item, we found them a replacement; if they came to us with a problem, we solved it. In Antarctica I couldn't look after everyone all of the time. The women would have to take responsibility for themselves.

As the light faded, I sent someone out to fetch Steph and bring her back to the hostel. When she arrived I gathered the team together in the breakfast room. I sighed inwardly, feeling like a headmistress. I talked about the consequences of the broken stove and the lost jacket, adding drama to emphasize the point. 'I know you think I am being harsh but Antarctica will be far less forgiving if we make these kinds of mistakes during the expedition. In Antarctica there are no second chances. I know you feel terribly sorry now – but it is too late, the damage has already been done. I want you to remember how sorry you feel right now and use it to stop you making mistakes. Imagine how awful you would feel if you make a mistake in Antarctica that sends the expedition home, a mistake that stops us reaching the South Pole. Use that thought to scare yourself into being more careful and more conscientious than you have ever been in your life. Every time you are tempted to cut a corner or rush a job – and believe me, when you are cold and tired, you will be tempted – remember how awful you feel now and use it to make yourself go that extra mile. I need you all to feel sorry before you make a mistake, not after.' There was a glum silence and I was tempted to lighten the mood, to focus on how well we were doing, but I fought the instinct. I needed this message to sink in.

The doctor from ALE called. He had offered to give the team a talk about cold injuries. The women had been taught about symptoms and prevention of cold injuries repeatedly by a number of different experts but I didn't see that hearing it once more would do any harm. The girls sat around the doctor's laptop in the breakfast room of the hostel as he went through the basics and showed pictures of hideous injuries suffered by previous expeditions. I watched the girls carefully and saw the faint glimmer of panic grow on their faces. They started to ask questions that I knew they already had the answers to but were asking out of nervous fear. As the questions got more basic I could see the concern grow in the doctor. He shot me a number of alarmed glances and I wondered what would be reported back to Steve. I finally interrupted the session, 'Guys, this is all really valuable information but you can't let yourselves panic. This is all information you've had since your first day in Norway. You not only know this stuff but you have put it into practice in both Norway and New Zealand. None of you came away with any kind of injury. All you need to do is keep doing what you have been doing and you are all going to be fine.'

'Yes, there's no need to panic,' agreed the doctor, 'But Antarctica is very different to Norway or New Zealand. We get teams down here who have been to Greenland and think that means they know it all. Antarctica is dangerous and you mustn't let your guard down for a second.'

He was right of course but scaring the team at this eleventh hour wasn't going to make them more careful, it was just going to make them panic. I didn't want to appear flippant but neither did I want my team petrified of leaving the tent.

That evening everyone put on all their Antarctic clothing and I gave them a military-style inspection to make sure that vital adjustments had been done, such as sewing fleece onto the bottom of goggles to protect the nose, tying tabs onto zips to make them easier to pull when wearing mitts, and the all-important colour coding. All these tiny details seemed so insignificant and yet in Antarctica I knew they would take on critical importance.

Reena shocked everyone by returning to the hostel with her hair, which normally fell a long way down her back in a near-permanent plait, cropped in a bob just below her ears. She was grinning but had tears in her eyes; it had clearly been an emotional ordeal. Most of the team had decided to cut their hair short before the expedition. We all knew that we had two months ahead of us with unwashed hair stuffed under close-fitting hats. Long hair would be difficult to manage and would probably be so knotted and matted on our return that it would need to be cut off anyway. While for most of us it had been a trivial decision, for Reena it had a lot more significance. 'In India,' she explained, 'long hair is seen as a sign of virtue. In the films, if the woman has short hair and make-up it is clear that she is no good.' It was the first time in her life that her hair had ever been cut and although we all reassured her that it looked great – which it did – she was nervous about the reaction at home. She wouldn't let us send her picture to her husband. 'He will see it soon enough,' she said, but I suspected she was hoping that by the time she saw her husband again, her hair would have grown back.

Our flight from Punta to Antarctica was scheduled for 12 November but the flights from South America to Patriot Hills, the ALE base camp in Antarctica, are notorious for delays. Safety is paramount and so it is not uncommon for the crew to wait days, sometimes weeks, for a suitable weather window. On the eve of our departure we were ready, but I secretly hoped the flight would be cancelled the next morning. The idea of having a completely free day was appealing. We got up early for breakfast and sat together drinking coffee as we waited for the promised phone call from ALE. I allowed myself to think about what I would do in my free day and considered the possibility of going back to bed or finding a sunny spot to sit and enjoy my book or perhaps indulge in some calorific coffee and cake at the inviting cafe I had spotted in Punta. The phone rang in the kitchen and the anticipation was so tangible, it felt as if the room was suddenly full of static. The hostel owner answered and held out the receiver to me. It was ALE.

'I've just spoken to the pilots,' said the voice on the line. 'It was a bit windy at Patriot Hills this morning but conditions this afternoon are looking good, so the flight will be leaving today on schedule.'

The voice paused, expecting a reaction.

'Oh good,' I managed feebly.

'So if you can get your guys ready, we'll be coming to pick you up in forty-five minutes.'

I was aware of the girls in the room, watching me for a response. Before the voice had finished I gave them a silent grin and thumbs up so that by the time I put down the phone most of them had already disappeared up the stairs. I could hear Kim chattering loudly in excitement and Reena's booming laugh. Steph stopped to give me a hug and Kylie whooped as she squeezed my shoulders on her way past. I sat down in the empty room listening to the chaos upstairs and finished my coffee. I took a deep breath. This was it, we were on our way.

CHAPTER EIGHT

THE GREAT STORM

The inside of an Ilyushin is reassuringly Russian, with deep carpeted seats, tiny myopic portholes and veins of industrial wiring running along the inside walls. The Russian loadmaster, with a comically bushy moustache and grey rings round his sagging eyes, watched us all fiercely from his perch beside a backdrop of twitching dials. Strapped into our seats, we were arranged before him in rows as if this was the opening act of a play and he was the only actor. The plane lurched forward and trundled down the taxiway. The roar and vibration of the engines enveloped us, making communication impossible. As the noise crescendoed, the plane lurched again and took off at such an angle that those of us inside were tilted backward like astronauts being shot into space. I got a glimpse of brown fields through our nearest window as the plane banked and then the ground was gone – we wouldn't see earth or greenery again for weeks.

About six hours later I woke the team just before we were due to land to make sure they were all prepared for stepping out into –20°C. It sounds paradoxical, but as well as needing warm down jackets and fleecy neck-gaiters for the cold, they also needed suncream and sunglasses for protection from the sun. The air temperature in Antarctica may be well below freezing but the sun is extremely strong and there is little natural ozone protection from harmful UV rays, so it is incredibly easy to get severely sunburned and snow-blind. The plane landed in a thunder of engines and as the crew prised open the door, we waited for our first glimpse of Antarctica.

Rather than a blast of cold air, it was the sunshine that hit me first. I squinted behind my sunglasses, trying to filter out the glare as I stepped onto the hard ice of the runway. Behind the plane and stretching in a long curve away to our left were the Ellsworth Mountains, a wall of angular peaks smothered with heavy drapes of snow. In places ice oozed imperceptibly slowly from high plateaux, so that it appeared suspended in mid flow; the flawless white fractured with crevasses that revealed a watery blue beneath. The steeper faces were ice free and the rocks reflected the sun so that they seemed to have a golden sheen. Beneath the mountains was a large area of bare ice so old and compressed that it was a striking powder blue. Kept clear of snow by the wind whistling down the mountainsides, it was this strip of ice that was used as a runway. The fierce sun made the ice look wet and highlighted the hundreds of fist-sized dimples that textured its surface. Beyond the ice, almost a kilometre away, was a small camp. At its centre, beneath a tall metal mast, was a small, square Portakabin strapped to the ice with wire rope. This was the communications box and the hub of ALE's operation on the ice. Surrounding it were a number of small store tents, rows of even smaller geodesic tents used for staff accommodation and a number of Portakabins on skis that were used as workshops or towed behind tractors as part of convoys across the continent. Large machinery trundled across the camp carrying cargo from the plane and staff zipped about on colourful snowmobiles.

It had been six years since I had last been in Antarctica but as I breathed in the familiar smells of the continent – a peculiar mix of aviation fuel and suncream – I knew that we had arrived. Looking around for the team I spotted them standing together in the shadow of the plane's wing. In their identical red jackets they looked like a huddle of disorientated schoolchildren who had been overdressed for an outing in the cold. They looked very small and very lost. I could hear Kim repeating 'Oh my God, oh my God,' over and over to herself like a mantra as she turned slowly on the spot to take in the view. Half walking, half skating in my grip-less ski boots across the ice towards them, I pointed out the flagged route that led from the runway to the camp and we followed the long line of ALE staff heading in the same direction.

As the sun blazed unwinking in the sky, we were soon sweating in our layers of fleece-lined, down-padded and extra-insulated layers and had stripped down to thermals and salopettes. A tractor with paddled caterpillar tracks towing large trailers full of cargo deposited our bags on the fringes of the camp and we busied ourselves sorting out our equipment and putting up our two expedition tents on Antarctic ice for the first time. Our bright red tents and sledges flecked with the green Kaspersky Lab logo looked violently colourful against the white and blue of Antarctica. We monopolised a small area, slightly set apart from the rest of the cluster of tents and buildings and it was soon being referred to as Camp Kaspersky.

We'd brought some wine and treats with us from Punta for our first evening, to celebrate not only our arrival but also Steph's 27th birthday. All eight of us squeezed into one tent, sharing cake cut with a penknife and handed around on a plastic lid, drinking red wine out of the lids of our thermos flasks and laughing too loud in the hushed base camp. I revelled in the glorious joy of the moment, a time and place, a feeling of euphoria that I stored up in my mind like a time capsule to remember in the days and weeks ahead.

When Kylie announced that it was way past 1 a.m., the sun outside was still blazing as brightly as at midday on a Mediterranean beach. I had forgotten how disorientating 24-hour daylight could be, and how easy it was to lose track of time completely. The announcement broke up our little party (I suspect to the relief of the rest of the camp) and the team shuffled over to the toilet tent in ones and twos. I stood with Helen and watched the trail of tiny women in huge jackets beetling across the site. 'They look like an invasion of little red munchkins,' she laughed. I wondered warily for a moment what we must look like to the rest of Patriot Hills. No wonder ALE was remaining cautious: we didn't look like a team capable of skiing to the South Pole. If we were to convince anyone that we were serious, I thought grimly, we couldn't afford to make any mistakes now that we were in Antarctica.

The same thought crossed my mind as we prepared to leave Patriot Hills for a day ski the following morning. Naturally, the team was slow to get ready. As a group the team had always struggled with personal administration and I often felt like a cross between a nanny and a headmistress. Nerves about our first day in Antarctica made everyone flustered and brought back bad habits. We had planned a week of acclimatisation at Patriot Hills for precisely this reason. The idea was to introduce everyone slowly to the Antarctic environment, one step at a time. I wouldn't have been concerned about our disorganisation that morning except for the need I felt to demonstrate to ALE that we were capable of looking after ourselves. I remembered the disaster in Norway when the Norwegian film crew had filmed our departure on the mini-expedition – I didn't want a repeat.

Once everyone was on their skis I gathered the group together and reiterated the importance of feeling sorry before the event.

It would only take a second of carelessness to get injured but any slight mistake could mean the end of the expedition. I went through a checklist, making sure everyone had spare gloves and goggles, easily accessible food and water, suncream and a warm jacket. We were going to ski slowly, travelling in single file and taking regular breaks. At each break I encouraged the team to check each other's faces for any signs that skin had been exposed to the super-cooled air and I made sure that everyone was still able to feel fingers and toes, that they weren't too hot or too cold, that they were eating and drinking at the breaks and still talking coherently. I felt like an over-protective mother hen, skiing up and down the line shepherding them all forwards. We had a few false starts but within an hour or so the group was moving well together and I began to relax.

The wind had picked up since the night before. It blew steadily against our backs, dragging loose snow across the surface in a continuous flow along the ground. The surface wasn't smooth but had been worn by the wind into sastrugi, wave formations carved into the snow. The sharp, clean lines of the ripples were as perfect as the petals of a flower. They caught the sunlight, creating shade and texture so that the ground was flecked with pale pink and purple as well as flashes of pure white. Above us the bold blue of the sky was ribbed with bands of cloud and while to our right we were accompanied always by the golden Ellsworth Mountains, to our left there was nothing but horizon.

Eight hours later, the wind which had blown the snow along the ground as we set out had risen in strength to fling the fine white powder into the air and create a haze that extended above our heads. The team emerged from the blowing snow to arrive back at Patriot Hills like a returning army. They looked magnificent and I felt as proud of them as I would if they had just conquered the South Pole in a day. As the girls defrosted I checked for any injury or mishap. Kim had a slight spot of frostnip just under her eye. Little more than a chilblain, it had risen into a tiny pale blister that stood out on her dark skin. It wasn't serious but as I gently pointed it out, her hand shot to her face in panic as if she had been stung. It was probably caused by a miniscule gap between her goggles and her balaclava. 'It will heal completely in a couple of days. Just make sure you keep it well covered and you can sew some extra material onto the bottom of your goggles just to cover any gaps,' I reassured her. The next time I saw Kim she had the largest plaster she could find in our first aid kit covering her cheek and had attached a huge section of neoprene to the bottom of her goggles. She was clearly not taking any chances.

The wind increased through the night so that we woke to find the tents dancing erratically above our heads, bulging and writhing with each gust. The noise was a constant roar and even when we were all sitting inside the same tiny tent, not more than a few feet from each other, we had to shout to be heard. I pulled on my hat, jacket and boots and ventured outside to find that the world had disappeared completely into a fury of white. It was like walking into a cross between a gale and a thick fog. Looking towards the base camp, I could only see the shady outlines of the tents nearest to us and one or two dark, indistinct figures struggling against the wind.

The plan had been to depart on a mini-expedition in the local area that morning but seeing the weather I decided to postpone for the day. While I accepted that the team needed to be able to deal with conditions like this without fear, I also didn't want our first tent routine in Antarctica to be in a 40-knot wind and risk something going terribly wrong. The vision of one of our tents flying across Antarctica particularly haunted me.

That night I slept fitfully. The wind had increased steadily throughout the day and was now punctuated by vicious gusts that pummelled the tent so hard that it strained against its anchors. We'd shovelled so much snow around the tent to weigh it down that it was almost buried and ALE had used a snowplough to build a wall of snow around our two tents for protection, but still the wind thundered over our barricades and blasted our shelters. The tents that had seemed so hardy now felt extremely fragile. Every few minutes a change in the sound of the tent would make me peer nervously out of my sleeping bag. Getting out of that personal cocoon of warmth is an absolute last resort when it is −20°C outside but the tent was our lifeline, and when I noticed one corner of the tent bulge inwards, the thought of it being damaged had me out into the cold in seconds.

Once outside I realised a lot of the snow that we had dug onto the tent had been blown away. Grabbing a snow shovel I called through the tent to Steph to come and help me. Together we shovelled snow onto both of the tents but it was clear we needed more hands. As I ducked into the tent to rouse the rest of the team a gust flattened the tent, breaking the poles in several places. Steph and I stumbled in the wind to find and isolate the broken ends of the poles to stop them ripping through the tent fabric – but we were too late. I shouted across to the rest of the team, 'We need you out here!' I didn't know if they could hear me but I knew Era and Sophia were desperately flinging on boots and jackets inside the collapsed tent, anxious to help. In the meantime Steph and I grappled with the billowing tent material. The gusts hit us at regular intervals and it was all we could do to keep a grip on the straining fabric and stop it flying away. My fingers cramped in pain as we pulled against the wind with all our strength and I yelled again to the team for help. Era emerged from the tent and stood in shock for a moment looking at our ripped and misshapen tent, not sure what to do. Sophia was right behind her and didn't hesitate. She flung herself prostrate across the tent just as another gust pulled at the material like a kite in a storm. I saw Era lose her balance and fall to the ground, the violence and force of the gust taking her by surprise.

Still cowering from the latest onslaught I felt someone fall against me. It was Kylie, closely followed by Helen; they'd both, thankfully, heard my calls for help. As the gust passed, the wind eased enough to be able to shout instructions to the whole team. 'After the next gust, get the poles out!' I shrieked over the noise of the storm, 'but when the wind blows, just hang on to the tent.' It was as much as I could say before the next squall hit us and we all braced ourselves, trying to stop the jagged ends of the broken poles tearing the tent fabric. We struggled together to get the shattered poles out of their sleeves without making the damage worse. It was awkward. We were working against the tension in the tent and every few seconds work was stopped by an explosion of wind, during which we could do nothing but hang on to the free material. Kim and Reena arrived and stood close behind me waiting for instructions. 'Grab the poles,' I yelled to them both before we were all forced to crouch on the ground by another blast of ice-filled wind. When I looked up I found Kim standing behind me expectantly waiting for further instructions with a ski pole gripped in each fist. I looked at her wide-eyed with incredulity for a moment. 'Not ski poles!' I shouted over the wind, 'Tent poles. Grab the tent poles!'

With the last tent pole extracted we simply rolled up the tent with all the equipment still inside and, placing the oversized bundle of material on two sledges, heaved our dilapidated shelter to the nearest of the camp's store tents. These well-anchored shelters, although only a dozen metres long, were tall enough for a person to be able to stand upright inside and were, thankfully, mostly empty this early in the season. We coaxed the rolled tent through the narrow door and followed in behind it, all eight of us standing around the pathetic remains of our broken tent, breathing hard. We stood in silence for a moment, our goggles steamed up from the exertion and each of us dusted in ice which had collected in clumps on our hair, clothes and faces. Kylie spoke first, 'What an awesome team!' There was subdued celebration but most of all a feeling of relief. My mind reeled. I had seen the damage to the tent, particularly the poles, and knew it was going to be a big job to fix, but first we had to get through the night.

The wind was still furious outside and rattled the store tent alarmingly despite the fact that it was securely strapped to the ground. Kylie, Helen, Kim and Reena needed to get back to our second tent to make sure nothing happened to our only remaining shelter. The rest of us would stay in the store tent overnight and the whole team would meet again in the morning to assess the damage properly. Steph and Sophia pulled our sleeping bags out of the rolled tent while Era helped me pile all the equipment into one end of the store tent to give us enough space to sleep and the four of us eventually lay side by side in one end, our ice-wet jackets hanging above our feet. I was lying down but I was about as far from sleep as it was possible to be. I watched our jackets dance with the vibration of the wind and listened to the primeval growl of the blizzard outside. Several times it felt as if the store tent was in danger of tipping over and I began to wonder if I should check its anchors.

The rip of Velcro interrupted my thoughts. The door of the store tent flew open and as I sat up in my sleeping bag, Steve's head appeared, framed with an ice-encrusted fur hood. 'Your second tent is being shredded!' he bellowed. Without a word the others were up with me, all of us scrabbling to get dressed in our outside gear as quickly as possible. I was first out of the door and was half blown towards Camp Kaspersky. I scrambled up the side of our protective wall of snow to see several figures desperately shoving equipment into the tent through a gaping tear in its side. I fell to my knees in what had previously been the porch of the tent and madly scooped up pots, mugs, stoves and fuel bottles into bags and boxes as quickly as possible to stop them flying away or being buried in the drifting snow. Together we rolled what remained of the tent and carried it to our requisitioned store tent. With another tight squeeze we forced the second tent through the narrow door. Steve grabbed my arm and tilted his hood-covered head close to mine. 'Come to the ALE tent for some tea,' he yelled. We closed the store tent and hobbled in groups of two or three across the base camp, hanging onto each other as we fought against gusts strong enough to knock our legs from under us.

We weren't the only refugees taking shelter in the ALE tent. There were several members of staff whose small geodesic tents had been destroyed in the wind. Even the doctor was there; he'd been woken by a rigid door from an old storage building on the runway being blown into the back of his tent. Luckily he was unhurt, but the door could have killed him and it had destroyed his tent. It made me feel slightly better that we weren't the only ones who had been evicted by the blizzard but it didn't lessen the severity of our situation. Without reliable tents, we couldn't start our expedition. I didn't know the precise extent of the damage but it had looked severe.

My mind ran through potential solutions. It was possible we could borrow a tent from someone at base camp or perhaps get spare tents flown into Antarctica on the next cargo flight in a week or two but neither option was ideal. We were a large team whose routines and systems revolved around the tents we had trained and practised with. To change such a large element of the expedition now would cause chaos. The only workable solution would be to mend the tents we had and at the moment, that looked very unlikely. As I slurped down warm tea and listened to the girls describing their experiences in the storm I felt hollow. I knew that, as the expedition leader, this was when I was most needed but suddenly the entire project seemed completely without appeal. I had been fighting for this team for so long that I didn't think I had any fight left. I felt as if I could have walked away at that very moment and never given the South Pole another thought.

I decided to focus on the immediate. For now what the team needed was some sleep – it had been an eventful and frightening night. We stumbled back to the store tent and feasted on a breakfast of biscuits before clearing as much space as possible so that we could all lie down. I found myself a small niche, perched upright by the door, my head leaning on the side of the tent. Despite the awkward position I fell asleep immediately for an hour or two, still fully clothed.

A particularly violent gust jolted me awake and I sat for a while listening to the wind outside the tent and watching the others sleep as I thought through our limited options. I needed a plan of action, something that would show there was a way forward, that we were not beaten yet. So far the girls had been remarkably calm. They were all a bit shocked but there had been no tears, no frightened questions about what the consequences of this blizzard would have been if we had been on our own, already on our way to the South Pole. They were calm because they all confidently expected a solution to be found and it was up to me to find it.

Absently I started picking through the equipment piled at the far end of the tent, putting like for like into separate piles to establish what had been lost. By the time I reached the back of the tent most of our kit had, miraculously, been accounted for. We had lost one of our stove boxes but none of the contents, the lid of a communications box, a few gloves and a windproof jacket. Our most serious loss was three skis. As the team woke up one by one I sent out a search party to Camp Kaspersky to probe the snow and see if the missing skis had been buried in the drift.

The rest of the team gathered in a second empty store tent to take a better look at the damaged tents. The poles were a mangled heap of metal bent into alarming angles. Kim made herself comfortable cross-legged on the floor of the tent and set about straightening what she could with nothing but the pliers of a penknife while Steph patiently unthreaded the elastic from inside the hollow poles to break them down into their shorter sections. The poles had snapped in more than a dozen places and at least a dozen more sections were bent beyond use. Kim and Steph re-threaded new poles from the sections they had salvaged but we were left with only four complete poles – enough for only one tent.

Meanwhile, Helen and Kylie had spread out the shredded tent material. One tent had numerous minor tears all over the inner and outer sections which, although messy, would be relatively straightforward to fix without greatly lessening the strength and reliability of the tent. The second tent was more serious. It had been almost torn in half lengthways, with a tear that crossed the bottom groundsheet and continued up through the doors at both ends of the inner tent. Even if we could repair the tear, the quality of those repairs would determine the durability of the tent. If we were to experience a similar blizzard such major repairs might see our tent once again literally ripped apart. As well as the damage to the tent fabric both tents had busted zips and had lost numerous tabs that kept the inner and outer parts of the tent together.

I sat quietly as Helen and Kylie pointed out all the damage to me. It was a huge job and we had very few resources. Our own repair kit consisted of tape to repair modest tears in the fabric, some superglue, strong thread and curved needles, but it was not enough to repair all the damage. Furthermore, if we used up all our supplies we would have nothing left for the expedition. Tentatively we scattered through the camp to beg and borrow materials from the mechanics, air crew and support staff working at Patriot Hills. Everyone was incredibly kind and soon we had amassed some reinforced thread, extra needles, several types of glue and some ripstop material scraps to start our repairs. In the cramped store tent, only six of us could work at any one time, and the sewing was both frustrating and time consuming. The work was too intricate for wearing gloves so we were forced to use bare fingers, which regularly became so cold that we would have to stop to re-warm our hands. The storm outside was still ferocious enough that the store tent we were working in vibrated constantly and no surface was ever totally motionless. The limited working space caused frequent mistakes, from sewing the wrong parts of the tent together, to finishing a repair to find it was inside out or even finding that it has been inadvertently sewn to a neighbour's trouser leg. The glue repairs were no easier. The mechanics recommended a particular type of glue known for its strength but the glue needed to set at room temperature. The store tent was significantly below zero, even inside, so we carried the fragile repairs to a garage building that was artificially heated. It wasn't quite room temperature but it was the best we could do.

Walking back across camp to our requisitioned store tent I spotted a dark figure coming towards me. He was being blown with the wind and so we practically collided. It was Steve. Shouting over the wind, which was still strong enough to make walking difficult, was impossible, so we ducked into the shelter of a nearby truck. He pulled down his face-covering so that we could talk and I saw the concern in his face. 'How are you?' he asked. He put a hand on my shoulder and shook it gently in encouragement. I gave him a brief synopsis of our situation: the ongoing repairs to the tents and the three lost skis. He nodded sympathetically and promised to look in on us later, before we both plunged back into the abating blizzard, him skidding with the wind, me fighting into it.

Later a member of staff from ALE called into the store tent. He had a present from Steve; eight complete tent poles. They were spare poles from a make and model of tent different to ours and so were slightly shorter and thinner than those we had lost but by putting two poles through each pole sleeve they would be strong enough.

We were soon helped by another act of generosity. Reena and Sophia called me out of the store tent in time to see a figure walking towards us, emerging from the blowing snow like a rock star making an entrance through dry ice. As he got closer some sunlight seemed to break through the cloud cover and even the wind seemed to die down a little. Laid across his outstretched arms were our three missing skis. As the figure reached us we all cheered in amazement, hardly daring to believe our good fortune. Like all good heroes, our saviour didn't loiter but handed us the skis and left with a wave, quickly disappearing back into the haze of the blizzard. It wasn't until much later we heard that he was one of the ALE staff members who had gone out into the storm to search for our missing equipment and had miraculously found the skis snagged on some sastrugi almost a mile out of Patriot Hills – so it seems chivalry isn't dead, even in Antarctica.

One day later than planned we headed away from Patriot Hills on a two-day training expedition around the local area. The wind had died down a little – enough for the loose powder snow to snake along the ground rather than be hurled through the air, and for the sky to have turned from white to blue. I led the group away from Patriot Hills in single file, each of us towing a sledge. We skied in a direction slightly out of the wind so that the gusts blew into our shoulders rather than into our faces. Kylie, Reena and Kim had sewed late into the previous night to finish the repairs to our tents and although our main priority during the next two days would be to test the repairs, it was also an important chance to prove to ALE that we were a safe and competent team. The light felt golden, like a summer's afternoon back home, and threw into breathtaking relief all the delicate sastrugi that had been worn into hundreds of overlapping concentric circles like the inverted tiers of a wedding cake. As I concentrated on the rhythmic squeaking of my skis on the hardened snow, my mind emptied and I felt a wave of relief. Breathing in the freedom of being on the move and away from the pressures of Patriot Hills, I felt something new and powerful. It dawned on me that this unfamiliar emotion was enjoyment. I was finally enjoying myself.

We skied haltingly for a few hours before setting up our camp just a couple of nautical miles from Patriot Hills. (Nautical miles are a little longer than statute miles and are easier to use when navigating in latitude and longitude.) Everyone had a fitful sleep as the wind remained gusty throughout the night. More than once I sat up in my sleeping bag nervously watching the tent, looking for any signs of weakness or imminent collapse, and several times I heard my tent-mates doing the same thing. Our anxiety was unnecessary: by morning the tent was as sturdy as it had been when we pitched it. I took a close look at the repairs around the tent. They still looked robust. I was proud of us; in less than 24 hours we had patched our tents back together again and saved ourselves from what had seemed to be a hopeless situation.

The sun of the previous evening had disappeared. It was still windy but the cloud had drawn in, wrapping everything in a uniform whiteness. The horizon was visible as a gloomy grey smudge but the surface of the snow had no shading to it, no contrast, so that all the sastrugi that had been visible the day before seemed to have disappeared. Such weather is known as 'flat light' because the ground seems even but the obstacles are still there, it's just impossible to see them.

We set off slow and steady, skiing for an hour before stopping for a break and taking it in turns to navigate. The cold, windy conditions meant that every scrap of exposed skin needed to be covered, but wearing face protection and goggles feels very claustrophobic. All the warm air that is breathed out through mouth and nose needs to be able to escape otherwise the inside lenses of goggles steam up. That steam turns to ice and suddenly vision is reduced to the tiny spaces in between patches of condensation. It's incredibly frustrating. Finding an arrangement that provides complete protection but also allows hot air to escape is a process of continual adjustments and something that even the most experienced find difficult.

Kim was having particular trouble. Still shaken by the tiny blister under her eye, she had overcompensated by wearing an additional layer of face-covering which left no skin exposed but which also meant her breath couldn't escape. Her goggles had been hopelessly fogged from the moment we set out. She could see enough to follow the sledge in front but not much more. Kim had never been the strongest skier in the team and she found the hard, uneven sastrugi challenging even when she could see them properly. Now, with flat light and fogged goggles she fell frequently and a gap appeared in the line ahead of her. I slowed the pace of the team and put Kim near the front of the line but she slowed down to the point where the rest of the team were getting cold, putting on big mitts and extra layers to keep warm. I skied alongside Kim to try to give her some tips on keeping control of her skis. She listened and tried everything I suggested but there didn't seem to be a lot of improvement. I could see that she was frustrated and angry with herself, worried that she was holding back the team. I tried to be encouraging, reassuring her that it was all a matter of practice, but I was aware that she was withdrawing into her own world and losing heart.

Our first break was a disaster. I watched glumly as the girls moved slowly and awkwardly to fetch snack bags and flasks out of their sledges, seemingly taking an age just to put on a jacket to keep themselves warm while we stopped. It was frustrating to watch but I bit my tongue, telling myself that they would get better, that this was still training. We were aiming for our breaks to be just seven minutes long. This was long enough to do everything we needed to do during the breaks but not long enough to get too cold. Ten minutes would have been acceptable but it was a full 20 minutes before we were ready to start moving again. 'This break has been way too long,' I announced as we moved off. 'Only do what is absolutely essential and think about being more efficient. Think about the time.' As I spoke Era moved to one side and started undoing her harness. 'What are you doing?' I demanded.

'I need to pee,' she answered, unzipping her trousers.

'Sorry but there's no time. You'll have to wait till next break.'

Era looked at me aghast and started bouncing on her skis, 'But I need to go. I can't hold it in.'

I sighed. It was clearly futile to make my point now but as we all waited for Era I lectured the team on getting organised.

The weather had closed in even further. The wind that had been simply cold now blew wet snow at us that encrusted our clothing with icy slush. The air was thick with snow and the grey streak that had indicated a horizon now disappeared completely. The ground was as white and formless as the sky above. Nothing was distinct except for the figure in front and the figure behind; everything else was a mere supposition. With nothing visible to aim for, it became difficult to follow a compass bearing. It seems that the body has no instinctive ability to move in a straight line and without any points of reference the mind can't be trusted. If your eyes are lifted from the compass needle for so much as a second, within a few steps you have veered off course to left or right, often without realising it. As I watched Reena lead the team in an arc to the right, several team members shouted warnings to her but she was adamant that she was skiing straight ahead. It was only when she turned to find the team spread out in a sharp bend behind her that she believed her mistake and pulled out her compass to re-check her bearing.

Our pace had reduced to a painfully slow shuffle in the deteriorating visibility and everyone was fed up. I wanted the team to practise tent routines and thought that if we stopped now, the weather might have cleared a little by the time we were ready to move again. As the team split into our two tent groups I played my part in the routine, rolling out the tent on the snow and then simply hanging onto it in the wind until the others had firmly staked it to the ground. I could hear Era and Steph shouting to each other at the far end of the tent and it was clear that tempers were rising. As the discussion got heated I called them all over. Still hanging onto the tent I asked them to huddle together and we talked through the routine. 'Right, is everyone clear what they need to do?' I asked when we had finished. They all nodded and within minutes the tent was up and secured to the ground. Steph shovelled a final heap of snow around the front of the tent while Sophia and Era were already inside laying out equipment.

I looked across at the other tent a little way off and was surprised to see that it still wasn't pitched. It was up, but had no tension in the material. Helen and Kim were kneeling over one of the tent poles trying to get the end seated in the tent fabric. I went over to help and heard Helen talking to Kim. 'Go inside, Kim – if you've got cold hands get inside.' I looked down at Kim's hands to see that she was wearing only her thin cotton liners. She'd clearly been using them for the fiddly jobs that were made harder by wearing mittens, which were warmer but clumsy. Her liners had snow clinging to them and I knew they would be wet.

I was annoyed as we had talked so often about not giving in to this exact temptation. I was even more annoyed that rather than look after her hands, Kim was insisting that she stay outside to help. 'Kim!' I shouted. She hadn't seen me approach and both Kim and Helen jumped as I yelled over the wind. 'Get in the tent and get your hands warm. You're no use out here in those gloves.' She left and I knelt down to help Helen but when I looked up a few minutes later I saw that Kim had returned – icy gloves still on. 'Kim, get in the tent and don't come out again,' I pointed to the tent door, really angry this time that she could be so stubbornly reckless. 'Go and get your hands warm.' Kim opened her mouth to argue, then saw the look on my face and changed her mind. I watched her duck inside the tent to make sure that this time she followed my instructions. I helped Reena and Helen secure the tent with big snow blocks until they too, ducked inside.

Returning to my tent, I looked around. The weather didn't show any signs of improving but to stop for the day would be disappointing. We had only travelled a few nautical miles; I had hoped to do a lot more. Era and Sophia had made a good job of sorting out the inside of our tent: it was warm and cosy with everything in its right place. I stripped off the worst of my icy layers before shuffling back to the first tent to check on Kim. As I slipped into the porch the contrast between the two tents couldn't have been more pronounced. Helen, Reena and Kim sat in a huddle in the middle of the tent still in their outside clothes and surrounded by all their equipment mixed together in a big heap. Kylie had lit the stoves at the far end of the tent but it was still so cold that ice clung to the tent walls and the whole place felt damp.

My mouth fell open in surprise. Helen, Kylie and Reena were the three most experienced team members and they should have known better. Regardless of their experience, we had trained better than this in New Zealand. Out of respect, I had always held back from being as dictatorial with Helen, Kylie and Reena as I had been with the other team members. The last thing I wanted to do was to insult half my team by telling them what they already knew but neither would I let them get so sloppy. 'Right, you need to sort this place out,' I announced firmly. I tore through the heap of equipment, telling them exactly where to put each item and reeling off a list of instructions to each of them. 'Kylie, switch off the stoves until you have all the cooking equipment and food up in the kitchen area. Helen, rearrange the sleeping mats so that they lie over each other and form a kind of carpet. Kim, get all kit and clothing off the floor and hanging on the washing line. Reena, nominate a corner for each person and put all their things together...'

For a few minutes, the tent was thrown into chaos but soon it was warm and tidy. With the stoves back on, I insisted that they take off their outer layers and bring the stoves right inside the tent so that they could thoroughly warm up. Kim sat on one side of the tent with her legs curled inside her sleeping bag. She was noticeably quieter than usual. 'How are your hands?' I asked her. She held them out and I gripped each hand for a second to check that they were warm. Kylie had given her a hot drink and she clutched it as we talked about her mistake with her gloves and her refusal to go inside the tent when she was cold. She apologised miserably but somehow I felt that she was still missing the point. 'I know you want to help but if your hands are cold you have to make them your first priority. Everyone understands that. No one will think you are abandoning your job.' There was nothing left to say so I let the conversation move on to other things. Gradually,

Kim became more talkative. By the time I left she was sewing some elastic to the nose piece of her balaclava and laughing along with everyone else.

The next morning I was strapping on my ski boots in the porch of the tent when I heard Reena at the door. 'Kim has a blister on her finger,' she called through the tent wall.

My heart beat faster in my chest and I felt sick. 'OK – I'll be over,' I answered, careful to keep my voice casual. 'Stay in the tent for now.' As I tied the laces of my boots and pulled on my hat I tried to look nonchalant so that my tent-mates weren't alarmed but inside, that familiar dread I had been living with for the past two years once again gripped my stomach. In Antarctica a blister really only means one thing and that is frostbite. Frostbite is caused by the cells in the skin freezing. As the frozen flesh warms up, it swells and protective blisters form over the injury. Even so, I clung to the vain hope that there would be an explanation that didn't involve cold injuries. 'Please, please be a normal blister,' I thought to myself. 'Please, please.'

Kim was still sat in her sleeping bag as she held out her finger to show me. The very tip of it was a pale colour and slightly swollen with an angry pink line running around the edge. It confirmed what I had suspected: it was frostbite. I had Kim put her hand back in the warmth of the sleeping bag but was aware that she was scrutinising my face for my reaction. I didn't want to use the word frostbite, partly because I didn't want to panic her or the rest of the team and partly because I didn't want to admit it to myself. 'I think you might have a cold injury,' I said finally. 'So I think we should call Patriot Hills so that a doctor can take a look.' She looked into my eyes for a second, then nodded silently. Helen handed me the satellite phone and I called the emergency number we had been given. Patriot Hills answered immediately. The voice on the line promised to send the doctor out to us and I gave our position. While we waited I tried to work out exactly what had happened.

'Did your hands get cold last night?' I asked her.

Kim looked down at her hands, shaking her head as if in amazement.

'I don't think so,' she said. 'It was warm last night. I woke up once and had my arms out of the sleeping bag but my hands weren't *cold*.'

'And did you see or feel anything last night? Any blisters or numbness?'

'No, nothing.'

It was clear that the frostbite must have struck the previous day while Kim was outside with cold hands and wet gloves and that I just hadn't noticed the injury that evening in the tent, but the fact that Kim had been sewing with what would turn out to be frostbitten fingers was extraordinary.

Leaving Kim in the care of Helen and Reena with instructions to keep drinking the hot, sugary drinks being prepared by Kylie, I left the tent to wait outside for the doctor. I wanted to be away from Kim in case my face betrayed my thoughts. I didn't know how severe the frostbite might be – only the doctor could tell us that – but I knew it was unlikely Kim would be able to continue on the expedition. If it had been anyone else there might have been the possibility that they could look after the injury themselves and continue but Kim was finding the challenges of the expedition difficult enough without this added burden. If she allowed her injury to get cold again, her finger would be permanently damaged.

The doctor smiled as he arrived but looked unimpressed. He crawled inside the tent and crouched next to Kim. As she pulled off her gloves to show him the injury, curls of steam rose into the air. 'Are your hands damp?' he demanded, clearly alarmed. He slipped a hand alongside Kim's thermal layer, under her smock.

'Her clothes are damp too,' he reported, shooting me an accusing look of disgust. Kim's clothes had not been damp earlier but in her anxiety to keep warm, she had clearly over-dressed and started to sweat. I felt a flash of exasperation at those looking after Kim for allowing her to get too hot; and at myself for not checking.

The doctor took Kim back to the base camp so that he could take a better look at her injury. Getting the tents down as quick as we could, the team followed on skis. I skied silently at the back of our line, my mind processing what had happened. I was furious at Kim: she knew better than to let her gloves get wet and now, thanks to just a few moments of carelessness, there was a good chance she would be going home. I was angry at her tent-mates too: why had nobody noticed her ice-encrusted liners and forced her to go inside? And finally I admonished myself for not taking better care of her. I couldn't be everywhere at once but now it was clear that I should have been sticking closer to Kim. Why hadn't I left Helen to deal with the tent pole and followed Kim into the tent to make sure that she warmed her hands properly? I felt foolish, too, for not noticing her injuries the previous day; I should have made a more thorough inspection of her hands that evening.

Arriving back at Patriot Hills I left the team to set up the tents while I went to find the doctor for his verdict. He was already on his way across the camp to meet me, 'She has frostbite in six fingers,' he announced as he drew close. It was clear he was angry. I put my hand over my mouth in shock. I thought of Kim and didn't know what to say. 'Where is she?' I asked. The doctor took me to a Portakabin that had been converted into a dormitory. Kim was curled in a sleeping bag on one of the bunks. When she sat up I saw that six of her fingers were thickly wrapped in bandages. It made her hands effectively useless and she was unable to do the simplest tasks for herself. She'd been crying. I sat next to her and gave her a hug. 'I've spoken to the doctor and although your fingers will heal completely at the moment, if you get them cold again it could be much worse. To continue with the expedition would be too big a risk – no expedition is worth losing digits.'

Kim nodded in silence. She wiped away her soundless tears with her bandage-free wrists but they kept coming. I gave her another hug. There was nothing I could say. I felt wretched not just for Kim but for the rest of the team, too. Despite the fact that we were from all corners of the globe and had got to know each other through emails and Skype, we had all become incredibly close and felt strongly bound together. Kim was a huge part of the spirit of our team and to lose her would be a huge blow. First Barbara, now Kim. It seemed bitterly unfair.

I walked slowly back across camp, breathing deeply. Kim had paid for her carelessness by sacrificing her place on the expedition but she wasn't the only one who had made sloppy and unnecessary mistakes since we had arrived in Antarctica. Perhaps I *had* overestimated the women's abilities after all. I wondered if I should have prevented Kim from coming south but, if I applied that criteria to the whole team, I also had concerns about Steph and Reena – something I pointed out as I gathered the team in one of our tents for a meeting. 'It's not that you are not capable,' I explained. 'It's just a general lack of self-discipline that you cannot afford out here. Steph, I am still picking up your kit which you scatter everywhere you go and Reena, several times I've had to stop you for such basic things as layers being untucked so that your skin is exposed. I am responsible for you guys but I need you all to take responsibility for yourselves, too.' The team looked shocked that I would single out individual members for criticism but it was time for brutal honesty. Something had to change within the team otherwise we wouldn't be going anywhere.

Having outlined my frustrations I left the team in the tent so that they could discuss it between themselves. I walked across the camp to a store tent where all our resupply bags of food and fuel were being kept. It was quiet and out of the way. All the bags needed resorting so I busied myself but really it was an excuse to be alone. Gradually, the tears came. I wiped them away angrily but they wouldn't stop. I felt like I had let everybody down, most of all myself. I had promised ALE and Steve that the team was prepared despite their scant credentials on paper. Now, after failing to cover more than half a dozen nautical miles I had brought a team member back with serious injuries. We looked like a joke and I knew it.

Reena found me eventually. She came into the store tent to collect some equipment and we worked silently together for a while. I knew I had upset her by singling her out in front of the team but it had been necessary. Eventually she spoke. 'Felicity I just wanted to tell you that I look after myself, I know when I am cold and I will tell you if I am.'

'That's good to know,' I replied. I looked at her face. She was close to tears and I felt a pang of remorse. 'I'm just worried about you,' I added. We turned back to the equipment, working in silence again for a minute before she spoke again.

'Felicity. We all love and respect you.'

Her words made me choke with tears. Reena saw it and put her arm around me. I didn't feel that I deserved her trust and regard. Kim had trusted me too and now she was going home. What was done was done and I had to find a way to move forward but it felt like the end. I wanted to slink away in shame but I knew I had to stay and somehow muster the gumption to prove that we were better than this, that despite appearances we could make it to the South Pole.

I met with Steve and the doctor in the medical tent. A heater blazed fiercely in one corner so that I was soon sweating in my full polar gear. Steve placed a chair for me in the middle of the tent. 'You can relax,' he said. I smiled but I was not relaxed. It felt like being pulled up in front of a headmaster or being invited into the boss's office to be given the sack.

'How are you?' he began.

'Awful,' I answered honestly. 'I'm mortified. I've led lots of people through cold environments and never has anyone in my care ever had any kind of cold injury. Now I bring someone back with six frostbitten fingers.'

It was the first time I'd summarised my thoughts out loud and the harshness of it brought tears to my eyes. I had sworn to myself I would not let myself cry but I couldn't help it. The tears came and wouldn't stop. I apologised, turning away. I hated myself for crying, it felt weak.

Steve was very fair. He asked about the team's training, what they knew about frostbite and how to avoid it, if they knew not to have wet clothing. Even though I understood that Steve needed to ask all these questions, I still found it hard to bear. As the leader of this team, it was my competence that was being questioned and it was hard not to find the pounding of my credibility acutely painful.

'I know this sounds ridiculous in light of what has just happened but the team is capable and competent,' I pleaded. 'This one incident is not representative of the rest of the team. They are well trained and they know how to look after themselves.'

Despite Kim's injury my instinct was that we just needed to get out of Patriot Hills. 'I know that I am asking you to take my word on this when our performance hasn't demonstrated it, but we are ready to go. We're just stagnating here, we need to get started.'

I looked at Steve. He and the doctor both looked unconvinced.

As I left Steve put his hand on my shoulder. 'Learn to relax again,' he said. 'And sleep.' I smiled half-heartedly and stepped out of the tent. The sun was out and there wasn't a breath of wind. As I crawled gratefully into my sleeping bag I noticed that the tent was completely motionless for the first time in a week. It was blissfully silent and my sleep was deep and dark.

We had been in Antarctica for seven days when, on 21 November, we were ready to go. I got up early to walk over to the communications box in the centre of the camp and heard the news that we were going to be able to fly to our start point on the coast that day. The plane had already been loaded so all that was left to do was gather the team and say our goodbyes. I walked across camp with Kim to where the team loitered beside the small twin-engined plane. She had sunglasses on to cover her tears and was listening to music on her MP3 player. 'We'll fly the Jamaican flag for you,' I told her as we joined the team and she was engulfed in hugs. As I said goodbye I could hear the music she was listening to. 'I still haven't found what I'm looking for,' sang the vocals.

It was time to get on the plane. Kim turned away and headed back to the medical tent to wait for her flight out of Antarctica in a day or two. Steve came to say goodbye. 'Remember to enjoy yourself,' he called as I got on the plane. I smiled and waved, 'Thanks Steve, thanks for everything.'

The engines coughed into life and as we bounced down the rough snow runway we sat strapped to our seats, staring out of the windows or grinning madly to each other. It was too noisy to talk but the big smiles said it all. The plane banked sharply and Patriot Hills was reduced to a series of dots on an endless sheet of white. We levelled out and could see the vastness of what would be our world for the next six weeks. The ground below was a greyish silver, streaked with pastel purples and dusky blues where the wind had scored its icy surface, like the scuffs on an old leather shoe. Sophia sat alone on the opposite side of the plane and stared downwards. I watched her expression for some clue as to what was going on in her mind. I wondered if she was thinking about her family or simply about the days ahead – it was impossible to tell – but something about the seriousness of her look made me feel sombre. I felt so confident in this team, so confident in our abilities, but what if I was wrong? We had already lost one team member but the consequences of anyone else getting injured now that we had left the security of Patriot Hills would be far, far worse.

CHAPTER NINE
LOUIS POO-UITTON

'This is it!' I shouted through my balaclava. 'We're on our way to the South Pole!' The team shook their ski poles in the air and I heard a muffled cheer from within their layers of face-covering. I turned away from the cluster of well-clad figures and faced the horizon. Glancing at the compass strung round my neck, my eyes followed the direction of the needle to pick out a prominent patch of shade cast by a lump of ice in the distance. As long as I headed for that patch of shade, I would be heading in the right direction.

I slid forward on my skis, feeling the tug of the sledge attached to the harness around my hips, and peered over my shoulder to check that the rest of the team were following. It was a momentous occasion, the first steps of our 900-kilometre journey from the coast of Antarctica to the Geographic South Pole and yet, despite my enthusiastic battle cry, at that very moment it all seemed very ordinary, as if we were starting out on just another training run.

Considering our tumultuous first week in Antarctica, the girls had all been extremely calm as we waved goodbye to the plane the night before. After it had dropped us off at our designated starting point, we had stood together in a huddle around our newly pitched tents and waved madly above our heads as the plane diminished into a tiny black blob in the sky and finally disappeared altogether. For the first time our unconventional team was completely alone. The nearest human being was hundreds of kilometres away and although we had a satellite phone we knew that if we called for help it was likely to be days, not hours, before a plane could reach us. The consequences of getting injured out here were severe. At best it would mean the end of our expedition and at worst, it could be fatal. To make sure the team had absolutely no misconception about what we were doing I had hammered home the precarious nature of our safety during our last team meeting in Patriot Hills. 'Think about the consequences of your actions every second of every day. If you are ever tempted to take a shortcut remember how sorry you would feel if your actions brought about the end of the expedition. We need sorry before; not sorry after.' Kim's injury sat fresh in everyone's mind and I think it was the memory of her face as she had said goodbye, rather than my lecture, that had made everyone noticeably more conscientious as we struck camp on our first morning.

As we moved off across the snow in single file, the world ahead of us seemed to be split into two equal halves. Above was the sky and below was the snow, the horizon separating the two like the divide on a domino. Back home, the sky seems almost incidental, dwarfed by buildings and trees that encroach around its edges, but in Antarctica the sky became half of our entire universe. As we slid toward first one patch of shade then another, the sky was the main focus of our attention and we became intimately acquainted with its nuances of character. The vibrancy of its colours seemed almost supernatural. Close to the horizon the sky was a turquoise blue, blanched by the glare of the sun reflected from the snow; but if I tilted my head to look directly above, the sky became the deepest blue-black, like the pictures taken by astronauts of the very edges of the atmosphere, where our planet's benevolent sky meets the blackness of outer space. Meanwhile, the other half of our world had the texture of a badly plastered wall, the snow pitted with small hollows and contoured with shallow sastrugi. The surface reflected the sun like wet sand, so that in places it looked silver and shone so brightly that the rest looked almost grey, like over-washed white laundry. It was impossible to look at this flame-bright world without squinting and even then the image of it was burnt onto your retina as if staring at the sun for too long. Without goggles we would have soon been snow-blind.

Above all, the most impressive aspect of this wilderness was its devastating emptiness. There was not one track, glint of metal or smudge of habitation in the distance; not a mountain or a tree or a single lichen-splotched rock; not a fly or a bird or even the vapour trail of a plane overhead. In every direction there was nothing. 'It's the same,' Reena had marvelled soon after the plane had left us. She turned on the spot, scanning the horizon with her eyes. 'Every direction; it's the same.' I smiled at her amazement and waited for her to finish her rotation. 'I love it,' she announced in summary. I was pleased. I'd wondered what this lady from the Himalaya would make of such a relentlessly flat universe and was relieved that she clearly found it special; they all did.

We were setting out from the 'coast' of Antarctica but there was no open water or rocky shores to be seen. The ice that covers Antarctica is constantly flowing outwards towards the sea. At the edge of the continent the ice flows seamlessly from rock onto the ocean and forms huge floating ice shelves. From the surface there is no way of telling the difference between ice over land and ice over ocean. The exact position of the coast has been inexactly mapped by geologists, so we knew we had been deposited at the very edge of Antarctica, but from where we stood, all directions looked equally solid. We weren't heading immediately south from the coast, instead we were travelling in a slightly westerly direction in order to avoid the Pensacola Mountains that lay unseen somewhere to our left. We needed to circumvent the mountains, not just because crossing them would be pointlessly difficult, but also because they tended to be surrounded by crevasse fields – so we were giving them a wide berth. It would be some 300 kilometres before we would be able to turn southward and head directly for the pole. Shortly afterwards we would come across our one and only resupply. Although our sledges bulged with food and fuel as we left the coast, they only contained enough supplies for 21 days. The three large red duffle bags that formed our resupply contained all the food and fuel we would need to complete our journey. They had been dropped on the ice by a plane heading for the South Pole, at a point roughly halfway along our route. We had been given the exact coordinates of the depot so that we would be able to find it.

As we skied the first few kilometres of our journey, the South Pole seemed impossibly far away and the distances hopelessly long; our progress sounded ridiculously small when compared to the number of kilometres we needed to travel. To think of Day 40 during Day 1 was enough to make the bravest heart sink. The challenge was too big to comprehend when taken as a whole and so I concentrated on just the first stage, on reaching our resupply, and this made it more manageable. I had calculated that we should reach the resupply in 16 or 17 days. This was a time period that was easier to compute and so in my mind it became the whole expedition; I couldn't, and wouldn't, let my mind dwell on anything more.

After our first 90 minutes I stopped in my tracks and crossed my ski poles above my head to let the rest of the team know it was break time. We relied on hand signals while skiing because verbal communication was so difficult. If the skier leading the line held out their pole to one side, it meant 'Are you OK?' where 'OK' covered a variety of possibilities but usually translated as 'Is this pace OK?' If you were fine you mimicked the same signal. If something was wrong, we had alternative replies, the most usual being a waggle of the arm which meant 'slow down'.

Our only opportunity to actually talk to each other was during our short breaks but with only seven minutes to spare, there was a lot to get done. Everyone's top priority was usually going to the toilet. Our bodies hadn't yet adjusted to the increased fluids we were drinking every day to prevent dehydration and so having to hold in a pee for 90 minutes was a challenge, especially in the early days. Quite often someone or other would barely have stopped skiing before they were pulling down their trousers with a sigh of relief. Despite everyone's initial nervousness about going to the toilet in front of each other, in practice all modesty vanished almost instantly and we very quickly banished any hint of embarrassment about bodily functions. Harnessed to a heavy sledge, attached to two skis and wearing several layers of clothing made going to the toilet extremely difficult without adding the extra burden of wandering a few hundred feet away from the group where there would be no cover anyway (you'd have to wait a long time to find a handy boulder or tree to hide behind in Antarctica). Instead, we all just got on with what we had to do – and quickly. We weren't at risk of frostbite while going to the loo as long as we didn't leave ourselves exposed for too long and remembered to turn ourselves out of the wind.

Eating and drinking during the breaks was no less difficult. We had a snack bag of high-calorie food to eat during the day, broken into bite-sized pieces, but the difficulty was getting the food into our mouths. While skiing the moisture in every breath we exhaled froze onto the material covering our faces so that even the softest fleecy fabrics would become as solid as a plaster death mask. We'd have to chip narrow openings in our masks to post food through to our mouths. It was a messy business often resulting in a liberal coverage of peanut husks and popcorn fragments stuck to our masks and faces. Drinking was even more perilous. Using our insulated wide-mouthed water bottles was next to impossible without half the contents being spilt down the inside of our balaclavas. Anything spilt or dribbled would quickly turn to ice and, being right next to skin, could cause frostbite. Luckily, we also had narrow-necked bottles which could be wedged through the front of our balaclavas and held in place by our teeth as we gulped but it was never a comfortable process and there were frequent accidents.

Helen had volunteered to be the timekeeper during our breaks. She'd start the clock as soon as the last in line had pulled up their sledge next to the group and would give us warnings as we neared seven minutes. I would be last to leave, hurrying up anyone who was running late. Unless it was my turn to navigate, I usually chose to ski at the back of the line. I felt more comfortable being able to see everyone and check at a glance that we were all still together. I knew immediately if someone was falling behind the person in front of them, meaning that the pace was too quick, or if someone was carrying a strain and therefore skiing with a limp and, later on, I was even able to tell from body language alone if someone was simply having a bad day emotionally.

Each member of the team had a skiing style as unique as a fingerprint. Despite the fact that we couldn't see each other's faces and were all wearing identical clothing we could tell, even from a distance, who was who. Helen was by far the neatest skier. Her legs only seemed to move from below the knee, with her arms making perfectly matched swings but only from below her elbows. Sophia was also a tidy skier, making tiny, purposeful steps that looked more like marching than skiing. Kylie had more of a swagger. She put her shoulders into each glide in a way that reminded me of John Wayne in American cowboy films. Reena looked permanently exhausted on her skis, seeming to lean heavily on her ski poles as if they were the only thing keeping her upright. Steph lacked any kind of rhythm or consistency as she skied. She was usually staggering along, too busy adjusting her clothing or equipment to pay much attention to an efficient skiing style. Every second we were on the move she spent searching through pockets, changing gloves, adjusting her hat or altering the volume of her music player. After my tough criticism in Patriot Hills of her lack of organisation she had spent several hours attaching lengths of elastic to every piece of kit she owned so that she could physically fasten everything together in an effort to avoid losing it. The result was a constant battle with metres of tangled elastic that continually wrapped itself around ski poles, compasses, other people's legs and even her own head. It's a testament to her skill that she was able to keep up with the rest of the team despite this self-imposed handicap. Era had the most memorable skiing style of all; it was more sashay than glide. Each step forward would be accompanied by a genteel waggle of the hips and a dainty tap of the snow with her ski poles. With every forward movement her foot and ski would lift clear off the snow, a most inefficient way to ski. I tried encouraging her to glide more until finally she announced, 'I've tried skiing other ways but they are not comfortable. This is the way I prefer to ski.' I had to admit that she kept up with the group well enough – her chosen style obviously wasn't holding her up in any way or causing her injury so I left her alone.

Despite our unconventional skiing, watching from the back I was impressed with the way we were moving as a team. We stuck together and had eliminated a lot of the faffing that had become frustrating during our training expeditions. I noticed that if someone needed to make a quick adjustment to clothing or equipment they stepped out of the tracks to allow the team to pass as they did what they needed to do, before joining the end of the line. We hadn't practised this or even talked about it – it just happened naturally and was extremely slick.

In all we were making great progress, so good in fact that by the end of our third leg we had already reached the 8-nautical-mile target I had set for our first day. I'd noticed that each leg had been slightly faster than the last until I had been practically running on my skis. 'We can afford to dawdle,' I told the team. 'We don't want to wear ourselves out too soon.' I had seen too many teams make that exact mistake; going out too hard and too fast only to crash and burn before the end. This was an untried team and none of us knew exactly where the breaking point for us as a group would be. It seemed prudent to take it slow and steady. To keep a consistent pace sounds like a straightforward task but it was to become one of the most contentious issues of the entire expedition.

As we stopped for the fourth break of the day Steph announced that she would need some extra time. She had started her period the day before and needed to sort herself out. Menstruating during an expedition isn't the greatest experience in the world but neither is it impossible as long as you are well prepared and get yourself organised. Unfortunately, it takes a bit of experience before you can perfect a system that works for you. I announced to the team that we would have a 15-minute break and had them put on their down jackets while we stopped. Even so, as we moved off a quarter of an hour later, several people were complaining of cold hands and feet and Era refused to take off her big down jacket. It was clear that we were not going to be able to stop for longer than seven minutes again, regardless of the problem. By the time we stopped for our next break, Era and Sophia were still cold so I decided we would stop for the day. We had only managed to ski for six hours rather than the intended eight but we had exceeded our mileage target for our first day, so the compromise seemed reasonable.

It was a perfect evening, clear and cold with a slight breeze, but the sun was still strong enough for us to feel its warmth through our clothing as we pitched the tents. Steph and I were the 'outside men' for our tent. After the tent was up our job was to stay outside to anchor the guy ropes and pile snow on the valences, while Era and Sophia got inside and started with the inside jobs. As we worked it was such a relief to be away from the near constant wind we had experienced in Patriot Hills. We were still careful to secure our equipment when unpacking the sledges (after all, the consequences of a sudden gust snatching a sleeping mat or an abandoned jacket were serious) but the calmer conditions allowed us to relax a little bit and focus on something other than fighting the wind.

Still slightly nervous about the reliability of our patched-up tents, we were very diligent about making sure the tent was well anchored, but Steph took our caution to a new level. Part of her job was to build a small protective wall around the windward end of the tent but when I glanced up from my own shovelling I saw that she had built a barricade worthy of the Bastille. It was quite a feat of engineering, involving carefully shaped blocks of snow arranged aerodynamically to protect not just the front of the tent but our narrow side entrance as well. Inside the tent Era and Sophia had named themselves the 'homemakers' and they had taken the term seriously. Era had not only sorted our belongings into our designated corners but had hung any damp equipment on the washing line and actually folded our jackets into neat little piles. It was spectacular.

I made myself comfortable in my corner by the door. I was by far the largest in the tent and made a particular effort to try to constrain my oversized arms and legs as much as possible, but I still took up far more space than anyone else. Sophia handed me my dinner. After a long search I had found a supplier of halal expedition meals but we hadn't had an opportunity to try them all. 'Kung Po Chicken' boasted the label on my packet. I opened it up, the steam burning my fingers, and gasped in surprise. There, lying on the top of a bed of noodles, were genuine chunks of real, crispy vegetables. I made the others look and we all whooped in delight. To have real vegetables in an expedition meal was unheard of and yet here they were. Unable to resist, I tried a long green bean while it was still too hot, breathing out the hot air as I chewed but with a huge, ecstatic grin on my face. Better than the taste was the texture – to have something that went 'crunch' when you bit into it was such a novelty; everything else we ate was the soft, mulchy product of chemical processes but this was genuine food. Less successful was the protein powder that we were to drink each evening to help our muscles recover for the following day. It didn't dissolve as normal in our water bottles but formed granulated lumps that had to be chewed before they could be swallowed. Helen pronounced her revulsion when she joined us after dinner, 'It was like floating dandruff. Disgusting!'

Even though it was now nine in the evening the sun was still high in the sky and warming the tent, the light filtering through the red fabric so that, inside, everything looked a homely orange and we felt warm enough to sit around without the additional heat of the stove. Era was preparing for prayer in the far corner of the tent. She had already spent half an hour silently washing her feet, arms and face with a baby wipe dipped in a dish of water. Pulling down the sleeves of her thermal so that they covered her wrists, she had put on a pair of gloves and pulled up her socks so that her legs were entirely covered. Then she pulled a neck gaiter over her head so that it formed a tight headscarf around her face and neck. As a faithful Muslim she had put a lot of thought into how to carry out the obligations of her religion during the expedition. Usually she would be expected to pray five times a day but while travelling this was reduced to three; once in the morning and twice in the evening. Finding east (the direction of Mecca that Muslims must face to pray) was easy enough with a compass but calculating the right time to pray was a little harder because it is usually determined by dusk and dawn – something that is a little tricky when living in 24-hour daylight. Taking advice, Era had been told to use the prayer times from the nearest landmass that experienced night – in our case South America. Fortunately, Patriot Hills chooses to operate on South American time and so we followed suit, which made Era's calculations just a little easier.

I had learned about Islam at school but I had never personally witnessed Muslim prayer before. With all four of us confined to the small space inside the tent it was impossible to give Era any privacy as she prayed and although it felt like an intrusion to be present, I also have to admit that it was fascinating. Sat on her knees, Era repeatedly bowed, touching her head to the floor. Sitting upright she turned her head first one way, then the other, all the while muttering prayer softly to herself. It was a little strange at first, all of us falling into respectful but awkward silence, but eventually it became just another daily occurrence.

The highlight of our evenings was undoubtedly our daily satellite phone call with Patriot Hills. We took it in turns to report our position, the progress we had made and our intentions for the following day. Usually there was then time for a brief gossip, hearing any news from the camp and passing on our own. The radio operator had requested a joke from us each day and promised one of his own in return. Steph made our first satellite phone call and was ready with her joke after the formalities were over. 'What goes white, black, white, black, white, black, white, black?'

There was silence on the line so she continued, 'A penguin rolling down a hill.'

There was a burst of laughter down the phone, revealing that there were a number of people standing in the communications box to listen to our first report. When the laughter had died down the operator asked if we had any issues.

'No,' answered Steph. 'We're all absolutely great.'

'Are you sure?' asked the operator. 'You have no issues to report?'

'No,' said Steph. 'We're all good.'

'No issues at all?' tried the operator one more time. He sounded almost disappointed, as if the fact that we had not suffered a major calamity in our first day was somewhat unexpected.

The nadir of our evenings, dreaded by all, was the inescapable call of nature. Most expedition teams simply wander a discreet distance from their tents and dig a hole in the snow but for us, things were made slightly more complicated by our decision to remove all our solid human waste throughout the entire expedition. A friend had kindly sourced bags for us designed specifically for the purpose. They were made from a silver, reflective plastic and were the size and shape of a large ziplock freezer bag. The bag was used like a toilet before being securely sealed and placed under our sledge bags, distinctly separate from any rations or equipment. The contents of the bags froze rapidly so that the system wasn't as awful in practice as it sounds in theory. For most of us this was a daily occurrence but Steph astonished us all by announcing that she only needed to go once a week. 'Once a week?' I repeated in amazement. 'Steph, that doesn't sound healthy.'

Adamant that she knew her own body, Steph had confidently brought with her only one bag for every four days but as Helen began to complain that she thought the protein powder was giving her diarrhoea, Steph began to panic, 'Oh no, I absolutely cannot get diarrhoea. I haven't got enough bags for that.'

As each of us left the tent at various intervals through the evening, clutching our little silver bags, Kylie joked that it looked like we were off for a night out with a glittery clutch bag. 'I still remember Era and Steph in Norway, wading through a blizzard clasping their designer Louis Vuitton handbags,' I laughed.

'These are our Louis Poo-uittons,' someone replied. It was the perfect nickname and it stuck. Popping out of the tent with a Louis Poo-uitton may have been unpleasant but what we all dreaded more than anything else was needing to get up during the 'night'. It may not have been dark outside but it was still far colder than the average home freezer. Once comfortably wrapped in the warmth of a sleeping bag, the idea of exposing yourself to the merciless cold outside seemed unnecessarily cruel but, unless you were willing to accept a sleepless night trying to ignore the inevitable, there was no option. On the rare occasions I was forced to sleepily put on hat, jacket and boots to head outside while the others were sleeping, I bizarrely found it quite liberating. Having safely stowed my Louis in my sledge, I would stand for a while with my hands tucked under my arms to warm them, facing out of the wind and gazing at the surreal world that surrounded us. These were the only moments during the entire expedition when I could be alone and I treasured them. They felt special, private and unobserved, a moment for which I had Antarctica completely to myself. Wearing just the thermals I slept in and a down jacket, I'd stand until I could feel the burn of the cold on the skin of my legs before reluctantly climbing back into the shelter of the tent and the delicious warmth of my sleeping bag.

We woke to a second day in Antarctica with clear skies and beautiful sunshine. There was a slight breeze but it was warm enough for most of us to ski in just a thermal top with a thin windproof smock over the top. I couldn't believe our luck to have such wonderful weather but not everyone was as pleased. I overheard Era expressing her disappointment at the lack of heroic weather. 'I'm worried it will be too easy if the weather is good all the way.'

'Don't worry, Era,' I interrupted. 'We still have a long way to go and I promise you it won't be easy.'

She thought for a second, 'Felicity, I think we should ski faster and for longer than we did yesterday.'

Helen was quick to respond, clearly alarmed, 'We need to keep it slow and steady so that everyone can keep up.'

I tried to reassure them both. 'We'll find a pace that suits everyone but,' I continued, addressing Helen to reassure her, 'we certainly won't be shooting off anywhere. We'll do exactly what we did yesterday, perhaps a little slower if anything.'

Steph led the first leg and kept a really even, manageable pace but I kept a particular eye on Kylie. The previous evening she had mentioned a pain across the top of her left foot. She wasn't overly concerned about it but it seemed a little early to be getting injured. When the pain got worse during the second day she tried cutting an insole from her sleeping mat to cushion her foot but this didn't seem to make much difference. By the end of the third day the pain was so bad that she sat in the tent in the evening with her foot propped up on a pile of kit, wrapped in ice. 'My heel is rolling off the ski with every step,' she explained. 'I've packed out my heel with sleeping mat and bandaged up my foot but it doesn't seem to be making a difference. I think it might be something wrong with the binding on my ski.'

We took a look at her left ski, comparing it to Reena's. The binding looked like it was in the right place and mounted in a correct, straight position on the ski. There were no signs that there was anything wrong but Kylie was adamant that it was the ski and not her skiing style that was causing the problem. Reena agreed to swap skis with Kylie. I was a little uncomfortable with the arrangement, worried that this was just passing on the problem rather than solving it, but there seemed to be little alternative. The snow was too soft to make walking a realistic option, and for now at least, the swap seemed to resolve the issue. After a day with the suspect ski, Reena was completely unbothered and Kylie reported an instant improvement in her foot.

The rest of the team were also starting to have problems with their feet. 'My official blister count is three on both soles of my feet and my fourth toe on my right foot,' wrote Era in our team journal. She wasn't the only one. I held a regular 'blister clinic' in the tent, making sure that I saw everyone's feet, and offered advice on how to look after them. I don't profess to have expert knowledge on the subject but over the years I've done a lot of miles with blistered feet and have learned a thing or two about dealing with them. They seem like such a triviality and yet without healthy feet, it is impossible to ski or walk. If blisters aren't looked after they can become infected or become major wounds that are excruciatingly painful. The humble blister can easily put an end to an expedition.

Each evening I encouraged the girls to take off their socks and make sure their feet were warm and dry. We'd tape up any hot spots, drain any blisters and let them air overnight to harden before padding them the next morning. For Era, Sophia and Steph, blisters were an entirely new experience and so I was extremely hands-on. Reena, Kylie and Helen were more experienced so, bar enquiring after their feet, I let them look after their own. However, it gradually became clear that Helen in particular was having trouble. She'd mentioned several times that she had a few blisters but had given the impression she was coping until one day she repeatedly asked the team to slow down using our agreed hand signals. It got to the point that we were moving slowly and yet Helen was still allowing a gap to open up between herself and the sledge in front. I skied along the side of the group until I caught up with her and fell in alongside. 'My feet are completely shredded,' she admitted and I could tell that she was close to tears. That evening I asked to take a look at her feet. They were still recovering from the long trek she had completed in Namibia just before the expedition; her heels were covered in dry, cracked skin and her toes were pink with scar tissue where she had had several blisters. The nails on her big toes were blackened and misshapen; it was clear that it was just a matter of time before they would peel off. Two new blisters had formed on the outside of each big toe, close to the knuckle. They looked sore but not critical. 'So are you going to drain them tonight so that the skin can harden for tomorrow?' I asked.

'No, I've been leaving the blister intact to protect the skin underneath,' she replied.

I was horrified. Leaving the blister in place would have been unnecessarily painful. 'Are you taking painkillers?'

'No, I'm not used to taking drugs so I don't want to take anything unless I absolutely have to.'

I encouraged her to drain the blister and take some paracetamol to make skiing less painful but she was steadfast in her objection. I could see that the conversation was making her emotional. 'If I had known I was coming here, I would never have gone to Namibia,' she admitted sadly. 'It just seemed like too good an opportunity to miss.'

Helen was paying the price for taking on two such serious expeditions back to back. It wasn't just the physical impact of Namibia that she had underestimated; it was clear that there was a mental and emotional price to pay as well. It gradually became obvious that Helen wasn't herself. Normally happy and positive, the laughter seemed a little strained and she became very negative about the smallest of details. I could see that the expedition was already harder, mentally and physically, than she had prepared for and I was worried for her. One evening I made a point of finding a private moment to ask her how she was finding it. 'To be honest, Felicity, I'm eighteen years older than some members of this team, and today I felt it.' I gave her a hug of encouragement. 'I'm just worried that I'm not giving you the support you expected,' she continued. It was true that I was surprised at how difficult Helen was finding the expedition but I tutted at her concern. 'Don't be ridiculous. It's our turn to support you. You just need to concentrate on maintaining those feet and getting to the South Pole.'

Helen wasn't the only surprise of the expedition. Kylie, normally incredibly self-sufficient and organised, was revealing herself to be a magnet for accidental disaster. She was full of energy and never deliberately careless but things just seemed to get broken around her. She was in charge of the stoves in her tent and within the first week she had managed to burn her sleeping mat, the tent, a thermos flask, a water bottle and even the leg of her own trousers – while she was wearing them. Each day she listed her latest stream of disasters and I couldn't help laughing in pure exasperation. She may have been terrible with equipment but she was a master with people. If I ever fell short on the pastoral side of things I knew that Kylie would be filling the gap, ever ready with a comforting hug and a cheering view of the situation.

Kylie always brought good humour with her but it was Steph who supplied the fun and was the vitality of our team. Her direct observations about the surrealism of our day-to-day life on the ice kept us laughing but as fond as I was of Steph, she was often the cause of intense frustration. Her natural state was one of disorganisation and constant crisis. She'd worked hard to implement some self-discipline and although I recognised her effort I still found myself having occasionally to be quite hard on her, particularly when her belongings began spreading too far out of her corner of the tent, or when she spent too long getting into her sleeping bag at night, procrastinating for hours as she pointlessly fossicked long after everyone else was asleep. Steph's habitual disarray was highlighted by the contrast with Era's unfailingly neat habits. Era took her responsibilities within the tent very seriously and was often the one to scold us if we fell below her high standards of personal administration.

In retrospect the early days of the expedition seemed to have passed in a flash and yet at the time we noted the passing of every moment of the day in exhaustive detail. It was as if we had entered a cosmological hall of mirrors where instead of our reflected images being affected, it was the seconds and minutes of our days that were distorted. Time appeared able to stretch to fill an aeon or contract to last no longer than a click of the fingers. We began talking about 90 minute legs rather than hours as if this was a new unit of time ('Lets stop in two legs' time...'; 'It will take us four legs to get there...') and in days since departure rather than referring to dates or days of the week ('We'll get there on Day 15...'; 'It happened on Day 3...'). It felt like we had truly stepped outside normal existence. The landscape supported this conclusion. The relentless emptiness was absolute, as if the whole of creation had been wiped clean and we were, quite literally, walking across the great white drawing board of the gods as it waited to be filled with their new handiwork.

The sky was as unchanging as the horizon. Although the sun moved, it described perfect circles above us so that there was no change in the colour and strength of the light throughout the day. Only the clouds gave any indication of the passage of time.

The skies were so big that we could see whole fronts of cloud in their entirety and watch as they slowly advanced towards us. Flat and uniform, like thin blankets cruising through the atmosphere, the shadow of a cloud layer would fall across us as dramatically as a biblical event and as suddenly as an eclipse. Steph stood next to me at one break, munching awkwardly as she peered upwards at the clouds above us. They seemed so low that it was tempting to reach out to try to touch them. 'I've never watched clouds forming before,' she said in wonder. I could see what she meant. The swirling mists above us seemed to coalesce in front of our eyes, forming and reforming over and over again until they drifted away in a single layer, like a blind being pulled over the sky. On the horizon the clouds had gathered into vast towers of light and shade. I watched them as we skied onwards and they appeared to grow like candy floss being spun at a fairground. Their centres were dark triangles of shadow surrounded by smudges of grey. As I continued to gaze at them absently my vision warped and wavered as if looking at a magic-eye picture. I grinned in sudden perception. What I was looking at weren't clouds gathering on the horizon but the tips of distant mountains. It was the first distinctive feature we had seen since leaving the coast ten days before. Leading at the front I turned round and pointed excitedly at the mountains to Kylie a few metres behind me. She looked up from her skis and watched my pantomime. 'Mountains!' I shouted, even though I knew she wouldn't be able to hear me and jabbed towards the horizon again with my mitt. She followed the direction of my outstretched arm, confused, then spotted the apparitions. She nodded at me enthusiastically before turning to Reena behind her to act out a similar pantomime. Surprise and delight rippled down the line, even though there was not so much as a pause in the rhythm of our skiing. I conjured the map of our route into my head and realised that these ghostly mountains to our south must be the Pensacolas, some 100 kilometres away.

That evening in the tent I pored over the laminated map we carried with us. Era had conscientiously marked the location of each of our camps with a small cross in neat black pen. There were now ten crosses forming a slightly wonky line from our starting point on the coast, stretching out boldly across the white expanses of the map. Our advance looked impressive until I folded out the map to show our entire route to the South Pole. In contrast to the ground yet to cover, we had barely taken our first steps. 'In four days' time we will reach the eighty-fifth degree of latitude,' predicted Era confidently. Era had been a mathematics teacher and she loved any kind of mathematical problem or puzzle. Each evening, after carefully plotting our position on the map, she would cover our tiny communal notebook in her calculations of mileage covered and distances to go.

We were now skiing six 90-minute legs in a day and had increased our daily mileage from just over 8 nautical miles to nearly 14 nautical miles. I was pleased with our pace: we had built up gradually and the team looked really strong. However, Helen was still anxious. 'We've just got to keep plodding, we don't want to go too fast,' she said. I didn't think we were in any danger of going too fast and suspected it was her feet, not the pace, that were the real problem. The nails on her big toes, which had been damaged in Namibia, were coming loose and moving around painfully as she skied. 'They throb at night and keep me awake,' she admitted as we sat together in the tent surveying the damaged skin.

'Take some painkillers, Helen – at least overnight so that you can get some decent sleep,' I cajoled. Eventually she was persuaded to take some paracetamol and ibuprofen.

Her tent-mates were also nursing their feet. Reena, who had been using Kylie's skis, had developed a pain in her left ankle.

They were both now convinced that there was something wrong with the ski and neither wanted to use it. This was a problem as walking was still not a viable option in the soft snow and if the problem really was with the ski, passing it on to someone else would just spread the injury around. Kylie reluctantly took back her 'evil' ski. 'I just need to make sure that with every step my heel hits the ski right,' she decided (with more optimism than I suspect she felt). 'At least it will be something to occupy my mind,' she added. Concentrating on every step sounded exhausting. It was clear that we needed to find another solution.

In the second tent a few metres away the issue was not injuries but hygiene. 'Women shouldn't smell like this,' complained Steph. We had now been wearing the same clothes for at least 11 days and our last shower, back in Punta, was a distant memory. We each did our best with our daily ration of a single baby wipe, scrubbing at our face and hands first before attempting armpits and finally feet, but it made little difference. Every now and again we'd catch a whiff of ourselves and it was shocking. Thankfully, even though we were living very close together, I can honestly say that it was very rare I'd notice the stink of anyone but myself. Steph decided it was time for positive action and devised a plan for doing some laundry. We didn't have fuel to waste on melting snow to make water for washing clothes but, undaunted, she tried a dry wash. Taking her underwear outside (held in front of her at arm's length like a diseased rat) she dug a shallow pit in some powdery snow and rubbed ice into the fabric until it was damp. Adding a dash of antibacterial handwash she scrubbed at the laundry for a while before coming back inside the tent looking very pleased with herself. 'I don't know how clean they actually are,' she admitted. 'But at least they will feel clean.' I didn't share her enthusiasm when, later that evening, I sat up in my sleeping bag to be slapped in the face by a pair of drip-drying knickers hanging on the washing line in the middle of the tent.

The next morning we woke to a particularly cold, windy day. We all opted to wear our warm fleece-lined smocks and pulled our fur-lined hoods close around our faces to keep out the worst of the icy gusts. The mountains we had seen the day before had disappeared into the cloud-covered sky and so, heads down, we set off in our long line, watching the back of the sledge in front, occasionally looking up to scan the horizon, before resuming our fixed, downward gaze. The rhythmic motion of the skis and their sibilance as they cut through the snow lulled me into a kind of meditation. My mind wandered away from Antarctica and took me home. I thought about what Peter would be doing at that exact moment. I worked out that he would be on his way home from work and tried to remember in exact detail his route along the sea to our tiny flat near Epple Bay with its whitewashed walls and 'sea glimpses'. I imagined him gratefully shutting our front door against the winter weather and dropping his bags in our kitchen, turning on the central heating and the radio on his way into the bathroom for a shower, then cooking a meal to eat on the sofa. At that very moment, the simple comfort of sitting with him in the warmth of our front room seemed to be the greatest gift the world could bestow.

A jolt sent me back to Antarctica. My sledge had caught on a lump of ice. I leaned forward in my harness without looking back. The sledges got caught a million times over in a single day but it was usually just a matter of pulling harder to free them. This time, there was no movement as I tugged at it. I turned around to find that my sledge had tipped over onto its side, the lip of the plastic sledge firmly wedged under a wave-shaped sastrugi. I glanced up at the team who, unaware I had stopped, were now a long way ahead. I called out to Era who was next in line. 'Era! Stop!' Seeing there was no response I called again, pulling down my balaclava so that my mouth was clear of material. My shoulders heaved with the effort as I yelled. The team marched on oblivious, my shouts carried away on the wind blowing in the opposite direction. Part of the travelling routine we had practised was that the person navigating at the front of the line regularly looked back to make sure that the team was OK – and still there.

I watched the line for a while as it marched away from me, confident that at any moment Reena at the front of the line would look behind her. Seconds passed. Nothing. It was incredible how much ground had been covered in the few minutes since I had been stopped. The team of six individuals had now shrunk in size to become a single indistinguishable mass with numerous flailing limbs, like an oversized millipede. Sometimes the legs worked in perfect time with each other, at others it was random but all the while mitts jangled from elastic tied to harnesses or sleeves, webbing flapped from waist belts and ski poles jabbed at the ground leaving a spray of bullet holes in the snow either side of our parallel tracks. As the team continued to move further away from me, I realised no one was going to look around. I unhitched myself from my harness and, working quickly, moved around the sledge, moving the sledge bag so that I could disentangle it from the ice formation still stubbornly holding firm. It took me a number of minutes to right the sledge and reattach myself to my harness so I was shocked to look up and see that the team still hadn't noticed that they'd left someone behind. I was angry: they knew better than this. I set off at a fast pace to try to catch up.

Even though I was sweating with the effort, the distance between me and the receding millipede didn't seem to be lessening. I had been marching for a good five minutes before finally I noticed Reena's hand outstretched at her side making our hand signal for, 'Are you OK?' I watched as she looked round at the team behind her and then did a double take as she noticed there was one missing. Era swung around on her skis in shock to find that I wasn't behind her, then looked up to spot me in the distance. Reena raised her ski pole towards me to check if I was OK. I paused in relief, crossing my poles above my head in reply so that they would all stop and wait for me. I ploughed on towards them as fast as I could but felt a little easier now that I knew that I would catch up. Pulling up behind Era I panted with the effort. 'You've all got to look behind you,' I gasped. 'I could have been in real trouble and none of you would have known. You could have left me behind.'

The girls all looked sheepish, shuffling on their skis. 'Are you OK?' asked Reena, concerned.

'I'm fine,' I puffed. 'Just remember to look behind you.'

I was genuinely annoyed but when we continued I found myself laughing quietly as I noticed Reena checking behind her after every few paces. In fact, for the rest of the day the team looked as if they'd developed a serious twitch, each of them glancing over their shoulder every few minutes. I was glad. We were approaching the section of our route that skimmed a large area of known crevassing. Planes flying to the South Pole from Patriot Hills had been able to see extensive holes and fissures in the ice from the air and recorded the coordinates. We were heading for a navigation marker that would lead us around the northern fringes of this crevasse field before we turned southwards. The dog-leg added a day, perhaps more, to our journey and I wondered if there was any room to cut the corner. 'Good question,' Steve had responded when I'd asked him during our regular call with Patriot Hills. 'And a really bad idea.' As he described the size and extent of the crevassing that had been seen from the air, I felt a chill crawl down my spine and clasp my stomach. Our only protection from crevasses was vigilance.

I briefed the team to keep an eye open for any suspicious slumps in the snow, linear features or anything unusual and as we set off the next day, I could see that the girls were all periodically scanning the surface ahead and around us. Privately, I held little hope of us being able to detect anything until we were literally upon it. The snow around us was streaked with sastrugi which had been getting more pronounced over the last few days. Looking to my right or left as we skied, the ground seemed to be corrugated into delicate ripples so that it looked like the sea on a calm day. Each rise reflected a different shade of light so that the ground was no longer a uniform white but a collage of muted tones like the brush-strokes of a watercolour. Larger sastrugi protruded from the ripples, forming ice-sculptures that kept us amused. To me the porpoise-like curve of these larger waves were motionless sea monsters slipping through the frozen sea of ice; to Kylie they were groups of turtles crawling on each other's backs, as if scrabbling to escape the snow beneath, and to Steph they were surrealist artworks worthy of Gaudí. When we passed close to one of these bigger sastrugi Reena would prod it with her ski pole, as if checking it was dead. 'I see them as fish,' she explained later. 'So I make an eye with the end of my ski pole.' Kylie was delighted with the idea and followed behind Reena drawing a smile on the ice fish beneath their new eyes. I watched all this from my place at the back of the line, amused by the thought of our route across Antarctica marked out by these animated imaginings.

'Whooooohmp.'

The sound of a muted thump rose from the snow beneath my ski and rolled away from us like the crash of thunder. I felt the snowpack move under my feet, as if the whole section I stood on had sunk. A surge of adrenalin shot through me like an electric shock, so sudden that it was physically painful. My mind silently yelled, 'Crevasse!' and I scuttled forward on my skis half expecting the ground to be falling away behind me. I turned and studied the snow – it all looked exactly as it had before, unchanged. I breathed deeply to calm my racing heart. This was not a crevasse opening up beneath me but the snowpack settling under the addition of our weight as we passed over it. Steph was in front of me in the line and had heard the same noise. She looked down at the snow beneath our skis before turning to me, 'What was that?' I could hear the panic in her voice.

'It's just the snow settling,' I said casually, deliberately hiding my own fright. I had warned the team that we might hear this sort of thing but I expected that experiencing it for real would be unnerving for everyone, including me. Twenty minutes later the same thing happened again. I noticed Steph suddenly speed forward on her skis, moving closer to the person in front. She looked round at me in fear but didn't say anything this time. I kept my head down as if I hadn't heard it. Over the next three days we experienced the same sensation repeatedly. Each time my brain calmed my instinct with logic but there was still a quiet voice of fear wondering why we had only experienced the snowpack settling now, along the very section of our route that we knew was so close to a crevasse field. No logic in the world could stem the surge of adrenalin that flooded through me each time I set foot on some snow and heard the same sickening thump. I was amazed at the calmness of the rest of the team. 'Doesn't it bother you?' I asked Era at a break.

'You've told us not to worry about it, so I don't,' she replied simply.

I didn't know whether to be flattered or alarmed at the faith she put in my assessment.

As the noises from the snow continued, the sastrugi got bigger and the weather closed in. We were close now to the navigation marker and I could feel the expectation within the team. It wasn't that there would be anything to see at the navigation point but after 13 days of simply travelling it was a novelty to feel that we would be arriving somewhere, even if it was just an arbitrary point on the map. The cloud had muted the light so that there was no definition or contrast in the snow. It was difficult to pick out the sastrugi if they cast no shadow so we found ourselves tripping over unseen obstacles of ice. Steph was the first to fall. Her right ski slid suddenly away from her, slipping down the back of an invisible sastrugi and she fell heavily, trailing her left ski through the air in an impressive arc. Those behind and in front of her in the line tried to shuffle forward to help but were hampered by their own skis as well as their sledges. Era was the next to fall. I happened to be looking across the top of our line when I saw two ski-tips, still parallel, flash in the space where Era's head had been. Era was leading so the line stopped immediately but she was quick to get back on her feet, brushing the snow from her hat as she let everyone know she was unhurt.

Not long after, Era stopped again. I peered down the line, assuming she had fallen, then saw the crossed poles above her head. I stepped out of our tracks and skied towards the front of the line to see what was wrong. Kylie was bouncing on her skis, arms above her head in triumph, 'We've arrived!' she whooped. Era had disconnected from her sledge and was shuffling about on her skis, hunched over her GPS unit. She stopped and looked up, 'The navigation marker is right here,' she announced, pointing down at the spot where she stood. I skied over and marked a cross in the snow with a gloved finger, 'X marks the spot.'

Now we had something to look at. As the team laughed and patted each other on the back, I gazed southward at the grey, smudged horizon and for a rare instant allowed myself to think of the South Pole. Our goal was still more than 600 kilometres away but in that instant as we turned to face the south, head on, for the first time, the pole felt closer than ever.

CHAPTER TEN

POINTING FINGERS

I squinted into the glare and tried to concentrate on the small black square that danced and flickered in the distance. I could see it clearly from the corner of my eye only to have it disappear if I looked at it directly. Frustration rose in my chest. We should have been able to see our resupply by now; could this be it? I glanced down at the GPS unit in my hand. Usually we navigated by compass because the batteries in the GPS ran down too quickly in the cold but this was a special occasion. We were within a nautical mile of our resupply. Somewhere out on the ice were three large red duffle bags and the GPS, unlike a compass, would be able to guide us straight to them. 'There's a big cairn of snow marked with flags,' the operator at Patriot Hills had told me over the satellite phone the night before. 'You will be able to see it from at least a kilometre away,' he reported. The display on the GPS told me that we were now only 800 metres away. Why couldn't we see the resupply yet?

A feeling of dread rolled itself into a fist in my gut as my mind blazed through worst case scenarios. It was all too conceivable that we had made some terrible navigational error; that we were actually miles away from where we thought we were; that some sub-space magnetic storm had thrown our satellite-fixed positions into disarray and we had unwittingly already passed our vital resupply depot. Locating three bags in the vastness of Antarctica suddenly seemed ridiculous and our failure to find them, inevitable. But then there was that slight flicker of black from the corner of my eye. Could it be a flag? I felt myself speeding up, lengthening my strides in my eagerness to find out.

I glanced behind me at the team. A gap was opening up in front of Helen and I knew she'd be angry at me for increasing the pace but I ignored the concern. If this was the depot then we had only 300 metres to go. I felt myself racing now, a flood of energy surging through my muscles, a wave of joy rising at the sudden feeling of freedom. Glancing over my shoulder I noticed Steph and Reena had broken out of our habitual single file and were pulling up beside me – they had seen the flag, too. I grinned at them from behind my balaclava and we pushed forward together. With 100 metres to go there was no mistaking that the black dot was indeed a flag. This had to be our resupply, what else would be out here? We charged, flat out, over the remaining ground as the girls whooped congratulations to each other, the words smothered by the wind and our face-coverings, but jubilant nonetheless.

The depot was no more than a pair of crossed flags above a heap of red bags partially covered in snow and ice. The flags sat just a few feet above the ground and I marvelled at the fact that I had seen their flickering forms from so far away – two tiny black dots in this universe of white. Era and Steph had kicked off their skis and were hugging each other. Steph was quick to pull the hated face mask away from her skin so that it hung to one side and revealed the coating of ice that had built up on the inside. Reena too had ripped her balaclava away so that it framed her face with a fringe of thick icicles. Usually we were careful not to disturb our painstakingly arranged face-coverings but arriving at the resupply we pushed them aside, knowing that we'd promised ourselves a rest day once we reached the depot. After 15 days of skiing, a full 36 hours of blissful lassitude stretched ahead of us.

Helen and Kylie arrived a little behind the others but were soon joining in the celebrations, pushing aside goggles and masks to grin at each other with ice-wet faces and snow-dusted hair. We gathered together by the depot, resting our team camera on a ski to take a group photograph. Looking at that photograph now you can see the glee radiating from our faces. It wasn't just the fact that we were looking forward to a long rest; the fact that we had reached the resupply (and a day earlier than expected at that) was a huge source of pride. Having skied over 200 nautical miles we weren't yet quite halfway to the South Pole but somehow it felt as if, by reaching this point in our journey, we had proved ourselves worthy of being here in Antarctica at all. So many people had expressed so many doubts, that reaching our resupply felt like a vindication.

Still grinning with elation, we pulled our sledges a short distance from the flagged depot and fell into our normal tent routine. The wind was no more than a cooling breath and the sun warmed our backs through our jackets as we worked. I caught sight of the splotchy forms of the Thiel Mountains away to our west and couldn't help pausing to run my eyes over their crooked faces. We'd first spotted them the day before and they had accompanied us ever since like benevolent guardians, shady forms making tooth-like indentations in the line between snow and sky. Rising no more than a thumb's width above the horizon, they appeared to hover just a little above the ground, sometimes floating over their own reflections so that they formed distorted diamond shapes sharpening to points resting on the snow. The near-permanent mirage made it difficult to ever get a true sense of what we were looking at. It was already difficult to pin down size and scale in this vast featureless plain but now even the light was unreliable, twisting and morphing to change the form of whatever we looked at so that nothing was ever still, nothing ever definite. It added to the surreal nature of our monochrome world, always more dream than substance.

As much as we were looking forward to slumping in our sleeping bags for the longest sleep of our lives, I was keen to get organised before we relaxed. Our first job was to strip our equipment and sledges of every scrap of rubbish, uneaten rations and unwanted or unused kit that we didn't want to carry for the second half of the expedition. Everything we planned to leave behind was collected together in an empty resupply bag. We would leave it at the depot to be collected by plane later in the season. As the girls dispersed to sort through their sledges I was shocked when Era produced more than 10 kilograms of uneaten day bags. 'I'm sorry Felicity,' Era apologised. Her eyes were lowered as she spoke and she looked sheepish. 'I do try but I just can't eat that much food in a day.'

'I know it's hard Era, but if your body doesn't get all this nutrition now you will suffer later on.'

'But I feel fine,' she began to argue. I cut her off, 'You might feel fine now but it's a gradual effect. By the time you actually feel low on energy it will be too late to do anything about it. You have to replenish your energy every day.'

'I know, I know,' she replied impatiently. She had heard the same lecture a hundred times – a fact which made it even more infuriating that she continued to ignore the advice. 'I will try harder,' she promised. I couldn't be too hard on Era as most team members had struggled to a greater or lesser extent to finish all our daily rations – even I had a kilogram of uneaten peanuts in my sledge that I hadn't managed to eat – but Era was the smallest, physically, in the team and I worried that she was the most likely to suffer from exhaustion if she didn't eat a proper intake of protein, carbohydrate and fat.

Steph, dressed in her thermal tights and elf-like booties, was the first to delve into the resupply bags. Her head totally disappeared within the cavernous bags so that her bum was stuck high into the air; she looked like an ardent sale shopper looking for a bargain. She eventually emerged, brandishing aloft a well-sealed waterproof bag in the air above her head like a trophy. 'Oh my God. Clean underwear,' she exclaimed, her voice wavering with excitement.

She delivered the various bags to their respective owners in the tents and I could hear the squeals of delight and exclaims of relief as they were gratefully received. It was our first change of clothes in three weeks. 'I can *smell* detergent,' I heard Reena enthuse as she ripped open her bag of undies. 'Mmm, it's like fresh flowers.' The fact that the smell of newly washed clothes seemed to hang in the air inside the tents for the rest of the evening is an indication of just how dirty we were. In the resupply we also found the modest treats we had packed for ourselves: a party pack of cheesy nachos, a block of cheddar and a fruit cake.

After eating exactly the same food, every day, for 15 days, the thought of something different to eat was as mouth-watering as the finest delicacy. We gathered together in one tent to gorge ourselves on the treats, as well as the choicest bits from Era's excess rations. While squeezed together, munching and laughing, we rang Patriot Hills for our daily call and triumphantly announced our arrival at the resupply. 'Well done, girls!' congratulated the operator. 'You've done really, really well. Everyone here is very proud of you!' The praise made seven already grinning faces beam even more.

The operator handed the satellite telephone to the doctor who was standing by to check on our medical condition. Helen asked to speak to him and as she started describing the difficulties she'd been having with her blisters I could hear her voice begin to crack with emotion at the memory of the pain she'd endured while skiing. Suddenly Helen let the satellite phone fall from her hand and covered her face as she broke into a loud sob. I passed the telephone to Era and pulled Helen towards me into a hug. I felt her body shake as she cried quietly and I hoped she was releasing some of the frustration she felt at the condition of her feet. When Helen recovered, she decided, after a long consultation with the doctor, that the blisters on her feet were infected and that she should take antibiotics. I disagreed with the diagnosis. Helen's toes were the pink of newly formed skin rather than the red of infection but I couldn't see what harm it would do to have Helen take antibiotics if she wanted to and so said nothing. I had no idea what a mistake this would turn out to be.

The satellite phone was passed around the tent as one team member after another gave a detailed account of their aches and pains. Listening to the report given by the women, it sounded as if we were all on the brink of hospitalisation. A sore muscle was described as a 'sprain', an aching hip as a 'strain' – neither of which was strictly true.

'There seem to be quite a few concerns,' the doctor warned me at the end of the call. 'I know you've been making great progress but you might want to think about slowing the pace and taking some more rest days. Remember you don't have to ski. It's OK to walk.'

I was grateful for the doctor's advice but also resented his insinuation that I was pushing the team too hard. I spent my whole day pondering the fitness of the team and the options available to us from walking rather than skiing (which so far hadn't been practical due to the soft snow), to having a rest day, to the redistribution of weight in our sledges, to stopping early, to starting late. Despite the bleak picture the team had painted of their condition to the doctor the reality was that they were actually in great shape considering the distance we had covered. All the injuries were minor, only one or two women were taking painkillers regularly and we were still moving well. To expect to be without any injury whatsoever after skiing more than 300 kilometres was simply unrealistic. The phone call made me realise that I had to make sure the team understood how well they were doing. If they began to think we were a hobbling bunch of invalids this would affect their confidence and fragile morale.

Later that evening I noticed Kylie standing apart from the tent looking absently at the mountains. The hood of her down jacket was pulled tight around her face to keep her ears warm but her tightly plaited pigtails still protruded from either side of her jaw, the ends dusted with snow. She smiled as I approached and we both watched the silver reflection of the sun that smeared the tops of the mountains. 'I hobbled into camp, literally hobbled,' she said.

I made a sympathetic noise but was confused. I had watched Kylie ski the last few hundred yards to the depot and although she had been slow, she hadn't been limping – but it was unlike Kylie to exaggerate. She seemed generally subdued and I wondered if there was something else on her mind. 'Is everything OK?' I asked tentatively. 'In the tent, I mean.'

Kylie looked at her feet which were smoothing rounds into the snow and hesitated before replying. I could tell that she was fighting her natural instinct to say nothing. She didn't want to complain or make a fuss. She looked up and I could see tears in her eyes. 'Helen is an awesome lady but if she isn't talking, she's snoring.' I saw her look at me to judge my reaction. Both

Kylie and Helen had made pointed comments about each other to me repeatedly since we had left Punta. They were never overtly critical of each other but it was clear that their relationship was tense.

I put my hand on her shoulder in sympathy and I could see the relief in her body language as she continued. I listened as she let go of the irritations that had been building over the last few weeks. 'From the moment we wake up we're hearing about her blisters and although I'm really sympathetic – it must be awful – I just wish we could talk about something else sometimes. There's just no escape.' Her eyes searched the horizon as if looking for the right words. 'I'm sorry Felicity, I'm just feeling a bit sorry for myself.'

I smiled at her and put my arm round her shoulders. 'That's OK. It's allowed.' I knew that Kylie was not being malicious. This was not a clash of personality, just the result of living so closely with one another for so long. 'Kylie, I can mix around the tent groups. I'll say that it was always in the plan to move everyone around at this stage so that no one will ever know that you have said anything but in the mix I'll make sure that you and Helen are in different tents.'

 Before I had finished Kylie was already shaking her head, 'No, I've realised that my challenge on this expedition is not physical, it's mental. For me it won't be the skiing or the distance or the cold that will be the struggle, it will be this.' I didn't entirely understand her reasoning and emphasised how easy it would be to make a reshuffle of the groups seem completely natural but she was adamant, 'This is my test,' she said. 'It'll be fine.'

I considered taking an executive decision and reshuffling the groups anyway, regardless of Kylie's protestations, but I hesitated. Reshuffling the groups would cause disruption to the systems and routines that were now working so efficiently and to switch everyone around would take time and organisation. In the other tent, Era, Sophia and Steph worked really well together and we enjoyed each other's company. I knew how much I myself relied on their camaraderie to keep me going each day and felt disappointed for Kylie that she wasn't having the same experience.

I opened my eyes the next morning but didn't move. Silently I watched the gloves, goggles and watches hung on the washing line above me dance in the gentle vibration of the tent caused by the low wind outside. Pulling my sleeping bag closer under my chin I luxuriated in the warmth and the knowledge that I could stay like this for as long as I wanted today; it was our rest day. My last instruction to the team the night before had been to sleep as deeply and for as long as possible. I let myself float in and out of consciousness, ignoring the gentle nagging in my bladder. By now our bodies had become so attuned to our normal routine that we were not to be allowed a completely uninterrupted lie-in. I heard Sophia ease herself out of her sleeping bag, slip on some boots and disappear outside. Era soon followed suit. I heard them both return and hung on for as long as possible before giving in myself and blearily tripping out of the tent. The abrasive cold of the breeze searing across my cheeks soon banished any sluggishness as I blinked in the intense sunshine. For a moment the landscape was obliterated in the concentrated light like an overexposed photograph. Despite my reluctance, it felt good to be up. Today I could enjoy the miracle of our surroundings without the pressing need to pack up the tent and rush towards the horizon. Today, I didn't even need to look at my watch. Today, I could take my time.

Back in the tent Steph still lay motionless in her sleeping bag while Sophia sat in her habitual cross-legged position at the far end of the tent. Bent over the kitchen area, she quietly lit stoves and put water on to boil for breakfast. Sophia was so efficient in her role looking after the stoves that I often worried that we took advantage of her but on the few occasions I asked if she wanted to swap roles for the day she looked horrified. 'No, this is my relaxation. I sit and listen to everyone else talking and am happy doing my jobs. Compared to looking after the kids at home, this is a holiday!' she laughed.

Today, Era sat close to Sophia and whispered conspiratorially as she sorted through the ration bags. Holding up three bags of instant noodles in wordless triumph, she grinned at me in excitement across the tent. It was clear that Era and Sophia were planning to treat themselves to noodles for breakfast rather than the normal porridge. No fan of porridge myself, I joined them. As we munched our Asian-style breakfast in companionable silence I took out our communal notebook and looked at my mileage calculations scribbled in pencil onto the back pages. So far we had done exceedingly well, meeting or beating our daily targets so that we had arrived at the resupply with a whole day to spare. We now had 300 nautical miles to cover to reach the South Pole and were expected to arrive on New Year's Day in 25 days' time. Using the mileage we had covered on a daily basis over the last two weeks as a guide I began to set daily targets for the rest of our journey, taking into account the fact that our sledges would get lighter as we progressed but also that we would be getting slowly more tired as time went on.

Polar travel is a war of attrition. Each day you spend in the polar environment your body will weaken just a little. You can slow the process by looking after yourself but nothing can entirely eliminate the gradual deterioration. While I favoured the slow and steady approach in order to conserve our energy and stamina for as long as possible, I was also mindful that the longer we spent out on the ice, the weaker we would get. I didn't want to rush but neither did I want to drag out our journey for longer than was necessary. I estimated that, even allowing for the team slowing due to tiredness and injury, we could cover the remaining distance in just 22 days. I allowed ourselves a rest day which we would take whenever the weather was too bad to travel or, if we hadn't needed it beforehand, to take on Christmas Day.

I explained my calculations to the whole team as we sat around in the sun-warmed tent later that morning. As the others munched absently on cheesy nachos, propped up against the tent walls with pillows made from sleeping bags, they gave their verdict. Sophia looked serious but shrugged as she spoke as if to indicate her compliance with whatever we decided as a group. 'I am a conservative person so my instinct is that we should cover as many miles as we can now while we are strong so that we have lots of miles in the bank. We don't know what will happen in the future.'

Era nodded enthusiastically as Sophia spoke. Having wanted to go faster since the very beginning it was no surprise that she favoured the flat-out strategy. Brandishing a pencil she outlined her own calculations. 'If we do sixteen nautical miles every day and go without a rest day we can be at the pole in just nineteen days.' She grinned at the rest of the team as their mouths fell open. I think even Era knew that her calculations were recklessly ambitious.

Helen was quick to give the opposite view. She still felt that we should set a slower pace. 'Some people go a lot faster than others. My feet were ruined on that last leg when Felicity went speeding off,' she said.

I felt a flash of offence at her unexpected criticism. I waited until she had finished her comments before I replied, choosing my words carefully and trying hard to keep the annoyance out of my voice. 'Helen, your feet were ruined long before you arrived in Antarctica. I want to be clear that nothing that has happened on this expedition has been the cause of the condition of your feet.'

I resented the insinuation that I was responsible for the condition of Helen's feet. 'I'm aware that pace is becoming a contentious issue,' I continued, addressing the team through the assorted gloves, hats and goggles hung in the centre of the tent. 'We've each got to remind ourselves that a lot of this is all in our heads. It often feels like someone is leading a fast pace on a particular leg and yet it was actually the slowest of the day. I make sure on a daily basis that no one goes outrageously slow or outrageously fast – that's my job. At the moment the slowest leg is around 2.6 nautical miles and the fastest ever was 3.1 nautical miles – that is not a huge difference. In fact, looking at our progress, we have been incredibly steady and our consistency is something we can be proud of – believe me.' I looked around at the team. Helen nodded in agreement but I wondered if she had really taken on board what I had said. Some looked down at their boots absently picking at threads or studied the faces around them. I decided this was a good time to broach the issue of morale that had worried me the day before. 'Guys, please don't lose sight of how well we are doing,' I continued. 'I know that most of you have some kind of niggling injury but considering how far we have skied, we are in rude health. I packed enough ibuprofen and paracetamol for every team member to be on maximum painkillers by this point. We've not even touched the stronger stuff and we haven't needed to unpack the painkillers from the resupply. We are doing a lot better than expected – you should be really proud of that.' The mood lifted a little in the tent and there were a few smiles but it was clear that the crux of the problem lay with Kylie, Helen and Reena. If I didn't address their dip in morale, it was going to spread to the rest of the team.

Now that we had arrived at the resupply the previous 15 days felt like they had been the ultimate training expedition. I was determined that we would use what we had learnt to make sure we were better prepared for the second stage of our expedition than we had been at the start. The biggest job of the day was counting out ration bags for the next 23 days, making sure each tent had the right number of dinner, breakfast and day bags. As Sophia sorted the ration bags for our tent into piles I counted and recounted them, asking Steph and Era to count them again as they packed them into our four sledges. Walking over to Helen, Kylie and Reena's tent, Helen ran through with me what they had prepared, particularly the number of breakfast, dinner and day bags that had been loaded into each sledge.

By mid afternoon all the jobs had been finished and everyone was enjoying a stomach-bloating lunch of leftover rations followed by an indulgent siesta. Having made myself a comfy nest from my down jacket and sleeping bag, every fibre of my body seemed to be compelling my eyes to close and to join the others in a snooze. I listened to the quiet breathing of my tent-mates and smiled as I realised I could hear snoring from the other tent even though it was pitched 10 metres away. As I listened it dawned on me that I could hear something else; a low mechanical whine. My eyes shot open as I recognised the sound. I flung on my jacket and slipped in my rush to pull open the tent door. Leaning out, I craned my neck to scan the sky. I blinked for a moment to be sure before ducking my head back inside. 'Guys, wake up. It's a plane!'

There were whoops of excitement as the suddenly awake team fought each other to put on boots and hats in the confined space of the tent. I shook the other tent awake too and soon there were seven red-clad figures jumping up and down on the spot and waving wildly as the brightly coloured Twin Otter flew low over our heads before circling dramatically to our south and landing in a puff of propeller-blown snow and ice. The plane emerged out of the haze and taxied towards us, its metal skis blasting a path through the sastrugi, sending large slabs of snow flying into the air.

The plane stopped, the engines cut and we gathered in a huddle beneath its wing as the doors opened and two pilots jumped from the plane. We recognised them from Patriot Hills: they worked for ALE and had dropped in at the resupply depot on their way back from the South Pole to pick up all our rubbish and unwanted equipment. As we said our hellos there was a certain amount of nudging and laughing among the team as one of the men turned out to be the young pilot Steph had particularly noticed during our time at Patriot Hills. He flashed a smile beneath his mirrored aviators and if we could have seen his eyes I'm sure he would have winked. 'I'd watch out,' Kylie warned him, 'you're the first men we've seen in over a fortnight.' The two pilots suddenly looked a little nervous at the seven advancing women.

We loaded the red resupply bags full of unwanted equipment, rubbish and leftover rations onto the plane. Last of all to be loaded was the large plastic sack full of bulging silver packets – our Louis Poo-uittons. The pilot looked confused, 'What are they?' he asked. He didn't seem impressed as we explained. 'Toxic material can't be flown like this,' he said. 'It has to be packed in a certain way so that it can be flown safely.' Slightly panicked at the prospect of having to carry the large sack of waste for another 600 kilometres, I started to reassure him how securely the contents were contained in the Louis Poo-uittons. Kylie backed me up until finally the pilot relented and allowed us to load the bag onto the plane.

'Hang on!' called Steph running towards us with a silver bag in her outstretched hand. She popped the bag into the sack, grinning cheekily, 'One last deposit before you go.' It was a good point. Anything excreted after the plane left would have to be carried. I noticed one or two other team members disappear quietly to follow her lead.

We all stood and watched as the plane took off, bouncing over the snow as it retraced its own tracks, picking up speed as it went. Soaring into the air, the plane made an impressive arc to face us and flew low over the tents once more – so low that we all reflexively ducked as the plane's shadow rippled over us. It slowly diminished to a black dot in the blue sky and the team fell strangely quiet. The arrival of the plane had been a reminder that another world did still exist beyond our daily routine of tents and stoves. It felt like being unexpectedly woken in the middle of the night to see something extraordinary. I felt pleased for the experience but somehow wished I'd been left alone. After the excitement it is always a lot harder to fall asleep again and similarly our white world suddenly seemed very lonely.

I carefully dialled the number of Tim Moss, one half of our support team back in the UK. He answered after just two rings. Tim's job while we were away was to update the expedition website each day with the news and podcasts we sent home over the satellite phone. Today we'd arranged to talk so that he could deliver to the team some of the messages that had been left on the website by family, friends and supporters. I relayed each message to the girls who wedged themselves into the one tent.

As I listened to the first message I noticed the expectant hush in the tent. Although in theory the satellite phone allowed us to ring any telephone number in the world any time we wished, we'd agreed as a team that we wouldn't contact our families. It was just too hard to be in the room with loved ones in one moment and then, in the next, be thousands of miles away. Instead we had agreed to have messages on our rest day and although nobody had spoken about it, I knew everyone had been looking forward to this moment more than they dared admit.

We each knew it was going to be an emotional experience and so, it was with a collective deep breath that I relayed the first message. 'This one's for Steph,' I began. Steph's face broke into an instant smile and I could feel her eyes on me. 'It's from your Uncle Dinja in America. He says they are following your progress and are very proud of you.' Steph's smile grew broader and she dropped her gaze, looking at the ground in an attempt to control the tears welling in her eyes. Kylie rubbed Steph's shoulder in comfort, all of us feeling the potent echo of Steph's private emotion.

'Reena,' I continued. 'Your friends say "Buck up, Reena!"' We all laughed at what appeared to be a rather brutal message but Reena explained that the meaning had been slightly lost in translation. 'Buck up' is a term of warm encouragement in India.

There was a message for Kylie but Tim seemed a bit confused. 'This one seems to be in code,' he said. 'AB12SA4.' I repeated the code to Kylie who laughed loudly before explaining. 'It's the rugby score! All Blacks twelve, South Africa four.'

In the morning the sky was as grey as the snow. The dark shadow of the mountains away to our west was the only indication of the position of the horizon. As I stood in the ruins of our camp, the tent already rolled and secured to the top of my sledge, I faced southwards and carefully pushed my balaclava and goggles into place, making sure that every layer overlapped to leave not the tiniest gap. The wind blew gently but consistently in my face, already pressing the cold material of my balaclava onto my skin. It was going to be a tough day and I sensed that the team thought the same. They were unusually subdued as they pressed their boots into their ski bindings, pulled on gloves and adjusted sledge harnesses. I gathered them together for a rallying cry, pronouncing each word carefully and slowly so that they would hear me over the wind. 'One day at a time. Let's make this the best day yet.' There was a muffled cheer and we led off, leaning ourselves forward in our harnesses to feel the tug of newly laden sledges for the first time. With rations and fuel for 23 days our sledges were heavier at that point than at any other on the expedition and we were all a bit nervous about what difference it would make to the exertion of the day.

We fell into line and moved forward slowly into the murk. The cloud cover had obliterated all contrast in the snow surface so that we tripped over unseen sastrugi and were forced to focus on the back of the sledge in front simply to give us an indication of whether we were stepping up or down. With nothing to look at and no possibility of talking to each other, each of us disappeared into our own internal worlds, lost in our own thoughts. It was a flat-light day of the worst kind that made time slow to a crawl. It felt like we were barely moving and I would have despaired if not for a few private glances at the GPS which showed that we were actually right on our target for the day.

After leading her leg of the day, Steph was keen to know how fast she had been going but I feigned ignorance. 'It's just that it felt like I was going really, really slowly,' she pleaded. Stepping out of the line and slowing down so that she was skiing next to me, she leaned forward conspiratorially, somehow guessing that I knew more than I was letting on. 'Was it less than two nautical miles?' she asked. I laughed but said nothing. 'Don't tell me it was less than one nautical mile,' she exclaimed, horrified. 'I'll shoot myself if I was going slower than that.' Concentrating too much on me and not on her skiing, Steph's probing was ended by a fall.

Reena, leading the line, paused to check we were OK but I waved her on as I helped Steph to her feet. Disentangling all her elasticated attachments took longer than I anticipated and, by the time we were moving again, the team were already quite a long way ahead. As we watched the ribbon of skiers ahead of us, the line seemed to bend in a curve to the right. The group stopped and even from a distance we could see there was some discussion going on. Skiing towards the team in silence Steph and I watched as the theatre unfolded. Two figures branched off to the left, while a third continued towards the right. The two remaining figures looked undecided, following the determined figure to the right before changing their mind and veering left. Realising she was outnumbered the determined solitary figure eventually gave in and followed the others on their bearing to the left. Steph and I laughed together at the performance. 'See,' shouted Steph, 'you leave them for five minutes and it's chaos.'

The weather stayed flat and gloomy for the rest of the day. Featureless cloud cover formed milky swirls around the sun so that it was as faint as the moon. At the end of the fifth leg we stopped for our seven-minute break and I decided to let the others in on the secret of our progress. Skiing to the front of the halted group, I ripped open the front of my face mask and unhitched my sledge. The team looked at me suspiciously; this was bizarre behaviour when we still had at least 90 minutes of skiing to go. 'Guys, I have some good news and some better news.' I held the GPS aloft, displaying the distance we had travelled since our last camp. 'We've already skied twelve nautical miles, which is four more than our target for the day.' I watched with delight as Sophia's mouth literally fell open in surprise.

'Wow!' shouted Reena, releasing a booming laugh of shock.

'And the better news is that I don't think we should go any further today, so this is camp.' There were cheers of agreement all round and a ripple of chatter as everyone pulled icy masks from their faces and fished warm jackets from their sledges. No one could believe that we had been travelling at our normal pace; it had felt so slow. I hoped the surprise had made a point about our perception of our speed – it could be very deceptive.

As we rolled out the tents and set up camp for the night the mood within the team felt buoyant. Helen had finally agreed to take the stronger painkillers along with her antibiotics that morning and the release from the pain in her feet was like an epiphany. She danced around the camp, laughing and joking like the Helen we knew. Kylie too was on top form. Before setting out that morning we had worked together on a new position of her boot in her ski binding. The unnatural position would eventually ruin the boot but it had given Kylie instant relief. It looked like we had found a solution to the 'evil ski' at last and Kylie was delighted. I smiled in pleasure to see Helen and Kylie arm in arm as they took pictures with Reena outside their tent. My chest swelled with sudden emotion. 'Everything is going to be OK,' I told myself with relief.

Ironic then, that the next day started with a crisis.

Sitting in the porch of the tent, my head still thick with sleep, I was working with cold, unresponsive fingers at the laces of my boots when I heard footsteps in the snow outside. With a blast of cold air and a flurry of snow, Kylie unzipped the tent door and perched herself on a ledge of snow in the porch opposite me. She pushed her hat back from a forehead creased with lines of worry. She looked nervous. 'I think we might have accidentally left some food bags behind,' she said in a quiet voice. A shot of panic flew through me like a lightning bolt. I paused to get my instant reaction under control before replying. It was too early to panic; I needed more information. I followed Kylie out of the tent to where Helen and Reena were already outside busy with their sledges. They came over as I approached and I noticed the expression on Reena's face. She looked heartbroken and already close to tears.

'I should have all the breakfast bags but I'm five short,' Kylie started to explain. Each bag not only contained breakfast for the three of them but also the sports drinks that we mixed into our water for additional carbohydrate and calories as well as the daily ration of toilet tissue. Five bags short would mean five days in which half the team would be starting a day skiing without having eaten; and five days in which they would have significantly less carbohydrates to keep them going.

'There's no reason why they shouldn't be here,' Helen interrupted. 'They were all in a pile at the back of the tent for Kylie to pack in her sledge.'

'I packed what was left out for me,' Kylie retorted quickly. 'I didn't leave anything outside the tent. There was nothing left behind.'

'It would have been better if we'd known about it yesterday. I don't think we should conceal things from each other,' Helen continued pointedly.

I saw the colour in Kylie's face change, 'I haven't concealed anything. I said to you in the tent last night that I thought there weren't enough food bags in my sledge but I couldn't check it out till this morning. There was no point saying anything until I knew for sure.'

I listened in silence but as the exchange got heated I stepped in.

'I don't care whose fault it was,' I said coldly. 'What matters now is solutions. I want to see every single food bag you have, laid out in piles so that I can see exactly what we're missing.'

'We've already checked. We have everything except the breakfast bags that Kylie was supposed to pack in her sledge,' answered Helen.

'I want to see for myself,' I replied firmly, glaring at the three of them.

They turned to empty their sledges and I returned to my tent, squatting in the porch as I asked the rest of the team to sort out any spare ration bags we had, particularly breakfast bags.

Reena, Kylie and Helen stood to one side like disgraced

soldiers as I counted the food bags they had laid out in the snow. 'Are you sure this is everything?' I asked without looking at them. 'Have you checked in the tent? Does this include today's rations?' They nodded glumly. They were missing five entire breakfast bags. Making rapid calculations in my head I worked out that we had just enough emergency rations to see them through to the end of the expedition – if our progress stayed on target – but it would mean that the team were without any spares whatsoever and just increased the pressure on us to reach the South Pole by Day 38 as planned. I let out a long breath of relief but with the relief came anger. This was exactly the kind of flippant carelessness that I had warned against from the start and it came from the most experienced members of the team who should know better. I turned to face the girls as they stood in a row like guilty schoolchildren. 'This is a major fuck-up,' I said in a steady but emphatic voice. 'This carelessness could have cost us the expedition.' I paused to study their faces. It was clear from their mortified expressions that I didn't have to press home the seriousness of the mistake.

'We left the bags outside the tent for Kylie to pack,' insisted Helen.

I cut her off. 'I don't care, Helen. You are all responsible. I'm responsible for not triple-checking what you told me you'd packed. What annoys me more than the mistake is that all three of you have stood here blaming each other.'

Kylie and Helen looked at each other. Reena started to cry. 'We're sorry Felicity,' she said in a quiet voice. I didn't want apologies. I was too angry for that. Sorry was easy after the event; what I needed was for these mistakes not to happen in the first place. I paused for a second, pressing my lips together. There was clearly no point in venting my frustration at them; they already felt bad enough.

'Now that we've found a solution, the worst possible outcome of this is that it causes a rift between you. Don't let that happen. You can't change what has happened but you can change how you deal with it. Each of you need to forgive each other, accept that it was a mistake and move on. We've still got a long way to go and I need you guys working together. OK?'

There were murmurs of agreement. Helen's shoulders were shaking and I knew she was crying behind her goggles.

'And for God's sake, be more careful. We can't afford any more mistakes.'

I turned away and busied myself with my sledge. I wondered if I had been too reasonable but there seemed little point in shouting and screaming. They knew what a lucky escape we'd had. I kicked myself for my own part in it. Thinking back to the day we had sorted the resupply I had let Helen talk me through what they had done but I hadn't checked for myself. I should have made sure I laid eyes on every single food bag. I sighed in frustration. It felt like I couldn't win. On the one hand I didn't want to be a complete control freak; it was important that the team did things for themselves and that I trusted them. But then, on the other hand, the expedition had nearly come to an early close because I hadn't personally checked on every detail. Perhaps I had been too trusting in my novice team. Perhaps it was me who was getting nonchalant.

As we set off towards another metal grey smudge of a horizon I tucked myself into my usual position at the back of the line and fumed silently within my hood and face-covering. I knew I had to concentrate on getting rid of the pointless anger that still gripped my insides.

My thoughts were interrupted by a sudden shiver. I concentrated on my fingers for a moment. They had got cold and needed some attention. I wrapped my numb digits inside my palm and shook the warm blood in my arm down into my fist by punching the air beneath me as I skied. I was usually warm enough when skiing but now I could feel the chill on my back and down my thighs. I shortened my stride, picking up my feet to make my body work harder and warm itself with the extra exertion. Glancing down the line I noticed that Kylie was wearing her mitts, which was unusual, and Sophia hadn't taken off her fleece, which she would normally have done by this stage in the leg. The cause dawned on me gradually. We were moving very slowly. The line was all bunched up so that I could hear the occasional tap of a ski-tip on the sledge in front and several members were shaking their arms or hopping on their skis to keep warm. I waved an outstretched ski pole to send a message down the line to Helen, who was leading, to speed up slightly.

The line stopped abruptly as Helen readjusted her clothing before moving on again at a noticeably quicker pace. We were skiing quite fast but I was warming up and I was sure the pace would settle before long. As the minutes passed I felt the stretch in my muscles as I struggled to keep up with the sledge in front. I noticed some gaps opening up in the line and felt myself breaking into a sweat. The pace showed no sign of slowing; in fact, it seemed to be getting faster. We were now skiing flat out, something we never did. What was going on? After ten minutes, with no let up in the pace and the line beginning to break up, I waved my outstretched arm giving the signal for slowing down. The line stopped abruptly and I saw ski poles being thrown into the snow by someone at the front. Alarmed, I skied past the team to the front of the line to find Helen in a state. 'I don't know what you want from me anymore,' she shouted at the team in general. 'I'm obviously completely incompetent to lead the team.'

I was shocked. I had never seen Helen so upset.

'Helen, what is the matter?'

'First you say to go faster, then I have to slow down. I don't know what to do anymore.'

She ripped off her mittens and threw them into the snow next to her ski poles. Lifting her goggles she covered her face with her hands and burst into tears. I blinked in shock for a few seconds before turning to the rest of the team who were looking on in stunned silence. 'Guys, let's have a break for ten minutes. Put on your jackets and have something to eat and drink. But don't get cold.'

I helped Helen unhitch her sledge and led her a small distance from the team so that we were out of earshot. She'd stopped crying and had clearly calmed down a little. 'I'm just trying to do what everyone wants,' she started but I interrupted. I felt let down by her outburst but realised that sympathy and some comfort was what she needed right now.

'Helen, this hasn't got anything to do with our pace. This is all about you feeling angry with yourself for the breakfast being left behind. Do you agree?'

Helen didn't answer but took a deep breath and studied the horizon behind me.

'It doesn't matter now whose fault it was that the breakfast got left behind. It's one of those things and now we've found a solution you have to forget about it. We all have to move on.' I paused before giving her a big hug. 'You've just had a bad day, that's all.' Helen nodded silently and wiped her eyes. I left her to drink some water and eat some food as I skied back along the line to speak to the team who were waiting quietly.

'I want to draw a line under all this rubbish about our pace. You each know what speed to set when you lead and you know what to do if you want the lead to slow down. No one is going too fast or too slow; so let's just get on with it.' I was addressing the team but I raised my voice enough so that Helen could hear me clearly.

There were nods of agreement along the line and as we moved off once more I felt like we had made a breakthrough. The unspoken disagreement about our speed had reached a climax and we were finally rid of it for good, I hoped.

CHAPTER ELEVEN

SASTRUGI LAND

My vision had been reduced to a tiny sliver just above my right eye. The rest had been obliterated by a creeping layer of ice forming on the inside of my goggles. It was a daily occurrence and on some days no amount of adjusting my face-covering or funnelling warm breath away from my goggles could prevent it happening – it was just a matter of time. During the last break I had tried removing my goggles and chipping away at the ice with my gloved fingers but it only seemed to have made the problem worse. If I tilted my head forward a little, I could still see just enough to follow the sledge in front and ski in the team's tracks. At the next break I decided I would have to swap to my spare goggles and hope that by the time they too iced up, my first pair would have cleared. Otherwise, I'd be as good as blind.

Despite my limited view there was nothing to hide the hill that lay ahead. With every step forward it seemed to bulge further out of the ground like an exaggerated boil growing out of a cartoon character's head. Without any features like trees and houses to give a sense of scale there was no way of knowing how big the hill was or how far away it might be. Sometimes we would march towards a hill all day never to reach it; at others the ground would seem to scoop into a near vertical wall ahead of us only to turn out to be a mirage. As I watched the slope in front tower ever further into the sky I prayed silently, 'Please be a mirage, please be a mirage.'

Since leaving the resupply a few days before it felt like we had done nothing but climb hills. From our maps we knew that over our 900-kilometre route we would need to gain considerable altitude from our start at sea level to the South Pole which sits at around 3,000 metres on a huge dome of ice – but we hadn't expected to do it all at once. During the first half of the expedition we had gained over 1,000 metres but almost imperceptibly. In a landscape that was more optical illusion than reality, often the only indication that we were climbing was a slight burn in our thighs, the suspicion that we were inexplicably slowing down and the nagging notion that our sledges felt a bit heavier. Once or twice we had stopped for the day with the unshakeable impression that we were camped on the top of a hill but without any evidence to back up our instinct. Looking behind us I might imagine that I could see slightly more of our tracks than usual slithering away to the horizon, or perhaps have a slightly higher prospective of the sastrugi that stretched away in all directions but there was no way of knowing for sure.

Over the last couple of days, the hills had been unmistakable. They'd show up on the horizon as a slightly darker band of snow before growing into a morphing giant blocking our path. The evidence of our rise and fall was all too clear in the Thiel Mountains that still hovered on the horizon to our right. As we climbed, the mountains would appear to draw closer, revealing new summits and plateaux, while at other times they'd disappear below the horizon completely. The first time I glanced to my right to find a blemish-free horizon and the mountains gone, I felt a kind of panic, as if discovering that we'd lost a vital piece of equipment. Then as they began to come and go, seemingly at will, I began to wish we could shake them off for good; their presence was a continual reminder of our ponderous progress.

'I can see a crocodile about to eat something,' Kylie mused as we sat on our sledges chewing in silence during a break. She pointed to the mountains with her ski pole. 'There is its head, its back and its tail.' While some of the team were too engrossed in the delicate process of breaking open their frozen face masks to deliver food to their mouths, one or two turned to look.

'Yes, yes, I see it!' Reena agreed enthusiastically. 'No! It is a man on his back. See?'

After a week of gloomy weather, it had become sparkling once again. The severity of the sun turned the sky a concentrated blue and threw shadows from sastrugi that were so sharp that you could pick out every detail in the snow surface for what seemed like miles. It was still cold but the calm weather made the skiing hot work. This meant that while our bodies needed the freedom to perspire, our extremities (ears, hands and faces) needed warmth and protection. This led to a number of strange clothing choices along the line. Most of us skied in just a thermal with our thin, ultra-lightweight smocks over the top but Sophia, feeling the chill on her front, wore a fleece jacket backwards so that her back was open to the air. Our warm salopettes could be vented by opening long zips that ran down the sides. Most of us looked like Sinbad the Sailor with our unzipped trouser legs flaring but Kylie went one step further by tucking the free trouser legs into her waist harness. Her skinny little legs in tight thermal long johns stuck out from underneath her skirt of salopettes giving her the appearance of a Shakespearean actor in period costume.

The clear, calm days made camping on the ice almost a pleasure. Pitching our tents without fear of them blowing away, we could lay our icy kit out on the top of the tents to dry in the sun or suspended from our skis, which were speared into the snow like upright javelins. Steph and I took our time securing the outside of the tent, enjoying the feel of the sun through our warm down jackets and stopping to lounge on the sleeping bags which had been laid out on the snow to air. It was good to feel the sun's rays on our faces as we tipped them towards the big blue above. Thin wisps of cloud scored the sky, drawing together towards a single vanishing point as if sucking the whole universe towards the horizon. It looked like we were watching the eddies of a stream in freeze-frame, the vast speed and size of the processes happening above us captured in a snapshot. Four small but vibrant rainbows flecked the points of the compass around the sun, leaping out at us from the streaky blue of the sky. They were perfectly formed but shortened as if a normal rainbow had been snipped into four equal parts and placed around the sun to frame it. They were sun dogs, the faithful companions of the sun who are only ever seen dancing around their master, never too close but never too far. Steph and I watched the dramatic skyscape unfold until she broke the silence. 'Thanks, Felicity.'

'For what?' I asked confused.

'For this,' she answered with a grin.

I couldn't help smiling. For all the stress and heartache and gruelling monotony I was glad that she was still able to see the miracle in what we were doing. I thought back to the first day I'd met Steph. She'd burst into the interview looking like she'd come straight from playing a sports match and I'd been impressed by her casual confidence. Steph laughed at my memory. 'Errr... I have an admission to make,' she said nervously. 'I was wearing trackpants because I'd been out all night and was terribly hung-over. I only woke up just in time to make it to the interview, which is why I didn't have time to get dressed into something more formal.'

We both laughed. I had been totally fooled. Knowing Steph as I now did, the story made absolute sense. Somehow the misunderstanding seemed rather fitting. Our first meeting in that over-heated glass-walled conference room two years ago felt like a different lifetime. It seemed impossible that there had been a time I hadn't known Steph or any of the other women. As we drifted back into our own thoughts I listened to the laughter and chatter coming from the two tents a short distance away. A wave of sudden clarity washed through me and I marvelled at this strange yet wonderful group of women I had gathered together. We were no longer Cypriot and Kiwi, Muslim and Hindu: we now had a common identity. I could feel the pride we each had in each other and the unspoken trust between us.

Laid out on our sleeping bags like overdressed sunbathers, it wasn't long before Steph and I both began to feel the chill. Even on a sunny, calm day like this one the cold gradually worked its way in through our layers of clothing and nibbled at the exposed skin of our faces. I stooped to enter through the curved door of the tent and was hit by a wave of heat from the stoves at the far end. Having followed me in, Steph was already stripping off her outer clothing so that she sat in just the thermal layer that we slept in. Obsessed with detecting any weight loss, she carefully inspected her hips and thighs. 'It's just not fair. I haven't lost any weight at all,' she moaned. I disagreed. I spent most of my days skiing behind Steph and had noticed a distinct change in her body shape. Her salopettes now noticeably hung from her hips. 'Believe me, Steph,' I insisted, 'your backside is my view most days, so I should know.' My own weight loss was rather less flattering. I'd noticed that there was a lot more room in my sports bra than there had been at the outset. I used my bra as a convenient extra pocket for the various batteries that Steph would share out between us every morning after re-charging them from our solar panel overnight. The batteries needed to be kept warm to conserve their charge, along with the lighter we each carried and our MP3 players. At the outset it had been quite a squeeze to fit one of the chunky video camera batteries down my front but I now noticed with disappointment that two fitted easily. Even so, I complained loudly when Steph handed me a third. 'If I can fit three video batteries down my front I really am in trouble,' I protested.

Era, like Steph, was disappointed in the results of our extreme weight-loss programme. 'I still have a fat face,' she said sadly, looking at herself in our tiny mirror. (The mirror was meant for looking for any signs of chilblains or frostnip on our faces but quickly became the most popular item in our first aid kit, closely followed by the tweezers.) I was concerned that this desire to lose weight might be a contributing factor in Era's continued struggle to finish her daily rations. Every day I made her show me what she had eaten and nagged at her to finish off her snack bags. I was aware that my nagging was getting on her nerves but ignored her glares across the tent as I insisted she keep eating. I risked pushing her goodwill even further by charging Kylie with the responsibility of being Era's break-buddy to check up on exactly how much she was eating each time we stopped. I didn't want to upset Era but the prospect of her failing to eat enough was just too serious to leave to chance. I'd noticed that Era wore her fleece-lined smock on days when everyone else was happy in a windproof and worried that her energy levels were already starting to wane, her lack of energy making her feel the cold more than everyone else.

That night I slept fitfully. In that strange state between alert and asleep I could hear footsteps in the snow outside and wondered absently why someone was walking around so much in the night.

Snow has an amazing ability to transmit sound. Even though the footsteps were perhaps a dozen metres away it seemed as if they were trampling the ground just a few inches from my ears. In the morning I wondered if I had imagined the mysterious wanderer until Reena mentioned that Helen hadn't been well. I found Helen already up and out of her tent, intently packing her sledge. I could tell from the slump in her shoulders that she was feeling down. 'I think it might be the sports drink powder that's upsetting my stomach,' she said unhappily. I thought it was more likely to be the antibiotics but Helen was unsure. 'I hope not because I've got to take the antibiotics for another ten days,' she said with a sigh.

That day, despite taking pills to stop the diarrhoea, every break turned into a toilet stop for Helen. That in itself was bad enough but it also left her with little time to eat or drink to keep up her energy. It wasn't long before a gap was opening up in the line ahead of her and even though the team slowed, she was still finding it hard to keep up. From the back of the line I watched her ski and noted with concern that she looked terribly frail, her padded clothing hanging limp from her shoulders. By the end of the day she was clearly exhausted. After completing five legs I stopped the team. Leaving my tent group to pitch our tent by themselves I joined Kylie and Reena, telling Helen to forget her jobs and get straight into her sleeping bag. My tone was firm as I expected her to put up a fight but her face looked drawn as she meekly conceded and lay down in the tent.

Emerging into the cold air the next morning I noticed that Helen was already up and about. She said that she felt better after a good sleep but her face still looked grey and her forehead was creased in a pained expression.

'I really think you ought to think about stopping the antibiotics,' I suggested.

'But what about my toe?'

I hesitated before speaking. I hadn't felt it my place to voice my doubts about her infection but now that the antibiotics were affecting her so badly, it was threatening the well-being of the team.

'Helen, I'm not sure your toe is infected. I think if it was infected you would have clearer signs by now.'

Helen answered lightly but looked thoughtful, 'Well, let's see how it goes today.'

I nodded but throughout the day my concern grew as yet more breaks saw Helen reaching for her Louis Poo-uitton. This added stress was the last thing her body needed, both mentally and physically. That evening I sat next to Helen in her tent, both of us peering at her blistered big toe. The adhesive bandage was still firmly stuck to her nail but as the damaged nail slowly came free we could see the skin beneath. There were none of the typical signs of infection; no angry red, no swelling or pus and although the newly formed skin was tender there was no pain.

With our inspection over, Helen sat back and looked at me in silence for a moment. 'I'm going to stop taking the antibiotics,' she said decisively. 'I can't be ill anymore. It's too draining.' I went back to my tent feeling relieved. Helen had made the right decision.

Without the antibiotics in her system her recovery was almost miraculous. The next morning she reported with pride that she had spent the evening fashioning a fake toenail out of a corner of our laminated Antarctic map to replace the nail she had lost. The fake toenail, complete with a snippit of latitude lines and the contours of a nunatak, stayed in place for the rest of the expedition.

We'd been warned about the sastrugi beyond the 87th line of latitude. There had been no shortage of tales about sastrugi taller than a man and so big that they could be seen from space. We'd had continuous sastrugi for the last four or five days but nothing that had warranted lifting the sledges by hand or any serious diversions from our habitually straight course. Even so, everyone was a little apprehensive about what lay ahead, each of us imagining our own personal nightmare.

It started with just one or two notably large sastrugi, clusters of perfectly curved, motionless waves all folded over each other to form large barrier-like sculptures. Sometimes they formed a ramp so that we were able to pass straight over them, like climbing over an ornate hump-backed bridge, but most of the time we were simply able to ski around them. Then, without noticing exactly when the change occurred, it seemed like one big sastrugi simply ran into another and by Day 27 we were completely surrounded by choppy peaks and miniature mountain ranges. Not only were the peaks and rises taller but the troughs were deeper and it became impossible to find a route between them that avoided the rough ground completely.

'It's like skiing across a giant, frozen meringue,' Helen commented flatly during a break. The metaphor made me laugh. It was a perfect visual description of the landscape around us but somehow seemed far too flippant for something causing us so much exhausting effort. 'We've entered sastrugi land,' she continued in the same flat voice.

I couldn't help but notice a ring of doom in her tone that made everyone survey the horizon sombrely for a second. Although the sastrugi were not as huge as those reported from previous seasons (and none of us could say whether they were big enough to be visible from space), they were certainly big enough to completely obscure Era from view on occasion and to make taking a turn at the front of the line even more demanding than usual. As well as keeping a close eye on our bearing southwards, the navigator had to pick a route through the never-ending obstacle course of sastrugi.

Most of us stuck to a relatively straight line, forging through the choppy ground and only deviating for the largest dips or rises. Kylie was different. She went to great lengths to lead the team around every lump and bump so that our tracks formed more of a squiggle than a dart. Although everyone appreciated her efforts to find the flattest route, it gradually dawned on us all that we were travelling miles further than necessary. I watched with private amusement as one day Era, skiing second in line, took decisive action. Ignoring Kylie's elaborate detours she crashed over the sastrugi creating her own, more direct route. At first the team weren't sure who to follow – you could almost hear the sound of critical thinking taking place – but eventually the entire line fell in behind Era taking the shorter route, unwilling to expend any effort skiing so much as one stride more than strictly necessary. Out in front, Kylie remained completely oblivious to the silent mutiny taking place behind her.

Unfortunately, no amount of careful route-finding could avoid all the uneven ground completely. We became used to coming across steep drops, our ski-tips protruding over the edge of the wind-sculpted ice like ski jumpers. The drops became known as 'penguin-jumps' because each of us in turn hesitated at the lip before committing ourselves, just like penguins leaping after each other into the sea. The drops were never more than a metre or two but they were never straightforward; there was often a second drop immediately after the first or a series of sharp fins of ice radiating across the run-out. Negotiating the penguin-jumps would be tough enough on skis without the extra burden of a fully laden sledge thundering at your heels. Mindful of the fact that until eight months ago few of the girls had so much as seen a pair of cross-country skis, I was anxious in case someone slipped and broke a bone or badly twisted an ankle. In fact, they each tackled the terrain with calm determination and – I noted with pride – surprising skill considering their lack of experience.

Skill there might have been but not grace. As sledges became jammed between ice formations, or slid off the sastrugi in unexpected directions, we scrambled to help each other but in our haste skis were often crossed, ski poles were jabbed into feet and harnesses became entangled. If someone's sledge was stuck after a penguin-jump it was often too late to prevent the next in line crashing into the back of them. It wasn't long before there were some spectacular falls. Steph launched herself from the top of one penguin-jump with a little too much enthusiasm and found her skis running up the far side of the trough. Unable to correct herself she fell, her head hitting the ground first with an audible crack. On another sastrugi Era misjudged the height of the drop and her ski-tips speared vertically into the snow beneath her, leaving her to fall woodenly over her own toes, face-planting spectacularly into the snowdrift.

Adding to the difficulty was the fact that the arrival of sastrugi land had not brought an end to the hills. As we closed in on the summit of the latest hill each of us would plead with our own deities to make it the last we would climb in Antarctica, only to be disappointed as another brownish strip of dirty-looking snow appeared on the horizon, signifying another hill in the distance. The repeated falls and the jerks of the sledges on our harnesses as we clambered over the uneven terrain put extra pressure on our already sore joints. It was clear to everyone that our bodies were beginning to feel the kilometres we had covered. We joked about the soreness in our muscles and the fact that we felt at least twice our age but the banter hid a deeper unspoken concern; we still had just under 200 nautical miles to cover and if we didn't reach an end to either the hills or sastrugi land soon, it was inevitable that something in our bodies was going to give.

Reena, at the front of the line, flung her ski poles into a cross above her head, stopping where she stood. The rest of the team

slowly concertinaed into a cluster around her, pulling their
sledges alongside them to form makeshift benches. I found myself
standing next to Sophia who was eating from her snack bag with
automaton determination.

'How are you doing, Sophia?' I asked casually.

She looked up and shrugged, 'The sastrugis are not so good. I
have to be careful of my knee.'

I had forgotten that the year before I met Sophia she had had
reconstructive surgery on the ligaments around her knee. It
had been a serious operation and although Sophia rarely made
reference to it, I got the impression that it weighed on her mind
much more than she allowed us to know. Sophia's face was hidden
behind her goggles and mask but her tone was full of concern.

'Every step I worry might be my last on this expedition,' she
said quietly.

It took me a moment to understand the meaning of her words
but the realisation was chilling. The rough ground was putting
such pressure on her reconstructed ligaments that every step she
took carried the potential of serious injury. Before I had time to
think of a reply our brief break was called to an end. There was no
time to probe further but as we reformed our line and began our
next leg, my thoughts dwelled on Sophia's words. I felt terrible
for not checking on her sooner. Sophia was so competent and
self-contained that it had been easy to assume that she was fine.
I had been watching others in the team so closely for any signs
of trouble that I hadn't appreciated the danger the rough ground
put on Sophia's relatively recent injury. The tone in Sophia's voice
had been unmistakeable. She was clearly seriously concerned
about the ability of her fragile knee to withstand the continual
punishment of the sastrugi. I knew Sophia well enough to know
that her words had not been dramatic for effect; she had stated
only the facts. I watched her ski in the line ahead of me and knew

that each placement of her ski-clad foot would be careful and deliberate. I had absolute confidence in Sophia that she would not be taking any chances but now I shared in her anxiety. I calculated that Sophia, with her shorter stride, took at least 30,000 steps in a day; each one carried the potential for harm. I couldn't imagine the mental strength required to concentrate so completely on one action for so long. That alone must have been exhausting. I kicked myself for not taking better care of her.

I took the opportunity to talk to Sophia in the tent that evening while Steph and Era were out with their Louis Poo-uittons. Sophia looked serious as we talked, resting her eyes on the stoves and pans of water at her feet as she spoke. 'I feel a lot of pressure from home and I don't want to let them down,' she admitted. 'The president will not be happy if I don't get to the South Pole.' Sophia had met the president of Singapore for dinner before she departed for the expedition. I knew that she took the expectations of her country very seriously but I had no idea that it weighed quite so heavily on her. 'Don't worry, Sophia. We will get you there,' I comforted her. 'Even if we have to put you in a sledge and pull you, we will get you to the South Pole.' She laughed at the image and I wondered for a second if she would let us do such a thing if it came to it. I felt immense admiration for Sophia. She had not found the expedition easy but she had approached its challenges with an unflagging strength of mind.

Sophia was quietly more focused and driven than anyone else on the team. She wasn't vocal about her determination but it burned within her, occasionally showing itself in flashes so fierce that in anyone else would be intimidating. With Sophia, the quest for the South Pole was clearly personal.

I met Steph outside the tent and together we sorted through the contents of the four sledges in our tent group, lightening the load for Sophia (to reduce the pressure on her knee) and for Era (to reduce the decline in her energy levels). With only 13 days' food and fuel remaining, Steph and I were able to split the rest of the weight between us so that neither sledge would be unmanageably heavy. I didn't want to load anybody, including myself, with so much weight that they couldn't keep up.

Back inside the tent I told Era and Sophia what we had done. I was worried that they would be offended. 'It's not that I think either of you is incapable but I want to make sure both of you get to the South Pole and with seven of us to share the weight it seems silly to have you both pulling more than necessary.' I waited for their reaction.

Sophia shrugged, 'It's not necessary,' she said turning back to the stoves as she spoke, 'but I don't mind if that's what you think is best.'

Era too was pragmatic. 'It's only the same as we did for Helen when she was not well.'

I nodded earnestly. 'Exactly,' I said. I was glad that they had both seen it this way. I had worked with teams in the past who had seen it as a weakness to accept help, even at the expense of reaching their goal. I was keen that our team maintain a very different culture, one where the success of the team as a whole went before any personal ego or pride. Even so, I wasn't sure that the reduced weight would have any bearing on Sophia's knee. The problem was more the danger of a sudden twisting or jarring than the weight of her sledge. 'At least I have something to think about while I am skiing,' she smiled.

After a month on the ice and having covered more than 400 nautical miles, it was becoming increasingly difficult to keep our minds occupied. All day, every day, we marched through an unchanging landscape, repeating the same movements again and again, surrounded by the same six people, following the same routines. Our existence was a video running on a continual loop. Smothered in protective layers and usually partially blind thanks to the ice in our goggles we were forced to spend the majority of our time inside our own heads. Thinking is an ability that we normally take for granted. It is something we are usually barely aware of and yet the expedition highlighted the vital importance of a busy mind to our sanity. During the first week I'd found the time to think as we skied to be a pleasure. After nearly two years of frantic preparation and planning for the expedition it was a relief to finally be able to mentally run through everything that had happened. My mind fizzed with the remaining logistical plans for the expedition, thoughts of loose ends in the UK that needed to be resolved and worries about what lay ahead for the team. I thought a lot about Kim and the day that had resulted in her frostbite. I scrutinised my memories to piece together what exactly had happened and whether in retrospect there was anything I should have done differently that could have prevented the outcome. I allowed my mind to analyse a whole range of decisions I had made throughout the expedition, agonising over some, reaffirming others and making resolutions about decisions I knew I would have to make in the future.

Eventually, the tempo of my mental fizz slowed to no more than background static. I became more aware of the rhythm of pushing one foot in front of the other, hearing nothing but my own breathing and occasionally the beating of my heart. Gradually, it felt as if I had entered a state of greater calm and clarity and I began to think about the bigger questions. Perhaps it is because there is so little to look at in the surrounding landscape that your mind begins to look inwards instead, into the rich landscape of your own soul. As is my nature, the first thing my brain focused on was all the periods in my life of which I am ashamed. I found myself inwardly squirming as I remembered conversations or actions that embarrassed me but which I could recall in vivid detail. Sometimes it was almost a blessed respite to be interrupted from my reveries by the arrival of a seven-minute break which provided a distraction from this mental self-flagellation.

Then I began to ponder the critical decisions I had made in my life, from the subjects I had read at university and the career I had chosen, to the man I want to spend my life with. I imagined whole other lives that might have been my fate if I had acted differently or made other choices. As Era put it, 'Antarctica makes you think of the forks in your life.' The process was engrossing but emotionally exhausting. I rarely allowed myself to think too deeply or for too long about my family. Memories of spending time at home were like finding a plump, juicy olive in a bowl of couscous. I'd fall on it greedily, enjoying the sensation of being transported thousands of miles to my home but then I'd reluctantly force myself to carefully pack the thoughts and memories away. Thinking of home made me feel lonely and homesick and I couldn't afford to be either.

Eventually, there was barely an episode in my 32-year life that I hadn't minutely examined and the tentacles of my brain reached out for something else to fill the hours and days. I listened attentively to the lyrics played through my MP3 player, invented sequels to films I had seen recently, constructed plots for novels I might write one day and even composed a few lines of poetry – but I was always aware that I was hovering on the edge of a black abyss. To be bored was a torment that seemed to gouge out my insides so that it took all my will to stop myself screaming into the cold air and striking out at the hovering landscape. Sometimes as we set off for another 90-minute leg, I would realise with horror that my brain was completely empty, that I could not find a single avenue for thought. I'd be seized with panic, scrambling through my internal catalogue of memories and ideas for something to catch hold of my imagination. It's difficult to imagine not being able to think of a single thing to think about but it was at these moments that the abyss yawned largest.

Each of us had our own methods for keeping our minds busy. Most of us had MP3 players as a basic first line of defence. Sophia had recorded the music she used for her kick-boxing classes and ran through her routines in her head as we skied. Watching her in line ahead of me, every now and again I would catch her punching the air or lifting a knee into her chest with lightning speed. She challenged Steph to a competition to see who could make their precious daily boiled sweet last the longest. (Sophia won by being able to savour her sweet for 46 songs.) Steph in particular was adamant that she wouldn't be able to get through the day without music and looked after her slim iPod religiously. Therefore it was somehow inevitable that the pampered iPod stopped working shortly after we left the resupply. Steph was distraught. 'I can't do it without music,' she wailed in panic. 'I'll go nuts.' But she had little choice. At the end of her first music-less day she was sullen; the day had dragged painfully. By the end of the fifth day without music her attitude had changed completely. 'I'm actually quite enjoying it,' she admitted. 'Sometimes I get lost in a tunnel of thought and the days just fly past.' She hesitated before adding as a hasty afterthought, 'I do miss it, though.'

In complete contrast to Steph, Reena had declined to bring music with her right from the start. 'I live in Delhi where there is noise all the time, there is no escaping it. To have six weeks of silence is going to be bliss for me,' she explained emphatically. I was worried that she might regret her decision as we moved into our fourth week on the ice but she found the shapes of the sastrugi kept her imagination busy. 'Today I saw fairy steps in the snow,' she wrote in the team journal.

We might have been worried about her sanity except, in truth, this was indeed a place where your imagination could run riot.

The sun dogs that had danced around the sun grew into a single circular rainbow, trapping the sun within a fortification of colour as if protecting it from the skein of milky cloud that slowly crept across the sky like advancing cataracts. Sometimes there were haloes within haloes, barely perceptible echoes of colour rippling across the sky in concentric circles. The sun and its haloes seemed to float beside us like our personal guardian angel.

It is easy to imagine that the divine live here; that the South is the only place on earth where it is possible to come face to face with your God. Era certainly found Antarctica a spiritual place, using the time to 'pray and think about how to make myself a better Muslim'. We'd all come to be very fond of practical and devout Era. She delighted in explaining the intricacies of her religion to us and took any opportunity in the tent in the evening to tell us an interesting, bizarre or notable fact about her beliefs. As a result, we often found ourselves falling into long discussions about our thoughts and philosophies. Sometimes we got so carried away that we'd realise with horror that it was way past our intended bedtime and that we had squandered precious hours of sleep. Jokingly, we referred to ourselves as 'the tent of Zen'. Hearing Era's views was fascinating because they diverged so completely from my own, but I found some of her ideas disturbing. 'It is quite extreme, but me and my husband feel it is better to have a short life because there is less opportunity to sin,' she told us one evening. I see life as the most precious gift and to resent it in this way seemed to me to be an insult to all those who have life so cruelly taken away prematurely. I sensed Era knew she had upset me. She tactfully acknowledged my view while making it clear her opinion had not changed. It was a practised response that I had noticed her use many times – a mix of good manners and resolute defiance that suggested she saw our discussions as a test of her faith. Our views were a temptation to be resisted. I suspected that if her views survived the expedition intact, Era would see this as a sign of her strength as a Muslim.

During one break Sophia sat heavily on her sledge and spoke quietly to Kylie who had pulled up next to her. I couldn't hear what was being said but from their body language I could tell something was wrong. When I skied over to them, Sophia waved away my concerns. 'My chest feels tight,' she explained. 'It's like a panic attack.'

'I think it might be the altitude,' Kylie suggested.

Our seemingly endless climb through sastrugi land had brought us to an altitude of just under 3,000 metres. This isn't very much in mountaineering terms but it is possible to feel the effects of altitude at anything over 2,000 metres. We had gained height so gradually over the last month that I hadn't expected us to be affected but I'd noticed that recently I found myself out of breath as we skied. It was difficult to be sure whether this was just general exhaustion or something more until I had woken up in the night with a feeling of being short of breath. I'd gasped in panic, gripped by a fear of not being able to breathe. It was a sensation I'd felt before at altitude, and it seemed that Sophia was having a similar problem. Kylie had spent more time than anyone else in the team at altitude and advised us all to concentrate on breathing out if we felt short of breath, rather than just focusing on inhaling.

As we continued to climb the air wasn't our only problem. On our map we could see that we were approaching the polar plateau, a vast expanse of high ground at the centre of the Antarctic continent that surrounds the South Pole. Our arrival on the plateau was marked by a noticeable drop in temperature and a strong wind from the south that seemed to cut straight through our clothing as if it wasn't there. The change caught us by surprise and we suddenly felt very vulnerable. The calm, relatively warm weather of the past month had allowed us to get away with sloppy habits. The new weather sought out our weaknesses and exploited them mercilessly. Steph had become used to unzipping her trousers up to the thigh for ventilation so that the skin beneath was covered by just her thin thermal leggings but now she found itchy red lumps appearing on her legs. The blood vessels in her skin had frozen in the exposure to the cold air to form nasty chilblains. Era found an angry red mark on her face where the cold wind had found a narrow gap between her goggles and mask. It was a reminder to all of us to double-check our face-coverings as we used to at the outset of the expedition. I noticed I found it particularly difficult to keep my nose warm and so fashioned some extra padding on the inside of my mask from some fleece scraps in our repair kit. Everyone found that the cold headwind exacerbated the difficulties with our goggles. The slightest moisture would freeze instantly until thick wedges of ice sat in the well of the lenses beneath our eyes and slowly crawled up the inside. We became used to seeing the world through a distorting film of ice crystals.

Our face masks too became instruments of slow torture. Frozen breath built up on the inside so that ice sat uncomfortably next to our skin and threatened us with frostbite. Unable to spare my hands as we clambered unsteadily over sastrugi I became adept at pushing frozen material away from my face with my tongue or making strange grimaces behind my mask to ensure my cheeks didn't freeze. Kylie mentioned that she did the same and soon the whole team were swapping techniques. Reena described how she blew hot air upwards, puffing like a steam engine, in an attempt to warm the tip of her nose or melt a small peep hole into the ice covering her goggles. I realised things had become desperate when I caught Steph using a shovel one evening to chip inch-thick blocks of ice from the inside of her face mask. 'I didn't want to bring it inside like that,' she explained. 'It would drip all over the place.'

The cold air seemed to freeze the clouds, too, so that they dropped out of the sky, filling the air with tiny flecks of crystal. Like fireflies, the diamond dust was impossible to look at directly but created an optical white noise around the edges of our vision. We had become used to sun dogs and haloes but this was new. 'It's like blessings falling from the sky,' said Reena. I loved the description; somehow it seemed comforting. However, later that day it appeared that our blessings had run out.

I sat in the tent with my knees pulled into my chest to keep them out of the way as my three tent-mates moved about preparing for bed. Above the noise of the stove I heard footsteps approach. Kylie called through the tent, 'Felicity, have you got a minute?'

I recognised her tone all too well: something was wrong. Outside Kylie had the hood of her jacket pulled tightly around her face with a hat on underneath. Her cheeks and nose were red with cold and her fingers were folded into the palm of her hands. It looked as if she had been outside in the cold for a while.

'Don't panic,' she started, 'but I've had a fuel leak in my sledge.' I took a slow intake of breath but followed her advice not to panic. Kylie led me over to her tent where the contents of her sledge were laid out on the snow. 'I've been through everything and it seems that the fuel has got into the ration bags but only affected the noodles. So I've taken all the noodles out and repacked the rest of the food and made sure nothing else was contaminated.' Kylie looked at me, waiting for a response. I wasn't sure what to say.

The fuel cans all had special tape stuck to the thread of the caps to prevent leaks and were wrapped in individual plastic bags as well as being placed together in a second strengthened plastic sack. The food was also in its own separate plastic sack and was divided into sealed plastic day bags. Therefore there were four or five separate layers of protection that should, theoretically, have prevented any cross-contamination. In a tent group of four, no one carried both food and fuel in their sledge but as Kylie was part of a tent group of three she was, unusually, carrying both. Only a few days before I had asked the team to check their fuel can every morning after Era had noticed that hers was dripping slightly. 'I did check it,' Kylie replied defensively. 'I swear it was fine this morning.' I reflected that we had crossed a lot of big sastrugi that day. It was quite possible that the cap on the fuel can had worked its way free as the sledge was bumped and bashed over repeated sastrugi and that the leaked fuel had then run between all the different layers of protective wrapping to contaminate the food.

'It's lucky that the main meals are in their own sealed foil packets,' I thought aloud. Kylie grimaced. 'Helen has been mixing a handful of noodles into her meals,' she said. 'So she got a belly full of fuel.'

'It was disgusting,' called Helen from inside the tent. I hadn't been aware Helen and Reena were listening. I lifted one of the bags of noodles and stuck my nose into the bag. The smell of fuel was unmistakable. 'Every bag is the same, except two,' said Kylie. The noodles had always been an optional extra in our rations, added after the resupply to give our bodies an extra boost of carbohydrates. It was unfortunate that Reena, Kylie and Helen would lose this extra input of energy, but we could share the noodles from the other tent to lessen the impact. The loss wasn't ideal but neither was it critical.

'Well, it looks like you've done what you can for now,' I said indicating all the bags sorted out on the snow. 'You're not going to run out of food as long as we get to the South Pole on time. It just puts a little more pressure on us, that's all.' I smiled flatly at her through pursed lips.

Leaving Kylie to repack her sledge I retired to my habitual corner of the tent and took out the team notebook to look at my mileage calculations. Despite the lack of noodles, we still had enough food to keep us on full rations until Day 38. If we maintained the mileage we'd been covering over the last week and stopped for one rest day, I calculated that it left us without much margin for error, but it would be enough. As I counted out the days for a final time, scribbling numbers into the margins as I worked, some sixth sense fell over me like a shadow. I had the abrupt conviction that something was wrong with the figures.

Sacrificing a clean sheet from the notebook I started afresh, using the GPS to double-check exactly how far we were from the South Pole. Adding up our target miles I looked at the final total in horror. Forcing down the panic already tingling in my fingertips, I added up the target mileage again and went through the sheet day by day to make sure there were no mistakes. I put down the notebook and ran my hands through my hair in frustration. There was no denying it, we had a whole 11 extra nautical miles to go to the South Pole than I had accounted for. Eleven miles doesn't seem like much but it was the equivalent of a whole day skiing. I couldn't understand how the miles had been dropped but here they were. On top of the lost breakfast bags and the contaminated food, this extra day of skiing squeezed our already tight schedule even tighter.

The next day I pondered our options as we skied. In order to make the South Pole before we ran out of food we would either need to cover more miles each day, reduce our rations and save the excess to create an extra day of food, or sacrifice the rest day we had planned for 25 December and use it to regain the additional 11 nautical miles. None of these options appealed. Although we had been skiing for more than a month, the team were still struggling to finish their rations every day, but I was keen for them to continue getting a full intake of nutrients for as long as possible. Already Era was showing signs of tiring and I was worried that Helen and Sophia would soon follow. I was also reluctant to abandon our rest day. It was a question of morale as much as our physical need for a rest. I knew that everyone was already counting down the days until our 'holiday' on Christmas Day. More than anything it was the idea of having a lie-in, a day when we didn't have to force ourselves from our warm sleeping bags into the subzero temperatures and frozen torments of our average day. I wasn't sure what the mental effects might be of taking away the carrot that dangled so tantalisingly ahead of us. That left the option of skiing just a little further each day. We had covered some 200 nautical miles since the resupply and the distance was beginning to show in our bodies. I didn't want to push too hard now that we were so close to the final stages. We'd all heard the stories of teams in years past being rescued from the 88th degree or beyond, less than 100 nautical miles from the pole and yet unable to go on. It was a spectre I kept close to remind myself not to get complacent or overzealous.

Around me what had started as a gloomy day of flat bluish light split open to let rays of sunshine illuminate the landscape like spotlights on a theatre stage. As the cracks in the cloud grew larger to reveal the indigo blue of the sky, a halo emerged around the sun, glowing with particular ferocity where it coincided with sun dogs. It reminded me of the glare of the sun reflected from glass buildings. At these brighter points, mirror images of the halo branched outwards like smiles in all four directions, meeting each other with a touch as light as a kiss. I was entranced and as I glanced down the line strung out in front of me I noticed that everybody's eyes were transfixed on this shimmering display. Once again diamond dust hung suspended in the air around us. I looked directly upwards through a tunnel of sparkles and noticed a new addition to our solar display. All the sun dogs and haloes we had seen until now had been split into prismatic colours but now a circle of white light stretched in a horizontal plane from the sun, as if the sun were the diamond in a colourless ring. I gazed in amazement at this completion of our light show and noticed that the horizontal halo was studded with pale globes of white light, like echoes of our star. I wasn't sure if perhaps I had looked at the sun for too long and that these were echoes in my retina rather than in the sky but as the team stopped for a break I asked Reena, 'Can you see that?'

She nodded enthusiastically. 'It is the most beautiful thing I have ever seen,' she said in awe.

That evening, with the whole team squeezed into one tent, I baldly outlined the problem of the missing miles and our options. 'I need you all to be absolutely honest with me, and yourselves, about how you are feeling and what our goals should be. We've come this far so it would be a shame to blow it now after a month of effort. It feels like we are close but there is still plenty of time for things to wrong.'

There was silence in the tent. Era looked around to see if anyone else was about to speak before taking the floor.

'I've actually been thinking that it would be wrong of me to celebrate Christmas with you. It is a Christian festival and I am a Muslim. So please everyone, do not give me presents or wish me Happy Christmas or give me special food.'

I frowned, taken by surprise. 'Era, we're not going to have a party in one tent and leave you alone in the other.' The idea appalled me.

'I've thought about that. I thought if I have the video camera I can film you. That means I have a reason to be in the tent but it is clear that I am not there to celebrate Christmas.'

I sighed. I didn't like the idea; it seemed divisive but I didn't feel I could argue. The discussion continued and seemed to boil down to whether or not to have a rest day.

'I just want to get on with it,' said Reena. 'A rest day seems like an unnecessary delay. I feel strong enough to continue without a day off.' As each team member in turn expressed their opinion, most seemed to agree with Reena.

Finally, I turned to Sophia. In many ways the expedition had been harder on her than on anyone else and I respected her judgement. She thought for a moment, eyes lowered. 'I think we keep going,' she said.

The conversation continued but I mentally withdrew, taking the opportunity to mull over what had been said. The eagerness of the team to abandon the rest day had surprised me. I was aware that it was my turn to speak.

'OK, this is what we'll do. We'll carry on without a rest day but if I think we need a break I will simply call a halt for the following day. Is that OK with everyone?' I looked at each in turn and waited for their nod of agreement. 'I want to be clear that we are in no hurry. We have plenty of food as long as we continue as planned. There is no rush and our primary concern, as always, is making sure we are all fit and healthy.' I looked at Era for a moment. 'And regarding Christmas, I don't think it is right to celebrate if not all of us can do so. I think Christmas should just be a normal day for us. We can eat together but it will be a celebration of reaching 89 degrees, or whatever, rather than Christmas so that Era can join in. Is that OK, Era?'

She seemed reluctant but nodded, 'OK.'

While the others chatted I took the opportunity to leave the tent with my Louis Poo-uitton. It felt good to stand up straight after the last few hours hunched inside the tent. I squinted, the combination of glare from the snow and the cold wind blowing in my face making my eyes water instantly. I glanced at the sun but the spectacular haloes I'd enjoyed all day had disappeared. The sun was alone in the sky, marooned in the endless blue just as we were alone on the polar plateau, marooned in the endless white.

CHAPTER TWELVE

THE LAST DEGREE

Still lying prone in my sleeping bag I gradually became aware of my surroundings and silently listened to Era and Sophia moving around in the tent.

'Happy Christmas, Sophia,' I called out eventually.

'Happy Christmas!' she replied.

'Happy eighty-ninth parallel, Era' I added, careful to make the point that I was not wishing her any unwanted Christian greetings. She laughed, appreciating the distinction. 'Happy eighty-ninth parallel, Felicity.'

'Happy Christmas, Sophia and Felicity,' croaked Steph, barely audible through the layers of her sleeping bag. We all laughed. By now we were used to the fact that Steph was not her best in the mornings. The tent was filled with a bright orange light, a sure sign that it was a sunny day outside. Taking a deep breath I flung the top of my sleeping bag aside and exposed myself to the cold air. It wasn't as bad as I had expected, much milder than we had become used to since we had arrived on the polar plateau. There was a crescendo of crunching footfalls outside the tent. 'We wish you a merry Christmas, we wish you a merry Christmas, we wish you a merry Christmas and a happy New Year!' three familiar voices half sang, half shouted through the still air.

Kylie's red cheeks framed with blonde plaits grinned through the vent at the end of the tent above the kitchen. 'It's already late Christmas Day in New Zealand now, so is it OK if I make my call home this morning rather than waiting until tonight?' she asked. Having agreed that Christmas was not going to be a rest day, the one seasonal gift we had decided to allow ourselves was a phone call home. Steph placed the satellite phone into Kylie's hand which appeared through the front vent. The hand and the phone disappeared, and Kylie's footsteps crunched in the snow as she retreated to her tent to make the precious call.

I glanced at my watch and worked out that my own family would be gathering in the narrow kitchen at Crofton for a late Christmas brunch. I could picture the scene, repeated exactly, year after year. There would be Handel drifting through from the front room accompanied by noisy complaints from my brother and sister, eager to play their own choice of music. My dad would be busy at the far end of the kitchen checking on the huge bird that had been slow roasting since the early hours while my mother, already elegantly dressed in something sparkly, would be flittering around the house lighting sweet-scented candles and dressing the large wooden dining table for lunch. I longed to be home with them. At that moment the simple pleasures of warmth and comfort and family appeared, unquestionably, to be the greatest aspirations in life. Our quest for the South Pole seemed, in comparison, to be an empty and worthless vanity.

Not for the first time I was struck by the irony of my perverse psyche. When at home all I could think about was the next adventure, the thrill of returning to Antarctica, the memory of the wonders of the South, but now that I was here my greatest wish was to be sitting in that wonderfully decorated room at Crofton with the warmth of a fire and the taste of good food, surrounded by those who are important to me. Compared to the scenes that I knew were taking place a thousand miles away, I felt cold, dirty and miserable.

'Hello darling.' My mother spoke quietly with a calm that told me how much the call meant to her. The sound of her voice made every emotion that I had subconsciously suppressed rise to the surface and fill my chest. For a moment I couldn't speak, it was like my breath had been taken from me. I tried to talk but there was only a staccato cough, I felt strangled. Aware of Steph, Sophia and Era in the tent with me, tactfully busying themselves with the morning chores, I turned myself towards the walls of the tent so that they couldn't see my face.

I regained my voice, 'Hello Mum. Happy Christmas.' I wiped away the silent and unwanted tears that I couldn't stop. 'I wish I was there with you all.'

'I know darling, we all miss you too.' Sensing my tears, Mum filled the silence with news of the family's day.

My brother was handed the phone and he croaked a Christmas carol in his low voice in which I could hear the excesses of the night before. My sister interrupted, fizzing with excitement about the expedition, 'We've been following the website. You are all doing so well. We're all so proud of you, Felicity.'

I wanted to reply but my voice had been replaced with a swelling, pulsating pain in my throat. The tears rolled down my face quicker than I could wipe them away and my nose began to run. The phone call ended and I sat for a moment staring blankly at the phone still in my hands. Wiping my face I turned back to the tent, swinging my legs into the porch to pull on my boots. Steph squeezed past me pausing briefly to ask if I was OK. I grinned at her gratefully and nodded. It was hard to be transported home but speaking to my family had filled me with new determination. They had reminded me of the real Felicity that existed beyond being the leader of this expedition. 'Five more days,' I told myself. 'Keep it together for just five more days.'

Christmas Day, Day 34 to us, turned out to be a long day on skis. At the end of it, the team pitched the tents in silence, each of us concentrating on getting our jobs done as quickly as possible, anxious to be in the warm where we could finally remove the ice-encrusted face masks and clothing that had felt like our own personal prisons all day. Nobody had the energy for much celebrating but we gathered in one tent to eat together. I had saved my favourite meal as a treat – probably the only time in my life that I will eat chicken tikka masala for Christmas dinner.

Helen surprised us all with a Christmas tree made out of sleeping mat and hung with tiny stockings of dark blue fleece, stitched together with red cotton from our repair kit. Each stocking had an initial embroidered onto the front of it and a small roll of paper inside. 'There is one for each of you,' said Helen with obvious pride.

'When did you do this?' asked Reena in awe.

Helen shrugged off the question, 'Each night I've been doing a bit in my sleeping bag.'

Reena looked at her wide-eyed, mouth open. None of us could imagine how Helen had had the energy to stay awake any longer than necessary, never mind do something as mentally taxing as sew tiny pieces of fleece together with such care. Most of us were asleep before our heads hit the ground each evening and barely had the brain power for conversation much less for being creative. It was an extremely touching gesture and the team were delighted.

'Aww, look at the tiny little stockings!' cooed Steph.

I looked anxiously at Era, worried whether this gesture would contradict her strict rules regarding Christmas, but she was clapping her hands together impatiently, her face alight in excitement. 'Have I got one?' she asked as the tree was slowly turned so that everyone could see.

'Helen, this is awesome!' enthused Kylie.

Sitting closest to Helen, Kylie enfolded her in a big hug on behalf of the team and I noticed Helen welling up. 'Well, I have been such a monster this trip, I just wanted to say a big thank you to everyone for putting up with me.'

Era was the first to open the roll of paper inside her stocking. In pencil Helen had written sentences about her, each one beginning with a letter of her name:

E – Era simply glides over the top of any sastrugi in her path

R – Radiant smile at all times under her mask, goggles, down jacket etc.

A – Antarctic arithmetician who counts our every nautical mile

We all listened, munching on our dinner as each of us read out Helen's careful observations, alternately nodding in agreement or laughing at the ridiculous truth of her words. I felt myself relaxing in the warm glow of our camaraderie and was struck by the surrealism of seven women sitting in a tent on Christmas evening laughing together in our 40-day-old clothes and plaster-patched feet. Despite the distraction of Helen's gift, the thought of the next day's exertion was never far from our minds and we were all anxious to be in bed. After a quick group photograph outside the tent, bunched around the miniature Christmas tree, we drifted away to our sleeping bags.

The polar plateau hadn't lived up to its name. We were still climbing hill after hill although the slopes weren't as obvious as they had been. The undulating ground made Era furious, 'They should call it the Polar Bowl or the Polar Hump,' she fumed. 'This is clearly not the polar plateau.' At least we had left sastrugi land behind. None of us could remember exactly when the sastrugi had disappeared but the ground was definitely smoother now. It felt as if the snow was more granulated, the carpet of white glittering brilliantly as if scattered with crystals. If I squinted I could almost imagine that we were skiing across a vast Caribbean beach of white sand rather than snow. Small lumps of crystals began to appear on undulations in the snow, like bobbles on an old woollen jumper. Soon these ice flowers spread to cover the entire landscape so that the ground had the texture of a cat's tongue. The wind continued to blow directly into our faces and chilblains began to appear despite the careful face protection. Everyone wore the fleece-lined smocks which earlier in the expedition had barely been needed.

Struggling with the ice around her face mask Steph missed her mouth while trying to drink during a break and spilled some water down the front of her face mask. A few legs later she complained about having a cold chin. Kylie, next in line, solved the problem by tucking her spare glove into Steph's face-covering so that it formed an extra couple of layers around her jaw. Seemingly satisfied, Steph continued with a Bruce Forsyth profile; it looked ridiculous, but she didn't care. Era too was struggling. From the back I noticed that she was repeatedly falling behind. I stepped out of the team's tracks to ski alongside the line and catch up with her but the sudden exertion left me breathless. The altitude still occasionally took me by surprise. Pushing my thighs harder I slowly caught up with Era. She was wearing her windproof under her fleece-lined smock and the down mitts I had lent her the day before. 'I'm OK,' she said in response to my question as I drew level with her. 'Just a bit tired.'

Fishing inside my jacket I surreptitiously switched on the GPS and checked on our progress. It had been a slow day and although it was already late afternoon we had only completed half of our target distance for that day. 'We need to push on a bit if we are going to hit our target for today,' I said gently. 'Do you think you can do that without exhausting yourself?' Era nodded, already starting to close the gap in front of her.

Where we had used to count down the minutes in anticipation of our next break, the cold now made breaks an unwelcome interruption in the business of keeping warm. We each dreaded the moment we would stop skiing and instantly begin to freeze. Laboriously pulling on the down jackets that were kept accessible on the top of our sledges, the breaks were a series of unpleasant tasks, from disturbing our temperamental face masks to eat and drink, to baring our bottoms for a pee and finally, being obliged to remove the delicious warmth of the down jacket as we set off once more. Knowing that we would eventually warm up again as we skied was no consolation for those first few minutes after a break when fingers were numb and joints were stiff with cold.

I was glad it was Reena out in front for the last leg of the day. She had a peculiar knack of being able to set a pace that felt slow and steady and yet covered more ground than anyone else. I knew I could rely on her to cover a solid 2 nautical miles in the next hour – it was what we needed to reach our target for the day.

Reena didn't let me down. I glanced at the GPS as we finished the leg – we'd travelled 15.2 nautical miles since our last camp. If we could manage another four days like this, we would be at the pole. Steph slumped on her sledge beside me as we stopped, leaning back with her arms and legs hanging wide, head back in a flamboyant expression of exhaustion. Later on, as we pitched the tent, she pulled back her face mask to reveal her chin and neck, which had got cold earlier in the day; her skin was an angry crimson. The water that had spilt from her water bottle had turned to ice next to her skin and given her a cold injury. The skin hadn't blistered, so it wasn't serious frostbite, but it spread like a birthmark over a large area. She would need to look after it to stop it getting any worse. As Steph inspected her injury in our tiny team mirror she was at first horrified, then worried and finally surprisingly relaxed about it. The next morning as we prepared to leave the tent I helped Steph bandage up the affected area which had been left to air overnight. Most of the bandage tape in our first aid kit had been used up to cover blisters, which left us with only gaffer tape. Placing some gauze over the discoloured skin I taped it into place as best I could. The gaffer tape was reluctant to stick to her skin ('It's probably all the layers of dirt,' joked Steph) so I had to place layer over layer until it finally stuck. As the bottom half of her face was gradually covered in tape we couldn't help laughing. It looked like she had a bad case of lockjaw. We were distracted from the taping by a sudden outburst from Era at the other end of the tent, 'Shit! My mask has dry-frozen.' Steph and I looked at each other, startled, before breaking into laughter. Era looked up confused.

'I don't think I have ever heard you swear,' laughed Steph. 'What is your husband going to think when we send you back swearing like a soldier?'

Era smiled with pretend menace. 'He has already seen me angry.'

Even though, rationally, I knew it was too early to expect to see any evidence of the South Pole ahead of us, I still couldn't help scanning the horizon. The South Pole is not an unmarked spot on the landscape; it is now the site of one of the largest scientific research stations in Antarctica. The American-run Amundsen-Scott Station has operated year-round at the South Pole since 1957. During the summer over 300 people work on the base, a population that diminishes to just 100 during the winter. It was Day 36 and I hoped that, even though we were too far away to see the station itself, we might see outlying research sites, storage buildings or perhaps even the tracks of vehicles. In fact, we saw nothing.

I wasn't the only one watching the horizon restlessly. We were all experiencing the most frustrating case of being 'so near and yet so far'. On the map we were barely a finger's width from the South Pole and in our minds we were already there. We had passed the 89th parallel and after skiing six and a half degrees since leaving the coast, covering the last degree seemed to be little more than a formality. And yet the last degree was still a full 60 nautical miles that we would have to ski, mile by painful mile. We were impatient now to be finished and that was the source of the frustration. I knew that the team were already day-dreaming about our arrival at 90 degrees south. We had already been warned that as a non-scientific expedition the rules were that we were not allowed to use any of the facilities at the station but it didn't stop us fantasising about flush toilets, fresh food and perhaps even a shower. There were more practical reasons to be anxious to finish, too. We were beginning to run low on essential supplies. We had started rationing toothpaste because it had run so low, toilet paper was being carefully watched and some people were now using empty zip-lock ration bags in place of the Louis Poo-uittons because they had run out.

The next day felt like the last day of school. There was a euphoria running between us, an irrepressible excitement. At just 20 nautical miles from the South Pole, we all expected to see some sign of the station in the next ten hours of skiing. It was a calm and sunny day, the sort of weather that would usually have us stripping off layers and cursing our steamed goggles but it was noticeably colder than ever. After a break I barely had time to warm up completely before it was time to stop again. I worked my fingers inside my mitts constantly to ward off frostbite and wriggled my toes in my boots as I skied, just to make sure I could still feel them.

Nobody talked to each other during the breaks; everyone concentrated on keeping warm. I stood scanning the horizon as I munched on mouthfuls of popcorn. My chewing slowed as I realised what I could see. On the horizon was a dark rectangle and a little distance away from it, a white dome that was catching the light. I looked away for a moment before finding the shapes again to reassure myself that this wasn't a case of wishful thinking. During the expedition we had seen distant sastrugi form all sorts of shapes but this time there was something different. The rectangle was too perfect to be shadow or mirage, the white dome too prominent to be merely another block of ice. The shapes were definitely man-made. I was looking at the South Pole.

I spoke to no one in particular, 'Guys, can anyone else see something over there?' I pointed towards the shapes with my ski pole, holding it steady as the others followed my line of sight. With my other hand I switched on my GPS. The South Pole was a little over 12 nautical miles away.

Kylie was the first to react. She flung her arms in the air and let out a huge cheer. She shuffled towards me on her skis and flung her arms around my neck. 'We've made it!' she bellowed.

Reena was frustrated, 'Where? I don't see anything.' I leant over her shoulder so that her eyes followed the line of my ski pole and I guided her gaze towards the right section of the horizon. 'Oh, oh, oh, yes! I see it!' The three of us tried to pick out landmarks near the shapes so that the others could find them too but by the end of our break they had still seen nothing.

Helen was silent. 'It's easy to mistake sastrugi or shadows for anything out here,' she said sceptically as we skied on.

I watched the shapes as we moved. After a while they disappeared and I worried that perhaps I had imagined it after all. Eventually they reappeared and I realised that in fact we were skiing over unseen undulations and gentle hills. We could see the distant station as we reached the high ground but it would disappear from view as we crossed the shallow valleys in between. As our view of the South Pole returned I noticed another white shape on the far side of the rectangle. It was too equally spaced to be a coincidence, it had to be another building. My eyes were so transfixed on the ephemeral vision to our left that my neck began to hurt. I forced myself to look away, promising that I would only take a peek in the base's direction once every ten minutes. I lasted about 30 seconds before my eyes automatically flicked towards the rectangle. It looked more solid now with defined edges and what appeared to be a tower, or perhaps a cloud, hovering above it. During our fourth leg the dark rectangle had disappeared but we were heading directly for a tall plume of smoke or steam that rose from the ice. As we approached our fifth break of the day there was not only a clear line of buildings ahead of us but several spherical communication domes and at least one outbuilding, which appeared to have a chimney belching steam into the air.

'So, is there anyone who can't see that now?' I exclaimed loudly as we pulled our sledges together for a break. Era had made a mental note of her exact position when she had first spotted the base; she had been just over 5 nautical miles from the South Pole according to our GPS. 'So, tall people can see it from twelve nautical miles away; short people from only five nautical miles away,' she stated matter-of-factly.

Despite the sunshine, Era had been cold all day. She had permanently adopted my big down mitts that had been packed for emergencies but I had noticed that she still spent a good five minutes pumping the air with her fists as we continued after breaks to encourage the blood to circulate and warm her hands. Helen had let gaps open up in front of her in the line several times during the day and I could tell from Sophia's brittle body language that she was concentrating hard on her knee. I considered what to do.

We had one more leg of skiing before we would normally stop for the day but if all went well we would be barely 3 nautical miles from the end of the South Pole station's VHF antenna, a long cable hung above ground on regularly spaced steel masts. Once we reached the end of the antenna we would have to ski into the base itself to reach the actual South Pole. Estimates on the distance from the end of the antenna into the base were a bit sketchy but Steve in Patriot Hills thought it to be approximately an extra 4 nautical miles. To extend our day by another 7 nautical miles didn't sound like a lot but it represented another three hours' skiing at least. It seemed like an unnecessary pressure to put on an already cold and exhausted team and besides, I wasn't in any hurry for the expedition to be over. I wanted us to enjoy our arrival rather than collapse on the finish line in a lifeless heap.

However, if we were going to stop short of the South Pole I didn't want to be camped in the station's backyard. We would need to keep our distance. As our GPS flashed that we were 3 nautical miles from the end of the antenna I skied along the line to stop next to Steph, who was leading the final leg of the day. The buildings were now large on the horizon and unmistakable.

'I don't want to get too close tonight, so what do you think? Is this a suitable spot for our last night?'

We both simultaneously glanced up at the sun blazing in an indigo sky surrounded by wisps of milky white cloud. To our left were the unfamiliar colours and angles of the station, while to our right was the same uninterrupted division of blue and white that we had become used to.

'Perfect,' she replied.

As I reported the news to the team that we were stopping as usual there wasn't a single murmur of disagreement; the team seemed to be pleased with the decision. 'I could not go further today,' said Sophia. 'This is far enough.'

'I think it's nice that we have one last night on our own,' added Helen.

Even so, as we fell into our well-rehearsed tent routine I couldn't help glancing up at the distant station buildings and wondering if we should have pressed on.

It was very rare that Sophia wrote in our team journal but Day 37 was special. She was prompted not by our proximity to our goal but because it was her 37th birthday. 'Counted my blessings for having such great weather for our last day of long skiing, although body and mind are feeling exhausted. Can't ask for a better way to celebrate my birthday in Antarctica and a great team to be with,' she recorded.

We woke on Day 38 knowing that it would be the last day of our expedition. After a lazy morning indulging ourselves in that thought, by the time we began to pack up it seemed that the team were suddenly in a hurry to be moving again. There was a buoyant atmosphere as we packed away the tents and attached ourselves to our sledges.

Despite the banter and laughter, I noticed the others occasionally stop to stand and stare at the station buildings. I couldn't help doing the same myself. The cloud of steam still bellowed above the base but I couldn't detect any movement. I felt a knot of anxiety in my stomach but couldn't isolate why I should be feeling so nervous. Once we had packed up, we moved off as normal. Helen was navigating and still following the GPS arrow pointing us towards the end of the antenna.

The station buildings away to our left didn't seem to be getting any larger but to our right a large black splodge appeared in the sky. As, one by one, the team ahead of me spotted it a few ski poles were raised to point it out but there was no halt to our forward progress. We all watched as the dark shape slowly lumbered towards us, revealing itself gradually as a large Hercules, a fat-bellied cargo plane similar to the one that had flown us into Antarctica. It seemed to pass right in front of us as we skied but was probably in reality a few dozen kilometres away. It glided ridiculously slowly, leaving what looked to be the narrowest band of blue between the snow and its greyish hull. I wondered if the crew flying the plane had spotted us, a line of seven black dots far below them. We heard the faintest of mechanical thunders as the plane merged into the base and was gone. I noticed with annoyance that my goggles had steamed up so that I couldn't see the base properly. I pushed a gloved finger awkwardly under the rim of my goggles to try to clear my vision before realising that it was not my goggles affecting my sight but a fine mist that had descended like a fog over the base. The mist grew, crawling across the sky until sun dogs appeared around the sun in the way that cartoonists emphasise the sparkle of a diamond. The sight made me smile to myself: I liked the fact that our arrival at the South Pole would be accompanied by the sun dogs and haloes that had patiently watched our progress over the last 38 days.

We stopped for a break and Steph took over the lead. She didn't need the GPS anymore; we could see fine black marks in the snow ahead marking out the antenna we had been told to aim for. Steve had given me clear instructions for our arrival at the South Pole station. Once we reached the end of the antenna we were to follow the green flag markers to the ceremonial pole, but as we neared the antenna Steph slowed in confusion. I skied towards the front of the line and stood next to her as we both lifted our goggles for a better look. To our left the antenna stretched away to a cluster of buildings in the far distance but it was clear that the main base lay quite a way ahead of us and slightly to the left. In front of the buildings was a wide area of groomed snow, presumably the runway, but between us and our destination was a multi-coloured forest of flags. Starting with the closest green flag I tried to trace a route through the perplexity of flapping markers but found every discernable route was interrupted with another line, a large gap or groups of crossed flags which seemed unrelated to any others. Slowly the rest of the team drew around us and we all looked on together in bewilderment. Looking down at my feet I noticed a set of old ski tracks in the snow roughly following the line of the antenna away to our left. It seemed as good a direction as any so we followed the tracks.

Now skiing directly towards the base for the first time, the scale of the buildings became clear and we could see vehicles moving around. It was hard to be sure but I thought I could see figures on the balconies of some of the buildings. It all looked very industrial; the buildings were square blocks of blues and reds encased in what looked like scaffolding. Old shipping containers were lined up in rows in front of the buildings as well as large wooden cable-rolls looking like oversized cotton reels. It became obvious that the large building to our right was the main base. The closer we got, the larger it loomed out of the snow. Raised above the ground on stilts it appeared to be at least three storeys high, its annexes arranged to form the shape of a capital E. The plane we had seen earlier was standing next to the side of the building closest to us and thrumming impatiently. I'd heard that the engines of these big planes were never switched off at the South Pole because it was so cold that there was no guarantee they would start again. Instead the plane was unloaded and reloaded on the runway with the engines still rolling. As we marched forward, another large cargo plane appeared in the sky and for a moment seemed to hang in the air alongside us before landing with a roar, its engines kicking up a large plume of snow.

Steph stopped the line and beckoned me to the front. 'Felicity, I think it should be you that leads us in,' she said. 'You're the one that started all this.' I looked at Era and Reena who had stopped behind Steph. They both nodded in agreement. I felt touched at the gesture and, lifting my fist in our habitual signal, checked that everyone was OK before I forged onwards towards the base at the front of the line. As we skied, my eyes searched the buildings for any sign of the ceremonial South Pole. I had seen pictures of it a hundred times; a silver sphere on a red and white striped barber's pole surrounded by the flags of the Antarctic Treaty nations. Instead I noticed figures moving about the base, the all-too-familiar smell of aviation fuel and even the faintest hint of rock music coming from somewhere.

We'd come to the end of the antenna but I still couldn't see a clear line of green flags to follow. It seemed obvious that we would need to veer right towards the main building at some point so I followed my nose, leading the team vaguely towards the runway. I'd barely turned in that direction before I became aware of a snowmobile heading towards us at high speed. Riding pillion was a passenger waving at us frantically. I stopped, leaning on my ski poles as I waited for the snowmobile to reach us. The passenger leapt from his seat, trotting to a halt in front of me and sticking out his bare hand in greeting. I struggled for a second to shake my mitt free of my ski pole before pulling out my hand and shaking his. The stranger's hand felt very warm.

'Congratulations! I'm Sean,' he introduced himself. I'd been told to expect to meet Sean, the ALE representative at the South Pole whose job it was to look after us once we arrived. 'You've got everyone here in a bit of a stir,' he continued. I looked at him in confusion, unsure what we could have done within our first five minutes of arrival to upset anybody. 'You seem to be heading straight for the science buildings and tourists aren't allowed near that part of the base,' Sean explained. I noted our description as tourists.

'We're just trying to follow a flag route to the ceremonial pole,' I explained. 'But there are so many flags it's a bit confusing.'

Sean pointed away to our right and I recognised it immediately: a semi-circle of flags arranged around a shiny metal sphere not more than 100 metres in front of the main base building. The South Pole.

Sean walked with us as we crossed the runway, the team still skiing in single file behind me. He chatted companionably as we moved but my attention was transfixed on our goal. We were less than 100 metres away and a sense of the enormity of the moment started to build within my chest. I knew it was ridiculous to think that I wouldn't cry.

Sean sensed my thoughts and faded into the background, moving down the line to shake hands with the rest of the team and thoughtfully collecting our team cameras to take some shots as we drew close to the end of our journey. I glanced behind me at the six women skiing neatly ski-tip to sledge-back as we had done for the last 900 kilometres. I raised my arm in our accustomed communication to check that everyone was OK, more in sentimentality than necessity. I couldn't see the faces of my team but I knew exactly what each was feeling. One by one, they raised their arm to mirror my own signal. I noticed with a familiar pain in my throat that without exception each of the girls had steamed up their goggles – like me, they were all shedding a private tear. Searing affection for this incredible, unconventional, unlikely team flashed through me, burning like a shot of adrenalin.

Covering the last 100 metres stride by stride, I made myself think back to the very beginning, to the interview at the Winston Churchill Memorial Trust, and dragged my mind forward through my memories of Ghana, India, Jamaica; I saw the faces of the women I had interviewed and of all those people who had given so generously of their time to help me. I remembered the late nights agonising over proposals and emails, the nerve-wracking elation of our first contact with Kaspersky Lab, the desperate early-morning Land Rover journeys through Norwegian blizzards and the twisting mountain roads in New Zealand. For a moment I allowed my ego to soar as I thought of those who had been disparaging or sceptical, those who thought we were a joke. 'And look at us now,' I thought to myself with satisfaction.

I stopped a metre or two from the silver orb and waited for each member of the team to catch up, so that we stood side by side. I stretched across to hug Era and Steph, both next to me in the line. I noticed Kylie waving her arms in triumph and heard her muted cheers from behind her face mask. She threw her arms around Reena, who had already lifted her goggles and was weeping openly, unable to speak. A group of employees from the South Pole base had come out to watch our arrival. They all cheered and applauded as we took the last step together in a confused mass of tangled sledges and crossed skis. The seven of us hugged around the silver ball, arms around each other, leaning forward like a sports team discussing tactics. I looked around at the six faces beaming at me and pulled my face mask away from my mouth so that they could all hear me clearly. 'If ever in life someone tells you that you can't do something,' I began, 'or you take on a task and you're not sure that you're up to it; think of this moment. This moment proves that you can do anything you want, and don't let anyone make you believe otherwise. We may be at the bottom of the planet but in the last thirty-eight days we have conquered the world.' I paused to look around at the faces of my team. 'Always be proud of what we achieved today. Always.' We hugged each other tighter for a second before breaking away to acknowledge the spectators that now crowded around to pat us on the back and take pictures.

'Do you know,' said one of the women who had come out to congratulate us, 'that it was exactly forty years ago that the first women arrived at the South Pole.' I hadn't known about the anniversary but I remembered the story. Five researchers working at another American Research Station on the coast, McMurdo, had been flown into the South Pole in a Hercules. Not wanting any one woman to claim precedence the five had decided to walk off the back loader of the plane side by side with arms linked so that they all set foot on the snow at the same time. The accidental coincidence of the anniversary pleased me. I was glad that this time the women arriving at the South Pole had skied the whole way, every step, right from the edge of the continent.

I felt slightly removed from the scene as I hugged and congratulated and cheered, trying to soak in the fact that our journey was over, that we were standing at the South Pole, all seven of us. Inwardly I tried to analyse my feelings. I felt relief, I decided finally; overwhelming mental and physical relief. I seemed almost to float through the scenes playing out around me. I had the strange certainty that I could just drift, that nothing could hurt us now, that we were safe. Then as I posed for photographs with my team I realised how proud I felt to be skiing into the South Pole with this spectacular group of women. The thought brought fresh tears to my eyes and I hugged the team around me even closer. I knew that from this moment this team would never be quite the same again but that we would remember the camaraderie we had shared over the last 38 days for the rest of our lives. Even at that moment, at the zenith of our celebrations, I was already mourning the beginning of the end.

Freed at last from our skis and sledges we all wrapped ourselves in our down jackets and were led the few hundred yards to the 'real' South Pole. The silver sphere was for ceremony but the actual point of 90 degrees south appears to move as the thick ice layer it sits on flows steadily northward. Therefore the 'real' South Pole is measured every year and marked with a small brass-headed pin and a large signboard. The board displays an outline of Antarctica. On one side is a quote from Amundsen, the Norwegian explorer who was the first man in history to reach the South Pole. It read 'So we arrived and were able to plant our flag at the geographical South Pole' and is dated 14 December 1911. On the right-hand side of the sign is a quote from Robert Falcon Scott who arrived at the South Pole more than a month later but who died on the return, 'The pole. Yes, but under very different circumstances from those expected.'

I thought about Scott and his team of men who had stood at this very spot nearly a hundred years before and considered the gulf of difference between our experiences in getting here. Scott's journey had been longer, and once at the pole he knew he had to return. We didn't have to ski any more. We simply had to wait at the pole until a plane was available to come and collect us. I wondered what those men would have thought of this multicultural team of women who had followed in their footsteps.

I dialled the number of the voicemail that would automatically upload my message onto the expedition website so that everyone who had followed our progress, from anywhere in the world, could listen.

'Hello, this is Felicity reporting that at nine minutes past eleven on the twenty-ninth of December the Kaspersky Lab

Commonwealth Antarctic Expedition arrived at the Geographic South Pole. We're all standing around the mirrorball that sits at the South Pole and surrounded by the flags of all the Antarctic Treaty nations with the South Pole base in the background. Standing next to me is Era Al-Sufri, the first Bruneian ever to ski to the South Pole.' As I spoke her name I looked at Era who grinned at me, squeezing her hands in front of her face in excitement.

'Next to her is Stephanie Solomonides, the first Cypriot ever to ski to the South Pole.' I deliberately looked at Steph as I spoke. As our eyes met I could see the disbelief in her face at her own achievement, which was still so at odds with her own self-image. The others cheered and Era put her arm around her.

'Next to her is Reena Kaushal Dharmshaktu, the first Indian woman to ski all the way to the South Pole.' Reena wore her unforgettable smile, with tears in her eyes.

'Next to her is Sophia Pang, the first woman from Singapore to ski to the South Pole.' The team cheered and Sophia, as imperturbable as ever, looked unruffled.

'Next to her is Kylie Wakelin, the first woman from New Zealand to ski to the South Pole.' Kylie cheered and waved her arms in the air like a boxer in triumph.

I met Helen's gaze who stood next in line and smiled as I chose my words. 'Next to her is Helen Turton who has fulfilled a long-held ambition to ski to the South Pole.'

I paused as I realised I was next. 'And I've also fulfilled an ambition: to take a team of inspirational women all the way to the South Pole.' The team hugged each other in silence.

'I'm incredibly proud of the team and I think the feeling that we all have right now is that if we can do this then you can do anything that you'd like to, and that's the message that we really want to send to everyone. We're all incredibly happy and we're standing here, seven women at the bottom of the planet with the biggest smiles on our faces. Thanks to everybody out there for supporting us and getting us here.'

I rang off and breathed deeply. I looked around at the girls. They still had their arms around each other and their faces were a mixture of smiles and tears.

Sean gently shepherded us away from the pole to a base camp some 50 metres away where he had already set up a mess tent. We crowded inside, perched on small stools forming a horseshoe around Sean as he produced mugs of hot tea and soup as well as dense chocolate brownies. We gratefully hoovered up the goodies and I munched as I listened to the team relate tales from our journey like seasoned professional explorers. I pulled the satellite phone from my jacket and handed it to Sophia who was next to me. Steph dug out our back-up handset from her sledge, slid a warmed battery into the back and switched it on to make a call. For the next half an hour there was an amalgamation of foreign languages in the tent as my teammates called their loved ones to let them know that we had made it safely to the bottom of the planet. Sophia finished her call and handed the satellite phone to Kylie. 'I rang my mother,' she told me. 'She is happy now that she knows I am safe.'

I let myself sink into the atmosphere. I knew that there were still things I needed to think about: publicity for our sponsors back home, delivering images to the right people, calling the journalists who had followed our progress, confirming our flights home, and sorting through our equipment. But I knew all of that could wait; there was nothing that needed to be dealt with immediately. For now I allowed myself to hang in limbo, to sit and enjoy the moment with an empty head. I could pause and rest – just for a moment. As the calls in the tent came to an end I began to think of my own family. The girls had begun to drift away to pitch the tents nearby and prepare for the sleep of their lives. Before I followed them I tucked the satellite phone in my pocket and walked alone to the South Pole. I stood in front of the infamous silver sphere and looked away from the base to the distant horizon we had just travelled over. More than ever before I understood the truth in the saying that it is the journey and not the destination that matters; the travelling not the arrival that is the true gift.

My fingers were already stiff with cold as I carefully dialled my home number hoping that my boyfriend would answer. I tried to work out what the time would be in England but my brain refused to even make a start on the calculation. I forced the handset awkwardly between my hat and the fleecy neck gaiter that was pulled up over my nose. Straining against the noise of the wind and my own breathing I could just hear the ringing of a phone. There was silence as the phone was picked up and then I heard my own voice telling me there was no one home. I hardly recognised myself. The voice was cheerful, full of energy, warm. I left a message, aware that my words were drawled as my jaw struggled to operate in the numbing cold. I sniffed loudly as I thought for a second before ending the call. I wiped my nose on my glove, laughing at the irony of leaving a message on my own answerphone from the South Pole, before laboriously pressing the digits of my parents' number at Crofton.

The phone picked up instantly and as soon as I spoke my mum guessed the implication of the call. 'Are you there? Are you at the South Pole?' she asked in excitement. I described our arrival, aware that my dad had picked up an extension elsewhere in the house so that he could hear. 'And how do you feel?' she asked when I had finished. I paused for a moment and looked at my reflection in the silver sphere in front of me. I looked into my own eyes and noticed how tired I looked. 'Now that it's all over are you happy?' she asked again. I searched for an answer, glancing around thoughtfully at the circle of flags and the endless blue above. What was it that I felt?

'I don't know,' I answered honestly. 'I really don't know.'

EPILOGUE

RIPPLES INTO WAVES

Perhaps the reason I didn't know how to feel when I arrived at the South Pole was that in many ways, completing the expedition was only the start of the challenge we had set ourselves. I had created the expedition in order to say something about what women are achieving around the world but also to make the point that there is a long way to go before all women enjoy the equality I have been fortunate enough to experience. Now that the team had made it to the South Pole, we were determined to apply ourselves to the task of sharing our story with as many people as possible.

This was a mission that we were all eager to start but first we had to get home – and that proved to be more difficult than expected. Leaving Antarctica was easy enough, but half an inch of snow on the runway at London Heathrow left us stranded in Spain. We sprawled on the hard marble floors of the airport terminal in Madrid, counting the hours that passed without a flight and growing ever more desperate. An audience of 100 guests, including the Commonwealth Secretary-General, were due to arrive at the Commonwealth Club at 6 p.m. that evening to hear the team give a presentation about their experiences. As morning turned into afternoon the chances that we would make our own welcome-home event looked increasingly unlikely. In an act of stubbornly blind optimism I asked the team to write and practise their talks as we waited in the terminal, even as the latest batch of flights appeared on the information board followed by their status: DELAYED, DELAYED, CANCELLED.

Our last hope was a 4 p.m. flight that would get us to Heathrow just an hour before we were due to be onstage in central London. The girls crowded around the gate, brandishing their passports menacingly as an inscrutable airline official tapped at her computer to determine the status of the flight. 'The plane will go,' she announced finally, handing us our boarding passes. We breathed a collective sigh of relief as we boarded the plane but it wasn't until the aircraft was actually rumbling down the runway and we were airborne that I finally allowed myself to believe we were on our way.

My family were waiting for us at Arrivals. They greeted the whole team like long-lost relatives, presenting each of us with a large helium balloon in our team colours. With the balloons tied to our wrists, and still excitedly hugging our hellos, we ran together from the airport terminal to the Heathrow Express which would take us directly into central London. Inside the subterranean station, the ticket clerk eyed us suspiciously as only a hardened Londoner can. Once we explained that we had just skied to the South Pole she treated us to an unexpected smile and a free upgrade to first class. 'It's the least I can do after what you girls have done. You are all amazing,' she enthused, passing us the tickets. Mum produced her *pièce de résistance* as we took over the entire first class carriage on the train: a make-up bag bulging with cosmetics, some new vest tops to replace the ones we had been wearing for the last 48 hours, and a round of sandwiches for each of us. The carriage suddenly resembled a girly slumber party as we peered into pocket mirrors, passing on mascara and blusher to one another in an attempt to make ourselves look presentable.

I rang Tim, who was already at the venue. 'They're all going into the auditorium now,' he reported. I estimated that we were still half an hour away at least. 'Don't worry, the Commonwealth Secretary-General is giving a speech and I've asked him to string it out a bit. We'll keep the audience busy until you get here.'

We leapt off the train as it arrived and ran along the platform to the nearest exit where a line of black cabs sat waiting. Our frantic party filled two cabs, complete with seven large green balloons pressed against the windows. 'We're in a massive hurry,' I called to the cab driver but I needn't have worried. He seemed to relish the challenge and soon we were lurching from one side of the cab to the other, screeching through the backstreets of London.

Grasping my mobile as I was flung around the taxi I called the venue and spoke to Kate, who was taking care of the expedition PR. 'Tim's just gone onstage to introduce you,' she whispered down the phone from the back of the auditorium.

I peered out of the window of the cab to see Admiralty Arch fly past at an alarming angle. 'We're in Trafalgar Square, we're almost there.' Finishing the call, Kate held up five fingers to poor Tim who had to fill five whole minutes on stage in front of 100 people. The two black cabs pulled up in front of the Commonwealth Club almost simultaneously. As we entered the building I could hear the applause which was our cue to go onstage. The auditorium doors were pulled open and we walked into the room, down the aisle dividing the audience – still trailing the green balloons tied to our wrists – and onto the stage.

That night at the Commonwealth Club the team gave our first ever talk about our journey. Each member spoke about a different part of the expedition and I was struck by how confidently the girls engaged the audience and how eloquently they spoke, despite having no training or previous public speaking experience. They were brimful of enthusiasm, each word saturated with the emotion of our experiences. It was clear that the adventure had had a profound effect on us all but also that the girls were going to be able to communicate that strength of feeling to others in a meaningful way. Over the next couple of days as we sat on the BBC *Breakfast* red sofa and flew to New York to appear on the NBC *Today* show, the team were equally unfazed, taking all the attention in their stride and remaining focused on the task of reaching out to anyone willing to listen to our story.

I had always hoped that there would be enough excitement surrounding the women's achievement to provide each of them a platform when they returned to their own country but I don't think any of us were ready for the level of celebrity that awaited them all when they returned to their home countries. Reena was completely overwhelmed by the mob of press, well-wishers and family that welcomed her at the airport when she returned to India, as she described to me in an email:

Members of the press, radio and TV, folks from my neighbourhood, friends, family and many people from my husband's home town, turned up with flowers and banners to receive me. There was also a band of traditional musicians. At my home a lot of women and children had gathered at the gates to greet me and I was accompanied by a procession all the way to my home, my neighbours sprinkling flowers on me on my arrival.

I felt I needed to visit Darjeeling, since that was the place I grew up and I was invited to my old school, Loreto Convent, to give a talk. I stood on the stage and was taken back to my school days. I used to watch my classmates and other girls going to the stage for debates and dramatics with awe, wondering when I would be able to do the same. Now I was a celebrity standing on the stage and talking about my experiences and inspiring the girls. I told them, 'Education gives you wings. You can use it to do whatever you want to do in life. If you follow your dreams then there is great power in it.'

Like Reena, Era too was met by a number of journalists when she arrived home and her story covered the front pages of the major newspapers in Brunei. Soon after, she was accorded the ultimate honour of a dinner which was attended by the Crown Princess of Brunei. But a greater joy was to come. Era is now expecting her first child. Nobody in the team was surprised when we heard the news. She had talked often in the tent during the expedition about starting a family. We may not have been surprised but of course we were all thrilled for her – in some way we all feel like distant aunties.

Sophia was contacted by the president's office soon after she returned to Singapore. The president was keen to arrange a dinner so that Sophia could relate her experience to him personally. She was shocked and humbled when a few days later he used her achievement as a rallying call to the whole nation in his speech to mark Chinese New Year, the most important speech in the president's annual calendar.

Kylie may not have been welcomed home by heads of state but her countrymen afforded her a uniquely Kiwi honour. After complaining during the expedition in her podcasts from the ice that she was craving marmite on toast, she arrived home to find parcels of marmite and bread piled up on her doorstep that had been sent from all over New Zealand by well-wishers who had followed the expedition. Kylie was delighted. Shortly after, the Sir Edmund Hillary Alpine Centre got in touch, asking Kylie to donate the skis and boots she used to reach the South Pole to their national exhibition. They will now be displayed alongside the ice axe used by Sir Edmund Hillary, an honour that makes us all proud.

I heard from Kim shortly after our return. Her injury was healing well and the feeling had returned to her fingers. Surrounded by friends at home, she had found a way to cope with her disappointment. I emailed her the picture we had taken for her of the team at the South Pole – flying the Jamaican flag on her behalf, just as I had promised.

As a team we have spoken to literally thousands of people about our adventure but have reached out to many more through media appearances, press articles and the web. As a result, the expedition has received a steady stream of emails from men and women who have been inspired by our story to make a decision in their own lives. It might be that they've decided to run a marathon, start a business, volunteer their skills to a cause or simply encourage someone else to achieve their dream. Whatever the decision, the fact that our actions have had such a direct impact on the lives of others and the choices they make is astounding. This is what I feel has been the real success of the expedition and our greatest achievement.

At the South Pole my mum asked me 'How do you feel? Are you happy?' Thinking back over the expedition I'm still not sure how to answer that question. I feel pride. I feel pride in the girls and I feel pride in myself for pulling it all together – but am I happy? Am I finally content? That is a harder question to answer.

When I was in my early teens a woman who had climbed Everest came to speak to our school. I don't remember much about her talk except that she had once been told that there were two paths in life and that taking the harder path would always lead to greater fulfilment. There and then I decided that I would always seek out the 'hard path' and I think, more or less, that that is what I have done ever since. As I write, new ideas for new adventures are forming in my mind and being rolled around. If they don't fade soon I'll be forced to do something about them. So, you see, I'm already seeking the next 'hard path' and I have a suspicion that it might always be that way.

FINAL THANKS

During my original interview with the Winston Churchill Memorial Trust, I promised that the WCMT would always be acknowledged as the seed from which the rest of the expedition grew. I willingly fulfil that promise here. I received more support and encouragement from the trust than I could have ever hoped and I can't thank them enough for their belief in me throughout (www.wcmt.org.uk).

I also feel incredibly fortunate to have worked with Kaspersky Lab, a global giant that welcomed us into their close-knit and inspiring community. Kaspersky Lab were more than just our dream sponsor, they became partners in our ambition, and friends. Particular thanks to Harry Cheung, Suk Ling Gun, Maggie Yu, Roger Wilson, Jennifer Jewitt, Christine Gentile and, of course, the irrepressible Eugene Kaspersky.

The expedition simply would not have been possible without the support of a number of key suppliers whose products and equipment saw us safely to Norway, New Zealand and the South Pole. Heartfelt thanks to Montane for the clothing; Iridium and Wright Satellite Connections for the airtime; Pilotur.dk for the watches; Hilleberg the Tentmaker for the Keron GT tents;

Chocolate Fish for the Merino wool thermals; Ellis Brigham, Buffera, Mountain Equipment, Multimat, Leatherman, Rab, Applied Satellite Technology and Bloc for the specialised clothing and equipment; Fuizion Freeze Dried Foods, Healthspan, High5, Power Porridge and Herbalife for the nutrition products; Anteon for the 'Louis Poo-uittons'; John Lewis for audio-visual equipment; Commonwealth Foundation, Visit Norway, DFDS Seaways, The Gordon Foundation, NSB, Hollock Waine Design, S. A. Brains and Wineaux for your services and support.

We also wish to gratefully acknowledge generous assistance from Medcon Constructions Limites, Ministry of Justice and Public Order in Cyprus (National Machinery for Women's Rights), Bank of Cyprus, Cyprus Computer Society, TSYS International, Caramondanis Group of Companies, Piraeus Bank, BPW Cyprus, (Louis Tours Ltd) Cyprus Airways, Tototheo Ltd, CYTA Cyprus, Komanetsi Fitness Center. Indian Mountaineering Foundation, Bajaj group. Technological University, Trailblazer Foundation Ltd, Singapore Sports Council, Singapore Sports Medicine Centre. BAG Networks, Bank Islam Brunei Darussalam, City Neon, Women's Council (Brunei Darussalam), Royal Brunei Technical Services Ladies Club, Ministry of Culture, Youth and Sports (Brunei Darussalam), Ministry of Foreign Affairs and Trade (Brunei Darussalam), Brunei Adventure and Recreation Association, Brunei Sports Medicine and Research Centre, Coach Rana and Dr Danish Zaheer.

There have been many people who have gone out of their way to give generously of their time, energy and enthusiasm to help the expedition in any way they could. I cannot begin to express how much your involvement has meant to us, for your laughter and friendship, as much as for the practical support you have selflessly volunteered. I sadly cannot mention everyone here who has played a role but I would like to particularly thank Dr Kapo

Simonian of Comtrack Services PLC who made the Norway training possible; Victoria Holdsworth for your dedicated championing of our project within the Commonwealth Secretariat and in the international media; Jim and Sarah Mayer for always being there, no matter how barmy the scheme; Jo Vellino for the laughter in Norway; Mark Priest for cheerfully accepting often bizarre or impossible jobs; Connie Potter for the scavenger hunt around London for Sesame Snaps and the endless rounds of phone calls; Paul Deegan for the no-nonsense motivation (and for calming me down before the launch!); Al and Elliott of Snowline Productions for working so hard on the expedition documentary; Kari Varberg Oydvin of Dyranut Fjellstove and her wonderful family for welcoming us to Norway; the snowplough drivers of Route E11 (I'm sorry we never learnt your names) for rescuing us on several occasions; Richard Woodhall of Mountain Equipment for your determination to find a way to help us; Rob Lewis of Mission Performance for introducing Red, Green and Blue to our team vocabulary; Dr Justin Roberts of Hertfordshire University for once again scaring us into action; Simon Meek and Anthony Slumbers of Estates Today for producing an awesome website; Danny, Joanna and Claire of the Royal Commonwealth Society; Phil H-B, Tori James, Chris Blessington and my lovely sister, Alex for the careful consideration of dozens of application forms; Amit Roy; Sandra Bodestyne of the British Council in Singapore; Satyabrata Dam and Namita Dam; His Excellency Burchell Whiteman; the staff of the British Council in Delhi; Soren Braes of Pilotur.dk for being such a dedicated friend to the expedition; Justine Jones; Steve Jones of Antarctic Logistics and Expeditions for putting on your 'friend hat' so often; Tim Butcher of Montane for literally saving the day on numerous occasions; Guy Risdon for being such a great support over the years and for showing us the value of good gaffer tape; Robert Hollingworth for the photographs that we shall all treasure for ever; Tim Moss for all the long hours and late nights waiting for our phone calls from Antarctica; Kate Gedge for coping with the world's press when you should have been enjoying Christmas – we are incredibly grateful; and Peter Martin for remaining unruffled by all the chaos I create (and for not telling me about the 360° slides along ice-covered Norwegian roads in the Land Rover). Finally to my wonderful parents, Jackie and Richard Aston, for allowing the expedition to take over their house so completely, for extending their hospitality so unforgettably to the team and for loving me despite the strife I bring. You are the reason I am free to do what I do.

ABOUT THE AUTHOR

Felicity Aston is a British expedition leader, public speaker and freelance travel writer from Kent. Her past achievements include leading the first British women's team across Greenland, completing the infamous Marathon Des Sables across the Sahara and working as a meteorologist in the Antarctic for three years.

www.felicityaston.com

A DIP IN THE
OCEAN
ROWING SOLO ACROSS THE INDIAN

'... obviously certifiably bonkers'
DAWN FRENCH

SARAH OUTEN

Foreword by
DAME ELLEN MACARTHUR

A DIP IN THE OCEAN

ROWING SOLO ACROSS THE INDIAN

Sarah Outen

ISBN: 978-1-84953-127-6   Paperback   £8.99

4,000 miles of unpredictable ocean
500 Chocolate bars
124 days of physical exertion
3 Guinness World Records
1 incredible journey

Each day as I pulled the oars in for the night, watching the water droplets drip off the blades and back into the ocean, I wondered at all the strokes they had taken and all the ones left ahead of us before we reached land. Thousands. Millions, perhaps? Each one was quite literally a dip in the ocean.

On 1 April 2009, twenty-three-year-old Sarah Outen embarked on a solo voyage across the Indian Ocean in her rowing boat, *Dippers*. Powered by the grief of the sudden loss of her father and the determination to live life to the full, Sarah negotiated wild ocean storms, encounters with whales and the continuous threat of being capsized, losing 20 kg of her bodyweight before arriving in Mauritius. She became the first woman and the youngest person to row solo across the Indian Ocean.

'*Sarah is inspirational*'   Mark Radcliffe, BBC Radio 2

'*Sarah's row across the Indian Ocean should be recognised as one of the most inspired and tenacious expeditions of a generation*'
                    Mark Beaumont, BBC Presenter and Round the World record holder

'*Sarah Outen's writing style is as charming as she is intrepid: as zesty as she is indomitable... her book sparkles and refreshes like the waves*'   Richard Dawkins

'*A story of true grit and fierce determination and dedication*'   Michael Morpurgo

Have you enjoyed this book?
If so, why not write a review on your favourite website?

Thanks very much for buying this Summersdale book.

www.summersdale.com